Also by Robert M. Hazen

North American Geology

The Breakthrough

The Poetry of Geology

With Larry Finger

Comparative Crystal Chemistry

With James Trefil

Science Matters

Science, An Integrated Approach

With Margaret H. Hazen

American Geological Literature

Wealth Inexhaustible

The Music Men

Keepers of the Flame

The New Alchemists

✧

The New Alchemists

Breaking Through the Barriers of High Pressure

Robert M. Hazen

TIMES BOOKS

RANDOM HOUSE

Library of Congress Cataloging-in-Publication Data

Hazen, Robert M.
    The new alchemists : breaking through the barriers of high
pressure / by Robert M. Hazen.—1st ed.
        p.   cm.
    Includes bibliographical references and index.
    ISBN 0-8129-2275-1
    1. Materials at high pressures.   2. High pressure chemistry.
3. Synthetic hard materials.   I. Title.
TA417.7.C65H39   1993
620.1′1—dc20   93-15703

Manufactured in the United States of America

9   8   7   6   5   4   3   2

FIRST EDITION

Design by Laura Hough

To
Hatten S. Yoder, Jr.,
mentor and friend

Contents

Preface

On a cold winter day in December 1955, Robert Wentorf, Jr., walked down to the local food co-op in Niskayuna, New York, and bought a jar of his favorite crunchy peanut butter. Back at his nearby General Electric lab he scooped out a spoonful, subjected it to crushing pressures and searing heat, and accomplished the ultimate culinary tour de force: he transformed the peanut butter into tiny crystals of diamond.

The triumph of Wentorf and his GE colleagues, who learned to turn just about any carbon-rich material, from road tar to snake oil, into sparkling treasure, marked the culmination of centuries of scientific study and technological breakthroughs—research driven by our fascination with nature's most romantic gemstone and by our awe at the power of high pressure to transform matter. Today, thanks to the work of generations of high-pressure researchers, scientists can use crushing pressure to explore the mysteries of the earth's deepest interior, to force materials into strange new forms, and to unlock the underlying structure of matter. The history of high-pressure research provides a dramatic tale of top-notch science, outright fraud, brilliant insight, and blind self-delusion. Yet in spite of the potential risks and possible rewards, most high-pressure pioneers were driven ultimately by an overpowering desire to explore the unknown. *The New Alchemists* tells the story of these scientists and engineers—their dreams of discovery and the powerful machines they built to unlock nature's secrets.

✧ ✧ ✧

Every scientific theory must be considered in the social and intellectual context of its time. Scientists find it tempting to view the history of science as a series of successes and failures, judged against our modern "correct" theories. Such an approach might seem especially applicable to the diamond story, for one simple test measures success: Was diamond made in the laboratory? But such a narrow perspective is at best misleading, and it ultimately serves no useful purpose. Science builds on past experience, and discovering what doesn't work often provides the key to finding what does. Those dedicated scientists who stumbled and fell short of our perception of truth cannot be viewed as failures, and their story also deserves to be told.

Some philosophers criticize scientists who believe in an independent, knowable nature. Reality, they say, is merely a human construct: there is no absolute truth in nature. Some scholars even deny the concept of "progress"; for them there is only change. I disagree. Along with most scientists, I am an unabashed believer in a universe with knowable physical laws, and I believe that we can measure scientific progress by our degree of understanding of those laws. To be sure, we have only come the tiniest fraction of the way toward understanding, but each advance marks a triumph for science and technology. The story of the diamond makers represents one such triumph. For centuries humans tried to make diamond; ultimately they succeeded. A few decades ago no one had ever done it; now, anyone with a few hundred thousand dollars and a big basement can make the gems at home. To me, that's progress.

This book is not a formal history of high-pressure science or even a comprehensive account of all the people who have contributed to this century's amazing advances in high-pressure research. Rather, I want to share some of the lore of science and scientists—the stories that never make it into formal publications. I was drawn into high-pressure research by these remarkable people, and I have shared the drama of their discoveries, as well as the frustration of their failures.

The first chapters of this book focus on the struggles of scientists to make diamond in the laboratory. The history of diamond synthesis cannot be divided neatly between pure and applied research, as is the case with many of the remarkable scientific discoveries that have transformed the twentieth century. With new diamond-making technologies have come both exciting new ways to study matter and extraordinary new uses for synthetic diamonds.

The book's later chapters chronicle high-pressure research of the past three decades, when diamond making has become routine. Today, the gems themselves are used to achieve record high pressures —pressures that exceed those at the earth's center—allowing scientists to unlock secrets of the earth's interior and explore matter at extreme conditions.

I have tried to present a fair and balanced history, but I cannot escape biases developed during seventeen years at the Carnegie Institution of Washington's Geophysical Laboratory, home to many central players in the high-pressure game. I am more intimately familiar with work done in the United States than elsewhere, so most of the book focuses on American scientists. Key contributions by researchers in Europe, the former Soviet Union, Japan, and Australia have perhaps received less than their fair share of space; I encourage scientists in those regions to recount their own personal histories.

I wrote this book for three reasons. First, the diamond has captivated human imagination for thousands of years, and the fascinating story of the gem's synthesis is not widely available outside the technical literature. Second, diamond making provides the ideal framework for describing high-pressure science—a field that has profoundly shaped our understanding of the material world and enhanced our ability to alter it. But most important, this book arose as an answer to a rhetorical question posed by my son in the winter of 1990. After a particularly frustrating textbook lesson in his junior high school science course, he asked me, "Why would anyone want to be a scientist?"

This book may provide a longer answer than Ben expected, but I hope it will help him see the drama that underlies scientific discovery. I hope it's not too late for him to appreciate how powerful science can be in helping us to understand our world, and, if used wisely, to shape it to our benefit.

The greatest joy in writing this book has been the opportunity to learn from so many high-pressure pioneers. Sadly, Percy Bridgman died before my years in Cambridge, Massachusetts, but many of his students and younger associates have vivid memories of his unique style and his extraordinary laboratory. Francis Bundy, Tracy Hall, Herbert Strong, Alvin Van Valkenberg, Robert Wentorf, Jr., and Hatten S. Yoder, Jr., all met Bridgman in his later years, and their recollections have enriched the story. I have also relied heavily on Maila L. Walters's recent biography of Bridgman, *Science and Cultural Crisis* (Stanford University Press, 1990), for biographical details.

Erik G. Lundblad, a member of the Swedish electric firm ASEA's diamond-making team, contributed much information on Baltzar von Platen's personality and inventions, as well as on ASEA's QUINTUS project. Lundblad also provided fascinating historical photographs of the ASEA effort.

Loring Coes, Jr., was remembered by many of his longtime associates at Norton: Neil Ault, George Comstock, Paul Keat, Alan G. King, and Osgood Whittemore all shared their reminiscences. Additional information was provided by Francis Birch, Francis R. Boyd, Eugene C. Robertson, Alvin Van Valkenburg, and Hatten S. Yoder, Jr., who were at the pivotal Norton meeting on December 4, 1953, and by Edward Chao, who discovered coesite in nature. Samuel Coes graciously provided details about his brother's early years.

All of the original members of the General Electric diamond-making team have contributed significantly to this book. Francis Bundy, Herbert Strong, and Robert Wentorf spent many hours retelling the story, clarifying details, and showing the site where the Man-Made Diamond process originated. Tracy Hall also shared his memories of four decades of diamond making and patiently explained the nature and origins of the disagreements that have arisen regarding the GE history. Harold Bovenkerk, the only member of the original team still working at GE, provided his unique insight into the history of domestic and foreign diamond synthesis. All of these men were generous in sharing historic photographs and documents, as well as unpublished anecdotes. I am also grateful to Mark Sneeringer and Anne Shayeson, who hosted a memorable tour of General Electric's Worthington, Ohio, diamond-making facility.

Joe Boyd, Ivan Getting, Julian Goldsmith, and Alvin Van Valkenburg, along with all the original GE diamond makers, provided reminiscences about the life and work of George Kennedy. Armando

Giardini, now mayor of Watkinsville, Georgia, contributed much on the unpublished history of diamond making at the U.S. Army's Electronics Research and Development Laboratory at Fort Monmouth, New Jersey. Henry Dyer of De Beers Industrial Diamond Division, and one of the original De Beers diamond synthesis team, shared the history of South African synthetic diamond studies. O. L. Bergmann of Du Pont contributed information on Mypolex, an explosively manufactured diamond.

Alvin Van Valkenburg, inventor of the lever-arm diamond-anvil cell and my friend for almost two decades, spent many hours before his death in December 1991 recounting the high-pressure history he knew so well. His son, Eric Van Valkenburg, contributed important photographs and other documents. Bill Bassett, who learned about the diamond cell from Van Valkenburg and thus became the first earth scientist to use it, shared memories of his research and his many colleagues in high-pressure research.

Raymond Jeanloz of the University of California at Berkeley provided much information on his life and research. I thank Arthur Ruoff of Cornell University, Isaac Silvera of Harvard University, and their students for stimulating discussions and informative laboratory tours.

Most of all, I am indebted to many present and former colleagues at the Carnegie Institution of Washington's Geophysical Laboratory. For almost ninety years, the Geophysical Laboratory has played a leading role in high-pressure research, especially in the earth sciences. Hatten S. Yoder, Jr., whose work began more than a half century ago, continues to provide inspiration and expertise to the next generation of high-pressure researchers. This book has been shaped by his wealth of firsthand historical knowledge.

Francis R. ("Joe") Boyd, who could have been the first to make diamonds when he came to the Geophysical Lab in 1953, is still making big presses and squeezing rocks. Joe's knowledge, based on decades of research on diamond-bearing rocks from South Africa and elsewhere, was invaluable in telling this story.

I owe a special debt to Peter M. Bell, who advised me in my first years at the Geophysical Lab, and his brilliant colleague Ho-Kwang ("Dave") Mao, who has transformed modern high-pressure research. Peter and Dave were the first to achieve 1 million atmospheres pressure in a diamond cell, and Dave, either directly or through his students, has instructed most of the handful of humans who have learned to duplicate the feat. Today, with Rus Hemley and a gifted team of junior colleagues, Dave Mao continues to make high-pressure history. All of these scientists have contributed immeasurably to my historical research.

I have received thoughtful and constructive reviews of the manuscript from many friends and colleagues. Those who have read and reviewed substantial portions of the manuscript include Orson Anderson, Allen Bassett, William Bassett, Harold Bovenkerk, Ray Bowers, Francis Boyd, Francis Bundy, James Cheney, Joel Fishman, Tracy Hall, Russell Hemley, Raymond Jeanloz, Dave Mao, Charles Meade, Charles Prewitt, Gretchen Prewitt, Herbert Strong, Robert Wentorf, and Hatten Yoder, Jr. Each of these readers made important additions and corrections, and to each I am indebted.

Finally, I thank Margaret H. Hazen, my greatest supporter and most perceptive critic, whose influence is present on every page of this book.

The New Alchemists

✦

Prologue

Pressure. To most people the word brings to mind the stress of our lives in a time of economic crisis. Yet to many scientists, pressure means something very different; it is an idea filled with wonder and power—a phenomenon unlike anything else we know. Pressure shapes the stars and planets, forges the continents and oceans, and influences our lives every moment of every day.

Three arenas of high technology drive our economy and propel us toward the twenty-first century. Information technologies link us to the world and its resources as never before, while biotechnologies hold the tantalizing promise of an era of health and plenty for all. But of all the advances that shape this age, none plays a more immediate and dramatic role in our day-to-day lives than the science and technology of new materials, and no technology holds more promise for creating and producing these remarkable new substances than the technology of high pressure. With pressure we can transform commonplace liquids into spectacular crystals, ordinary gases into exotic dense metals, and lumps of coal into precious gems.

Advances in high pressure, which until now were seldom mentioned and little known outside of obscure academic laboratories and secret industrial facilities, stand poised to change our lives with products and processes now unimagined. From exotic materials for building futuristic skyscrapers to exquisitely crafted microscopic electronics, superhard abrasives, and room-temperature superconductors, high-pressure technology holds unparalleled promise for shaping our world.

These emerging technologies come at a time of economic crisis in the United States. Our country must turn to new materials as a centerpiece in our efforts toward greater international competitiveness. Materials research and development has been highlighted as a key need in the Clinton administration's 1994 budget, and high-pressure research figures prominently in achieving their objectives.

A great deal of this research is funded by your tax dollars through the National Science Foundation (NSF). The NSF distributes a couple of billion research dollars annually to tens of thousands of scientists, who in a typical year ask for about ten times that amount to spend on new equipment and scientific personnel. Much of the NSF money supports individual grants to professors at universities or researchers at laboratories where people do "small science," research performed by one or two people working in a modest lab for a budget of less than $100,000 a year. More and more, however, NSF and other government agencies are asked to support "big science"—multibillion-dollar projects like the *Hubble Space Telescope* or the Superconducting Supercollider that require the coordinated efforts of hundreds of Ph.D.s. The debate between big and little science continues year after year; ask any scientist about it and you'll probably get a much longer answer than you wanted.

A few years ago officials at NSF recognized a middle ground between big and little: promising scientific and technological problems that require the cooperative efforts of a few dozen people. No one person is likely to learn how to predict severe thunderstorms, design new superglues, or identify bacteria that can eat oil spills. But solutions to these worthwhile problems don't require hundreds of millions of dollars, either. Without a mechanism for funding such midscale research projects, which might cost a few million dollars each, many promising avenues would be left unexplored. NSF responded to this situation by creating a new program to fund science and technology centers—facilities dedicated to tackling key problems in science and industry. Not surprisingly, high-pressure research was prominent on the list.

✧ ✧ ✧

On June 10, 1991, three dozen high-pressure scientists from Stony Brook, Princeton, and the Carnegie Institution converged on the campus of Washington College in Chestertown, Maryland, for the first annual meeting of the NSF Science and Technology Center for High-Pressure Research. Our consortium's goals were to develop new high-pressure techniques and discover new high-pressure materials. The study of superhigh pressure is so new, its effects so extraordinary, and its capabilities growing so fast that a collaborative effort seemed certain to yield dramatic and unexpected results.

I traveled to the meeting with Joe Boyd, a pioneer in the science of pressure. A strong man with a full steel-gray beard and wise brown eyes, his confident hands speaking of decades as a geologist, wielding a sledgehammer in the field and working with great, powerful machines in the lab, Boyd has left his mark on the scientists who study the transforming power of high pressure.

"There's still so much to do," he said as we sped across the sweeping silver arc of the Chesapeake Bay Bridge. The sky was bright blue, the sun hot as we passed far above the white-sailed boats on the Chesapeake. He opened the window of his tan Toyota truck and breathed deeply.

"You know, I used to race down there." He nodded out the window as we passed the highest part of the span. Below, free-flying racers cut sharp wakes. He fell silent, remembering times past and friends now gone. Forty years earlier Joe Boyd stood at the brink of one of our century's greatest scientific and technological achievements—the synthesis of diamonds. The breakthrough marked the beginning of an astonishing flood of discoveries in high-pressure science, discoveries that continue to change our lives with extraordinary new materials and to shape our understanding of the earth's present state and its dynamic history.

✧ ✧ ✧

We encounter pressure every day of our lives, whenever we push a button, press down on a pen, pump up a tire, or hear the explosive birth of popcorn. Behind such simple actions as inflating a party balloon or squeezing a tube of toothpaste lies a phenomenon that has captivated scientists, driven engineers, and transformed virtually every aspect of our physical world.

Pressure occurs when a force acts on an area. Your shoe applies pressure to the sidewalk, water presses on a skin diver, and the atmosphere weighs down on everyone and everything at the earth's surface with a pressure of about fourteen and a half pounds per square inch. Scientists call normal, everyday pressure—the weight of thirty or forty miles of air pushing down on you—one atmosphere or one bar.

Most of the pressures we experience in everyday life are rather modest. A pressure cooker generates about one and a half atmospheres, while the air in your car's tires is typically pressurized to about two atmospheres. A scuba diver thirty feet down experiences almost ten atmospheres of pressure, while a heavyset woman in stiletto heels could generate a pressure of about fifty atmospheres to the floor on which she walks.

But when researchers talk about high pressure, they mean vastly greater pressures of thousands or millions of atmospheres—kilobars or megabars. In fact, as pressure records have soared during the past three decades, new superlatives have come into play. "Superhigh pressures" (hundreds of thousands of atmospheres) and "ultrahigh pressures" (millions of atmospheres) are now standard jargon.

Scientists investigate these immense, often dangerous extremes because pressure causes matter to change in remarkable ways—much like the dramatic changes induced by temperature. Humans have known for thousands of years that liquid water freezes to a solid if cooled and boils to a gas if heated. We can now mimic these so-called changes of state at room temperature by using pressure: we can cause water to "freeze" at high pressure and turn it into gas in a vacuum.

Over the centuries humans have learned to exploit a remarkable range of temperatures, from a tiny fraction of a degree above absolute zero (the coldest possible temperature) to about one million degrees centigrade at the focus of the most intense laser beam. Over this temperature range we observe extraordinary changes in matter, from superconductivity to nuclear fusion. During the last few decades, scientists have learned to exploit a similar range of pressure, from a high vacuum—less than a billionth of an atmosphere—to pressures of many millions of atmospheres. Matter subjected to these extremes of pressure displays astonishing behavior, rivaling anything seen at exotic temperatures. Researchers have discovered that high pressure can turn ordinary compounds into superhard abrasives and transform everyday rocks and minerals into the dense materials that form the dynamic interior of our planet.

Prologue

Pressure alters matter by forcing atoms into ever smaller volumes. Every substance displays this phenomenon: as pressure increases, the volume of the compressed material decreases. At high pressures atoms must shift into more efficient, more densely packed arrangements. At high enough pressure any gas will become a solid, and every solid will adopt a new, denser form. To accomplish this volume reduction, the bonds between atoms—the interaction of the atoms' electrons—must also change. Pressure thus serves as a powerful probe of atoms and their electronic structure, helping us to learn how our physical world holds itself together.

Dinner was already in progress when we arrived on the Washington College campus. We picked up institutional green fiberglass trays, assembled our hearty cafeteria meal, and joined the group in our corner of the dining room. More than thirty scientists sat in small clusters, intently describing their latest experiments or debating recent theories of the earth's innards, underscoring their ideas with sharp gesticulations and vigorous scribbling on napkins and odd bits of paper.

At meal's end we reassembled in a commons room for presentation of scientific posters, more talk, and beer. The standard uniform on this warm June evening was shorts, T-shirt, and sneakers. Dozens of two-by-three-foot posters, dense with graphs, diagrams, and other symbols of scientific truth, were tacked to corkboards, taped to walls, or spread out on tables. Small discussion groups formed and dispersed and formed anew as the work of the meeting began.

All in all, it was a typical group of scientists: four out of every five were male, most were young pre- or postdoctoral fellows, most were foreign born. Joe Boyd sat in one corner in animated conversation with Hungarian geologist Tibor Gasparik, his scientific counterpart at Stony Brook. They gestured intently, sketching out ideas on the back of a photocopied campus map, no doubt hatching new ideas. Postdoc Jinmin Zhang and graduate student Yusheng Zhao debated a poster on a high-pressure mineral. Though native Chinese, both argued in fluent English. The room was filled with wonderful accents: Gabriel Gwanmesia's Cameroon lilt, Yue Meng's Chinese singsong, Tibor Gasparik's thick Slavic vowels, and David Palmer's proper British consonants. Russian, German, Indian, and Australian accents all focused on a common, consuming theme—the opportunities and frustrations of high pressure.

The central item on our first meeting's agenda was to establish our scientific priorities. With $1.1 million the first year, maybe twice that in coming years, we had to focus our efforts on the most promising research opportunities. Joe Boyd advocated building more big presses: we had only one among us and he thought we needed more. Dave Mao, holder of several high-pressure records, lobbied for spending the money to design a new pressure device, one that could take a big sample to higher pressures than ever before. Use computer modeling; try new materials; work on different samples—the competing ideas came fast, and there seemed to be enough possibilities to consume dozens of lifetimes. Science must always move forward, and we were faced with the challenge of charting its new direction.

Our debate could not be resolved quickly or easily, for there is no obvious way to ensure good science. History provides little direction: for almost a century one all-consuming problem drove high-pressure workers. Diamond synthesis provided their greatest challenge, their holy grail. In a sense we owe modern high-pressure science to diamonds and the men who learned to make them.

Like those pioneers, each of us sensed that we were about to begin a great adventure—an exploration with many pitfalls and dead ends, to be sure, but one that promised unimagined wonders and glimpses of nature that would take our breath away.

PART I

✧

The Diamond Makers

1

··

✧

Mysteries

The most highly valued of human possessions, let alone gemstones, is the "adamas," which for long was known only to kings, and to very few of them.

—Pliny the Elder, *Natural History*, Book XXXVII

Deep within the earth, diamonds grow. Diamonds the size of footballs, the size of watermelons—billions of tons of diamonds wait for eternity a hundred miles beyond our reach.

Thousands of years before the invention of science, humans treasured the glistening, hard stones they found among the gravels of exotic rivers, without knowing exactly what they were or how they came to be. Some said diamonds were pieces of stars fallen to earth, or perhaps the remains of water frozen for too long, while others spoke of crystals grown at ocean depths or formed in the path of lightning bolts. Despite people's curiosity, the true origin of diamonds would remain a mystery until early in this century.

Humans have always prized diamonds for their unrivaled physical properties. They sparkle as the most brilliant of gems, dispersing light better than any other precious stone. They are nearly indestructible, capable of withstanding the most corrosive salts and acids for aeons. Pure diamonds are superb electrical insulators, and they conduct heat energy more efficiently than any other substance. They boast exceptional purity among natural things, often being more than

99.9 percent carbon. And, of course, diamond is the hardest material known—almost twice as hard as anything else created by nature or man.

Ancient artisans were probably the first to study the stones' physical properties. If struck forcefully, they found, diamonds could be broken into chips and shards of great hardness and utility. Diamond-edged knives and engraving tools have been used by stoneworkers for millennia, and some ancient warriors are believed to have embedded diamonds in their edged metal weapons.

Yet as useful as they may be, diamonds have long been coveted as much more than mere physical curiosities. They are the stuff of magic and legends. Mystics and alchemists ascribed wondrous attributes to the stones, which seemed to grant the wearer a portion of their immortality. They were said to give their owners awesome strength on the battlefield, as well as potency in the bedroom. Wise men proclaimed diamonds to be a protection against evil, an antidote to poison, a cure for insanity, and a charm for women in childbirth.

Flamboyant stones possessing unusual size and quality have long had a special mystique. Large diamonds weighing a hundred carats or more (a carat being a fifth of a gram, or about the weight of a small pea) receive glamorous names, and some even developed reputations. The magnificent Orloff diamond, a 190-carat gem that now adorns the imperial Russian scepter, was stolen by a French deserter from the Indian Foreign Legion, in a sacrilegious exploit that has served as a prototype for countless dime-novel and adventure-movie plots. He disguised himself as a devout worshiper and plucked the gem from the eye socket of an idol of the god Sri-Ranga. The stone was smuggled to France and there purchased by the Russian Prince Orloff as a tribute to Catherine the Great.

The breathtaking, deep blue Hope diamond, now the most popular exhibit of the Smithsonian Institution, is said to carry its own curse. Brought to Europe from India in the seventeenth century (some say it too was stolen from the eye of a vengeful idol god), the striking 112-carat stone from which the Hope was cut had many unfortunate owners. Marie Antoinette and a sad sequence of wealthy, ill-fated Americans all possessed and wore the gem before New York diamond merchant Harry Winston acquired the Hope and sent it to the Smithsonian's National Museum of Natural History.

To these well-known stories can be added dozens more. The 410-carat Regent diamond was reputedly smuggled to Europe by an Indian slave who sliced open his leg and buried the diamond deep in the wound. The great stone adorned the hilt of Napoleon's sword and the crown of Charles X, and now serves as the centerpiece of the French crown jewels at the Louvre. And then there are the giant stones—the 726-carat Vargas, with which a Brazilian slave woman won her freedom in 1850; the 995-carat Excelsior, found in a shovel of gravel at Jagersfontein, South Africa; and of course the Premier Mine's fabulous 3,106-carat Cullinan, the largest gem diamond ever found.

Late in the afternoon on January 2, 1905, a mineworker alerted the Premier's surface manager, Fred Wells, to a brilliantly shiny object that caught the setting sunlight high on the wall of the diggings. Wells carefully inched his way to the spot and used his pocket knife to pry out the colossal stone. He then hurried to the mine office to have the epic find weighed, but the office staff was unimpressed. "This is no diamond," the inspector said, throwing the stone out the window.

Wells went back outside to retrieve the diamond, which was eventually authenticated and logged in at more than one and a third pounds—more than three times larger than any other known diamond. Upon examining the mass, awestruck geologists realized that the Cullinan was just a small piece from what must have been a much larger eight-sided crystal. For two years the giant diamond was exhibited to prospective buyers at a London bank in its natural state; in early 1908 the stone was cleaved to yield nine principal faceted gems. The two largest faceted diamonds in the world, both cut from the Cullinan, now grace the imperial scepter and state crown of Great Britain.

The natural diamonds that were hoarded by potentates of old have little of the visual drama that we associate with today's faceted gems. Deeply colored rubies, emeralds, and sapphires were far more prized as adornments. Owners accumulated the seemingly indestructible diamond pebbles, as found in their unpolished natural state, as talismans against defeat and symbols of their own "manly" virtues without ever seeing diamonds as objects of beauty.

When unearthed, most diamonds are roughly rounded with per-

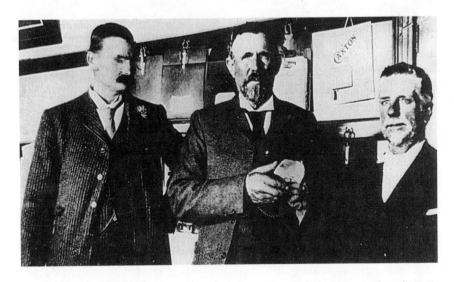

The magnificent 3,106-carat Cullinan diamond, the largest ever found, was at first tossed aside by a mine official who thought it a worthless piece of rock. The stone's discoverer, Fred Wells (right), stands with Premier Mine manager William McHardy (center) and owner Thomas Cullinan. (Courtesy of F. R. Boyd.)

haps a hint of regular crystal form. Many are colorless, but most are pale yellow; red, orange, green, blue, brown, and even black diamonds are sometimes found. Raw, uncut stones lack the exuberance of jewelry-store gems and can appear quite ordinary; Brazilian miners of the eighteenth century cast aside a fortune in raw diamonds while panning for gold. Diamond's familiar ornamental role represents a relatively recent development—a consequence in part of scientists' growing understanding of the nature of light.

A few scientific ideas have become part of our folklore. The equation $E = mc^2$ is one—a cultural icon as much as it is a statement of the equivalence of mass and energy. Another of these commonplace science snippets tells us that the speed of light is a constant. A popular T-shirt slogan proclaims "186,000 miles per second: It's not just a good idea, it's the law!" But as for many other legal systems, there's some fine print most people ignore. You have to add the rather mundane words "in a vacuum."

Anywhere else, light travels more slowly. The actual explanation, having to do with the way light interacts with the electrons present in every atom, is somewhat complex, but you can visualize the slowdown of light by thinking of rays having to make little detours every time an electron gets in their way.

Most clear and colorless objects slow light only a modest amount. The air we breathe has only a trifling billion trillion atoms per cubic inch. Spaces between atoms in the air are much greater than the size of the atoms themselves, so air reduces light speed by just a few hundred miles per second—not enough to notice under most circumstances. In water and ice, which have thousands of times more atoms per cubic inch than air, light travels about 140,000 miles per second —30 percent slower than in a vacuum. Window glass drops light speed to 120,000 miles per second, similar to the travel time through most common minerals, whereas lead-containing decorative glass, the kind used in chandeliers and cut glass, slows light even more, to about 100,000 miles per second (lead has lots of electrons that get in the way).

Diamonds can put the brakes on light like no other known colorless substance. Diamond is crammed with electrons—no substance you have ever seen has its atoms more densely packed—so light pokes through it at less than 80,000 miles per second. That's more than 100,000 miles per second slower than it travels in air.

The average person will probably never have reason to notice the variable speed of light, but one of its consequences can be experienced every day. Each time light passes from one clear substance into another with a different density, the light rays have a tendency to bend. You've probably noticed the distortion of people and objects in a swimming pool, which occurs when light waves change direction as they pick up speed coming out of the water. Ripples on the pool's surface compound the angular distortion. If you wear glasses or contact lenses, which "correct" the way light bends into your eyes, you're taking advantage of this useful optical phenomenon.

Light does not necessarily bend when passing between different materials. If light rays strike a clear substance head-on or at a modest angle, most of the rays will travel straight through. You can look straight down from a boat at the nearly undistorted bottom of a calm, clear lake or pond because sunlight enters the water from overhead and then comes back through the transparent water almost vertically to your eyes. But try as you might, you can't see the bottom of even the clearest lake standing on the shore, because you are at too low an angle to the water. Almost all the light reaching your eyes has reflected off the surface. That's why you can see the beautiful mirrored reflection of trees on the opposite shore of a glassy lake early in the morning.

Diamond plays this reflecting trick better than any other colorless substance. Light enters a faceted gemstone from all sides, but it may bounce back and forth several times inside before it finds a clean, straight shot out. All this changing direction accomplishes something very dramatic, because so-called white light actually contains all of the rainbow's colors. Each color—red, orange, yellow, green, blue, and violet—bends and reflects inside the diamond at slightly different angles. The farther the light travels, the more the colors separate. Bounce light inside a diamond just two or three times and the colors separate spectacularly. Diamond-like substances, including cubic zirconia, a crystalline compound synthesized from the elements zirconium and oxygen, attempt to mimic this light-dispersing property, though they fall short of diamond's brilliance and exceptional hardness.

If you look closely at a faceted diamond, you can see that it soaks up white light and breaks it apart like a prism, producing a rainbow of colors. Diamonds sparkle and dance with colored light; each of their dozens of facets produces its own dazzling display. Other natural gemstones disperse white light to some degree, but none comes close to diamond's ability to reveal the rainbow.

No one can say for sure when faces were first cut on a diamond. Diamond cutters, who cleave and polish natural stones, are thought to have been active in India a thousand years ago, while Parisian documents record such artisans working in France as early as the fourteenth century. Early diamond cutters probably chipped flat faces on rough and rounded stones simply to remove unsightly impurities. But, perhaps quite by accident, diamond finishers found that faceting accomplished much more than simple cleaning. Faces enhanced the beauty (and value) of their pebbles and ultimately transformed man's estimation of the diamond.

The shaping of a raw diamond into a pleasing geometric form is a painstaking and nerve-racking process. The diamond cutter first examines the stone for cracks and impurities, then designs a strategy for extracting the largest possible gem. Every diamond possesses some internal structures that are slightly weaker than others—cleavage planes that the diamond cutter hopes to find and exploit in shaping the stone. To cleave a gem diamond, the craftsman first uses a diamond-tipped instrument to inscribe a slight groove on the outside of the gem in the direction of the split. The cutter then places a sharp chisel on the groove and strikes the chisel with a swift, sharp hammer blow. Diamond cutters do not take their task lightly, for there is always a chance that a diamond, if improperly read or poorly struck, will shatter into small pieces. Cutters often study very large diamonds for years before they attempt to cleave them. Rough stones can also be sawed with a thin wheel coated with diamond dust and oil, but this tedious process requires many hours to cut even the smallest stones.

Once a gem has been roughly shaped by cleaving or sawing, the slow process of polishing facets begins. A metal plate, its surface impregnated with diamond dust, spins at high speed while the diamond is precisely positioned to create each of its many faces. In ancient times, cutters arranged their faces haphazardly, making little effort to compute the most favorable angles of reflection or even to achieve a pleasing symmetrical form. The oldest known cut stones, recorded and illustrated by the French traveler and pioneer diamond merchant Jean Baptiste Tavernier in the mid-seventeenth century, appear almost grotesquely crude when compared to modern jewels. But even ill-cut facets made diamonds more attractive, and people began to prize the gems for being beautiful as well as durable.

Popular history records that in the 1450s King Charles VII of France became the first European to give a gift of diamond jewelry to a woman, the beautiful Agnes Sorel. That the woman was his mistress, not his wife, may have delayed the adoption of the custom of the diamond engagement ring, but plenty of wives and mistresses proved willing and eager to display the new symbols of wealth and fashion. In a twinkling, the gemstone of choice for powerful men became the adornment of choice for powerful women.

Demand for diamonds soared and, for more than two centuries, India successfully met that demand. European diamond cutters sought to create ever more striking diamond jewelry by devising new ways to cut and polish the brilliant gems. Symmetrically faceted stones, championed by the Belgian craftsman Louis de Berquem, became the norm by 1500. Others added extra facets and introduced fancy new shapes—emerald cut, pear shape, marquise, and the popular fifty-seven-facet brilliant cut—to the diamond cutter's repertoire. More facets, they found, produced a more dramatic play of colors, while a variety of pleasing shapes let them make the best use of irregular stones. Carefully cut angles between flat faces—first discovered by trial and error, but eventually calculated with mathematical precision—increased a diamond's ability to disperse white light into colors and thus enhanced its beauty even more. Master diamond cutters learned the secrets of sculpting magnificent gems from crude, irregular pebbles. Spectacular rings, bracelets, necklaces, and pins gave the very rich a new kind of bauble on which to spend their money—and a new way to flaunt their wealth.

Making and selling diamond jewelry became a thriving business, so much so that by 1700 the demand for diamonds had outpaced the dwindling Indian output from the almost exhausted alluvial mines. But, as luck would have it, in 1726 miners discovered a major new network of diamond-rich streambeds in the Portuguese colony of Brazil. The diamond frenzy of the very rich continued unabated for another century.

Today, of course, the story has changed; now, almost everyone can own a diamond. Through a combination of new large-scale mining centers and brilliantly effective advertising, the once exclusive gemstone has become the symbol of love for people throughout the world. Today most people buy diamonds simply for their exceptional beauty, but the gem's particular mystique has not been lost. Diamonds are still sold as talismans by advocates of "crystal power," while seductive TV models look us in the eye and whisper, "Diamonds are love!" as though the hard, sparkling chips might somehow hold the power to alter our destinies.

✧　✧　✧

Even though the Western world was familiar with the diamond's strength and beauty, by the seventeenth century, the mystery of the gem's origins remained unsolved.

Two puzzles would frame the subsequent centuries of diamond research: Of what are diamonds made and how do they form in nature?

The first clues came from researchers who subjected diamonds to light and heat. Sir Isaac Newton marveled at the unique optical properties of diamonds during his attempts to understand the nature of the sun's radiation. The gem's well-known ability to break white light into rainbow colors—a trick diamond performed better than any other substance known at the time—provided Newton with a challenging puzzle. Assuming that oils possessed the greatest light-dispersing powers, Newton speculated that diamond was "probably an unctuous substance coagulated"—i.e., a solidified oil. He also came to the startling conclusion that diamond, like oil, would be combustible.

Newton's speculation resolved neither of the two central diamond questions, and none of his contemporaries were able to push any closer to the answers. A century later, scientists tackled the diamond mystery from a new perspective, using the young science of chemistry. All matter, they had found, forms from a few different kinds of building blocks, which they called atoms. Chemists had embraced the task of learning which combinations of atoms forms each fragment of the material universe, and they approached their mission like destructively curious architects who rip apart buildings to identify the materials used in their construction. Tearing matter apart also gave them hints about how to put it back together—the chemist's second mission.

Chemists devised many new ways of analyzing their world, but their first and best tool was fire. Many materials burn, leaving behind an ash residue that scientists could identify using simple chemical tests. And yet, despite Newton's conjecture about the flammability of diamond, attempts to ignite the hardest known substance seemed futile. Ordinary flame didn't work, nor did most ovens, but chemists kept trying. Finally, in 1772, the brilliant French chemist Antoine-Laurent Lavoisier confirmed Newton's prediction when he focused sunlight onto a diamond.

Lavoisier's private laboratory at his estate near Blois was a far cry from the high-tech chemistry facilities of modern research. He performed his experiments in elegant surroundings; his lab was filled with fine balances and microscopes and other instruments crafted of rich mahogany and polished brass. Hand-blown bottles with thick cork stoppers lined his shelves, and a sturdy wooden workbench supported an array of exotic beakers, burners, and other chemical apparatus. Lavoisier, resplendent in powdered wig and embroidered coat, conducted his experiments with great care while his wife, Marie, recorded the results.

The chemist prepared his diamond specimen by sealing it in a glass jar filled with oxygen. He selected a thick convex glass lens that could concentrate the sun's heat and mounted the lens on a pivoting metal stand that would keep the light focused on the gem as the sun moved. Lavoisier watched the diamond glow and burn like a piece of charcoal, not just to ash, but completely and totally away. The only by-product, identified in the laboratory as the gas carbon dioxide, suggested a close chemical relationship between diamond and charcoal, which also produced carbon dioxide when burned. Unfortunately, Lavoisier did not pursue this intriguing discovery, turning instead to other chemical studies in a distinguished career tragically cut short by the guillotine of the French Revolution.

The English chemist Smithson Tennant expanded on Lavoisier's work, demonstrating conclusively that diamond is nearly pure carbon, differing from charcoal only in its external form. By converting identical weights of charcoal and diamond to exactly the same volume of carbon dioxide gas, he established the chemical equivalence of the two dissimilar solids. Tennant's results, published in 1797, astonished the scientific world. How could it be that the toughest material on earth forms from simple carbon, the element of coal and soot? Scientists knew that carbon usually forms graphite, a material so soft that it is valued as a lubricant, so black that it is employed in the finest pencil leads. Many scientists, especially those who suspected that diamond must conceal a second, as yet unidentified element, were reluctant to believe Tennant's conclusions. Not until two decades later, after many careful researchers duplicated Tennant's observations, were these results accepted by the scientific community at large. Smithson Tennant, like Lavoisier before him, had little chance to enjoy this vindication; in February of 1815, while examining fortifications in Napoleonic France, he was killed in a bizarre accident when his horse fell through a decaying drawbridge.

Carbon taunted the chemists. Except in a few obscure streambeds in India and Brazil that yielded carbon in the form of diamond, carbon occurred as graphite. Why did nature produce two kinds of carbon? Could scientists reproduce nature's feat? For more than a century they tried and failed. Physicists and chemists used every trick to grow the gems. Some attempted to form diamond by evaporating carbon-rich solutions. Others tried electric arcs of intense heat to coax the carbon atoms into their most desirable form.

Nothing worked.

The discovery of primary diamonds —precious stones embedded in their host rock—transformed the search for the origins of the diamond. In 1866, children playing in a dry streambed in South Africa's vast central semidesert found the first tantalizing gem, a robin's-egg-sized blue-white pebble of more than 20 carats. Within a year of that find, the "shiny pebble" was known to the world as the Eureka. Two years later, the 83.5-carat Star of South Africa eclipsed the Eureka and captured the imagination of fortune seekers around the world. By the end of 1870 an epidemic of diamond fever had brought more than ten thousand miners to places with names now embedded in mining history: Jagersfontein, Bultfontein, Dutoitspan, and, of course, Kimberley.

For a time diamond mining was a haphazard affair. At first it appeared that the South African deposits centered around river- and streambeds, as did deposits in India and Brazil. The first large diamonds came from surface workings, such as those in the Vaal River Valley northwest of Kimberley. But prospectors soon located concentrated deposits of diamonds in the soft yellow rock that proved to be the weathered necks of ancient volcanoes. A new kind of diamond mine had been found, and new methods were imposed to exploit it.

Each miner at Kimberley was assigned one or two claims, each about thirty-five feet square. Each claim became a pit, sometimes as much as one hundred feet deep. As some claim holders labored more diligently, or more recklessly, than others, the Kimberley topography grew more and more chaotic. Historic photographs of the early workings show a nightmarish landscape of sheer rock walls and deep holes, festooned with a complex webbing of ropes and pulleys, each belong-

Kimberley Mine began as hundreds of separate claims. Different miners worked at different rates, producing a chaotic landscape of diggings. (Courtesy of F. R. Boyd.)

ing to a different claim. This unstable situation could not last long. Shallower workings collapsed onto deeper ones, and the deeper pits began to flood, forcing a more communal effort. By the 1880s, visionary entrepreneurs like Cecil Rhodes, who began his fortune by selling water pumps to the miners, had transformed the thousands of individual diggings into a centralized, mechanized South African diamond industry that surpassed the output of Brazilian and Indian diamond fields many times over. Millions of carats per year poured into a growing, middle-class, mostly American market, with the South Africans carefully controlling the supply and price of the precious stones.

Geologists eagerly scrutinized the distinctive matrix that held the precious crystals—a rock they called kimberlite. They had never seen such a deposit, and soon they began to understand the awesome testimony of the rocks. Kimberlite spoke of an origin deep within the earth, where intense heat and unimaginable pressures turn everyday stones into new, dense forms. The rock's cone-shaped masses, which cut across shattered layers of surface rock, attested to violent volcanic eruptions unlike anything recorded in human history.

Diamonds form when thousands of atmospheres of pressure combine with white-hot temperatures to coax carbon atoms into a particularly dense atomic arrangement. Natural diamonds are rare because they can grow only deep within the earth—one hundred miles or more down, where pressures reach hundreds of tons per square inch. But even though they understood how the stones were made, scientists were still at a loss to explain how diamonds reached the earth's surface. If they can form only at immense pressure—if soft black graphite is the only stable form of pure carbon at the earth's surface—how could diamond crystals have survived the epic journey from the earth's depths?

We now know that diamonds that take too long to ascend do in fact convert to graphite. Geologists have discovered incredibly rich deposits of what were once diamonds but are now diamond-shaped masses of ordinary graphite. These rock outcrops, which once held hundreds of millions of dollars of once-perfect diamonds in every cubic foot, confirm that many gems are destroyed during their long upward journey.

The small fraction of diamonds that do reach the surface unaltered make a fast and violent trip from below via volcanic eruptions —explosions of a fury and speed beyond our experience. A mass of partially molten diamond-bearing rock may sit deep within the earth for a billion years, but it can blast to the surface in less than an hour. Hot, upwelling magma weakens overlying rock; the molten rock, which contains water, carbon dioxide, and other pressurized gases, deforms and cracks the overlying rock.

Suddenly the rock gives way and the hot diamond-bearing mass explodes in a cataclysmic eruption. Magma from a hundred miles deep rises faster and faster, pushing through solid rock, rocketing to the surface. Hot expanding gases rush out with explosive force as the molten mass thrusts upward; the blast pulverizes much of the rock and its treasure of precious stones, scattering debris over thousands of square miles, leaving behind a cone-shaped plug of diamond-bearing rock that fills the cavity of the blast. The kimberlite, cradling its diamond hoard, cools in this near-surface environment. For millions of years wind and weather slowly erode the rock. Every so often a small, hard gemstone works its way free, washing into a nearby river or stream.

Kimberlite taught scientists what they had to do to make diamonds in the laboratory: squeeze carbon and heat it unmercifully, to mimic conditions in the depths of the earth. But how could humans duplicate the pressure of a column of rock many miles high? How could they provide the temperature of a blowtorch to pressurized carbon atoms?

Those were tricks worth learning.

2

$\diamond$

Attempts

"Diamonds," he began . . . "No one yet has hit upon exactly the right flux in which to melt up the carbon, or exactly the right pressure for the best results. . . . Suppose one to have at last just hit the right trick, before the secret got out and diamonds become as common as coal, one might realize millions. Millions!"

—H. G. Wells, "The Diamond Maker," 1894

Many men have tried their hand at diamond making—brilliant men, ambitious men, men driven by vision and men possessed by greed. The Frenchman C. Cagniard de la Tour claimed to have grown diamonds from solution in 1828, but his crystals were nothing more than aluminum and magnesium oxides—the fool's gold of diamond makers. In the same year, J. N. Gannal made a similar claim, but no one could reproduce his results. In the 1850s, Charles Despretz announced the synthesis of diamond in an electric arc; others disproved his findings. Within a century of Tennant's discovery that diamond is pure carbon, a dozen scientists had staked their claim in the diamond-making game. All of these early efforts attempted to use temperature alone to transform black carbon into diamond; before Kimberley, the central role of pressure was unknown.

Of all the men who tried to make diamonds—the gifted researchers and ignorant fools, the seekers of truth and the outright frauds—none failed more spectacularly than Scottish chemist James Ballantyne Hannay.

By the 1850s, chemistry had grown from its awkward infancy to an exuberant youth, buoyed by discoveries of magical wonder and extraordinary utility. New chemical elements, new compounds, new techniques for processing raw materials all added to the burgeoning repertoire of the chemist. New fuels, new pigments, new medicines, and thousands of other novel chemicals devised by curious scientists inexorably altered life-styles in the self-confident Victorian world.

The power of chemistry to transform matter had fascinated Hannay since his childhood in Glasgow, where as a precocious ten-year-old he had manufactured his own fireworks. Though largely self-trained in his modest home laboratory, Hannay acquired sufficient chemical expertise to be elected a Fellow in the Royal Society of Edinburgh in 1876, at the age of twenty-one.

Hannay became the manager of a Glasgow chemical firm, which allowed him to continue his chemical inquiries on the side. Much of this exploration focused on the solvent properties of fluids at very high temperatures or pressures. He found that, in general, the higher the temperature or pressure of a gas or liquid, the greater its dissolving powers. In these experiments, Hannay practiced classic chemistry— mixing chemicals in solutions to see what happened, in the tradition of centuries of laboratory study. But, as so often happens in science, one seemingly straightforward experiment led Hannay in a completely unexpected direction. While attempting to dissolve sodium and lithium metals in common liquids like melted paraffin wax and oils, he found that the liquids sometimes broke down, releasing hydrogen gas and depositing the carbon as a hard, scaly coating that could scratch glass. The tough layer looked to Hannay like diamond.

This surprising result gave Hannay the idea for a new strategy to synthesize diamond. His first synthesis attempts in the late 1870s, years before geologists understood the origins of Kimberley diamonds, relied on the tried-and-true methods of the chemist's craft. He employed the most basic and rudimentary crystal-growing technique, dissolving the desired chemical—in this case, carbon—in a liquid and waiting for the diamond to crystallize.

A variety of experiments employing simple liquids at normal pressures yielded only graphite. It was at this time that South African geologists discovered the importance of pressure in the formation of natural diamonds. Hearing of their discovery, Hannay decided to try to mimic the earth's conditions. His heroic and foolhardy attempts involved filling lengths of iron tubing with carbon-rich oil and lithium, sealing both ends, and placing the cylinders in a massive six-foot-long furnace with foot-thick masonry walls. The tubes were fired for many hours at red heat (perhaps 900°C)—usually until they exploded from excess internal pressure.

High-pressure research was terra incognita to Hannay and his contemporaries, and his first abortive experiments were hampered by many technical difficulties. His first concern was sealing an iron tube so that it would withstand high internal pressures. Screw fittings, the most obvious choice, invariably leaked. He then tried inserting an iron ball into the end of the tubes and crimping the ends shut to form a seal that became progressively tighter as pressure increased. Unfortunately, the ball seal became a lethal high-velocity projectile at extreme temperature, when the crimped barrel softened; he noted that "the iron yielded and the ball was driven out with a loud explosion." Reluctantly Hannay resorted to difficult welded seals for his subsequent experiments. It was no mean feat to obtain a complete weld while preventing the highly volatile hydrocarbons from escaping. "It is only one man in a hundred who can perform the operation with invariable success," Hannay wrote—a pronouncement that reflects the reality familiar to all experimental researchers, who understand that the most valuable laboratory asset is often the skilled technician.

No diamonds were found in experiments using ordinary one-inch-diameter tubes with half-inch bores, so Hannay began using thicker and thicker cylinders. A few experiments were tried with two-inch barrels, which burst with regularity, so three-inch tubes were tried. They too exploded or leaked. Finally he resorted to four-inch tubes, which blew up at even higher pressures, with even more violence.

In a typical experiment, Hannay wrote, the tube "exploded with a great noise, and knocked down the back and one of the ends of the furnace, leaving the whole structure a wreck." In the rare experiment that didn't leak or explode, the risk to the scientists was perhaps even greater. The highly pressurized welded cylinder had to be drilled open by hand; the technician was exposed to considerable danger when the pressurized gas finally escaped with a loud report and violent rush. Hannay expressed relief that one of his workers narrowly escaped injury when a tube ruptured and shattered in a spray of shrapnel as it was being drilled. "The continued strain on the nerves," he noted, "watching the temperature of the furnace, and in a state of tension in case of an explosion, induces a nervous state which is extremely weakening, and when the explosion occurs it sometimes shakes one so severely that sickness supervenes."

During one short period, Hannay lamented, "Eight tubes failed through bursting and leaking, and one of the explosions . . . destroyed a part of the furnace and injured one of my workmen." Of eighty high-pressure experiments, seventy-seven were failures. In most cases, the experimental products were lost through leakage or were scattered about the furnace by an explosion. The few runs that were completed produced only graphite—if they produced anything at all. But in early 1880, Hannay finally, joyfully, found traces of diamond. Tiny clear crystals, too hard to grind in a mortar and impervious to acid, were recovered from solid residues in three tubes. Chemical tests convinced Hannay that he had made diamonds. The weary researcher celebrated, wrote up and published details of his success in the Royal Society's *Proceedings* for 1880, and went on to other things.

At the time, most observers assumed that the problem of diamond synthesis had been solved. Hannay's triumph was accepted as just another in the flood of chemistry breakthroughs of the late nineteenth century. But we now know that something was wrong with his results. Recent analyses of Hannay's "synthetic" diamonds, which are preserved in the collections of the British Museum, prove without question that the crystals are natural, not synthetic. These tiny fragments of history, the only surviving "synthetic diamonds" from the many claimed before World War II, contain a telltale impurity. Natural diamonds, held deep in the earth for millions of years, can gradually develop thin plate-like concentrations of nitrogen atoms dispersed through the carbon crystal lattice. No rapidly formed synthetic diamond could display this feature, nor is it likely that such orderly impurities could form over any human time scale.

There can be no doubt that Hannay's diamonds came from a natural source. Some historians have denounced Hannay as a fraud, though others of more charitable disposition suggest that Hannay's workmen, fearing for their employer's safety as well as their own, planted the natural diamond bits to end the hazardous experiments. Chances are we will never know for sure.

Hannay's experience with exploding iron tubes and shattered furnaces was hardly unique in the search for synthetic diamonds. Many nineteenth-century researchers took grave risks in their pursuit of knowledge. Scientists are seldom portrayed as heroes who risk life and limb for a higher cause, but chemistry in the nineteenth century held many hazards. Ferdinand-Frederick-Henri Moissan, a Nobel prize–winning chemist and would-be diamond maker, almost died in his crusade to become the first to isolate the lethal gas fluorine.

Moissan and other chemists of the nineteenth century realized that just a few dozen different chemical elements form our world, and they placed the highest priority on cataloging and isolating those elements. Some naturally occurring "native" elements, like gold, silver, copper, and lead, had been known for thousands of years, while others, like oxygen, aluminum, magnesium, and hydrogen, were easily derived from common compounds as soon as a few simple chemical tricks were learned. Dozens of other kinds of atoms remained hidden and unexpected as trace elements in rare minerals. Fluorine was a maddening exception. Common "fluoride" minerals of calcium and sodium were loaded with the distinctive light element, but fluorine atoms were so tightly bonded to the others that it seemed impossible to separate and purify the stuff. It was as if the chemists had been invited into a fabulous castle, each glorious room containing a new precious element, except that one of the grandest chambers— the room containing fluorine and its treasures—remained locked and taunting, and booby-trapped, to boot. Many tried to unlock the secret of fluorine and paid a terrible price.

When Moissan began his most famous research in 1884, toxic fluorine and its compounds had already killed or injured a half-dozen respected scientists. Early in the century the famed English chemist and lecturer Sir Humphry Davy and the rival French team of Joseph Louis Gay-Lussac and Louis Jacques Thenard both tried and failed to isolate fluorine, only to suffer debilitating eye irritation and respiratory inflammation from their fruitless labors. The Irish brothers George and Thomas Knox also suffered horribly when they were exposed to hydrofluoric acid. Thomas almost died, and George spent three years recovering his health in Naples. George Gore of London managed to isolate a small quantity of the gas, but it almost immediately combined explosively with hydrogen, destroying part of his laboratory. And these men were the lucky ones. Jerome Nickles of France and Paulin Louyet of Belgium, though fully aware of the dangers, died horribly in their laboratories—asphyxiated as their lungs were burned and blistered by the corrosive gas.

It was a dangerous game these chemists played, but Moissan accepted the risks. In a crude, poorly ventilated laboratory in Paris he passed strong electrical currents through a mixture of hydrofluoric acid and fluorine salts in a costly apparatus constructed largely of platinum. He, too, suffered from fluorine poisoning, and shortly before his death at the age of fifty-four he blamed these chemical investigations for shortening his life by a decade. But in 1886, after almost three years of labor, he succeeded in purifying the corrosive greenish-yellow gas. Then, with his unique and steady supply of the element, isolated by the process still used in industry today, he was able to create a variety of totally new chemical compounds made possible by fluorine's unrivaled reactivity.

This work greatly enhanced Moissan's reputation and led to his appointment to a prestigious academic position (in toxicology, no less). But it also turned out to be an excellent foundation for his next research problem—the synthesis of diamond.

Moissan began his painstaking, and considerably safer, diamond work with the meticulous care of a craftsman. To make diamond in the laboratory, he reasoned, one must know as much as possible about how diamonds arise in nature. To this end, he gathered three very different samples of diamond-bearing material. He examined kimberlite from South Africa in detail, finding large numbers of previously undiscovered microscopic diamonds embedded in it. He dissolved almost five tons of Brazilian diamond-bearing gravel in strong acids to concentrate about two carats of fine diamond particles. Finally, he extracted two tiny diamonds from a piece of the Canyon Diablo iron meteorite, found near the great meteor crater in Arizona. In all these samples, iron was diamond's common companion. Perhaps, Moissan thought, a metal like iron was the key to diamond synthesis.

To find out, Moissan designed an extraordinary new oven capable of melting iron and most other metals. His electric arc furnace

Henri Moissan beside his electric arc furnace, in which he believed he had synthesized diamonds.

achieved record temperatures of 3,000°C (about 5,000°F) by passing a powerful electrical current through graphite, which glowed white with heat like the metal strips in a space heater.

The most famous photograph of scientist Moissan reveals much about the man. Taken early in the twentieth century, the image captures an elegant, keen-eyed academic, formally attired and studiously erect, standing in a crude brick-walled basement room next to a rugged laboratory workbench. Though his chief claim to fame was his Nobel prize–winning work on the separation of fluorine, Moissan was intensely proud of his furnace. The crude pile of firebricks and thick electric power cables dominate the central third of the photograph; its inventor stands to the left, one arm in familiar contact with his imposing device.

Moissan's thick full beard and grand mustache signify an honored professor's self-confidence, and perhaps an avowed experimentalist's pragmatism as well. The synthesis of crystals is as much an art as a science. You can perform the same crystal-growing experiments dozens of times; sometimes crystals form, sometimes they don't. The experimental chemist knows that one key to successful synthesis is often as simple as having a tiny bit of the right impurity to provide a starting place—a "nucleation site" for crystal growth. But how do you sprinkle your experiment with such microscopic catalysts? Experimental chemists learned long ago that nothing works better than a full beard for collecting and redistributing a laboratory's chemical dust. A beard like Moissan's, exposed to a long career in chemical laboratories, must have been full of exotic stuff. Maybe it's only a chemist's superstition, but Moissan did create a lot of new crystals.

In his first set of diamond-making experiments, Moissan used his furnace to melt iron and other metals in a crucible. He then dissolved carbon (in the form of burned sugar) in the liquid metal and let the carbonized mixture cool. The procedure must have been spectacular; at the extreme temperatures in the electric arc furnace, graphite glows intensely white and iron erupts in a shower of brilliant white

At full power, Henri Moissan's electric arc furnace, pictured in this illustration from his 1904 monograph *The Electric Furnace*, produced a spectacular display of sparks and flame as it reached temperatures of 3,000°C. Moissan believed that he had synthesized diamonds in his apparatus.

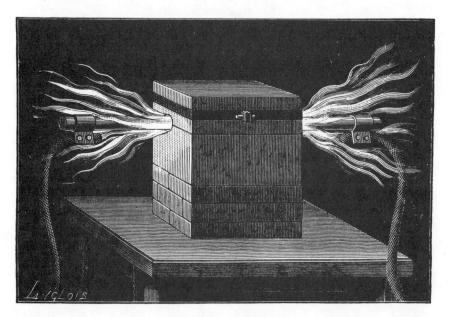

sparks. After the blasted sample cooled, acids were used to dissolve the metal away, leaving behind a residue of ordinary black carbon—graphite—in every experiment.

Moissan realized that pressure was a key missing ingredient, but he lacked the equipment to subject samples to simultaneous high temperature and pressure. His ingenious solution was to let the cooling, contracting metal provide the pressure itself. Carbonized liquid iron was prepared as in the earlier trials, but this time it was rapidly chilled in cold water, which caused the outer portions of the iron to solidify almost instantly. The sudden contraction of this cooling iron jacket, it was hoped, would generate the necessary pressure to induce diamond growth. To increase the cooling rate even more, Moissan dropped the iron into "baths" of molten lead—a substance hundreds of degrees cooler than the iron, and one that actually caused the iron's temperature to drop more quickly than in cold water.

Many of these primitive high-pressure experiments produced microscopic carbon particles, never larger than a few hundredths of an inch, that appeared to have the distinctive properties of diamond. The particles were very dense and scratched other hard materials; some even had the rough octahedral crystal form of natural diamond. Most important, Moissan's diamonds were said to burn, leaving a residue of carbon dioxide.

Henri Moissan went to his death in 1907 believing that he had made diamonds, and few challenged the distinguished chemist's assertion while he lived. But there were doubts, and within a few years, after several respected scientists failed to reproduce his claims, Moissan's experiments were dismissed as failures. Many years later, Moissan's widow expressed her belief that one of the professor's devoted assistants may have sprinkled the runs with a few natural diamond fragments "to please the old man."

Modern re-creation of the procedure produced several tiny, hard crystals, very much like the ones described by the Frenchman. Those crystals have been identified as silicon carbide—the primary ingredient in the commercial product Carborundum. Natural silicon carbide has been given the name moissanite, to honor the man who made it instead of diamond.

✧ ✧ ✧

Moissan firmly believed that his experiment had succeeded, and he meticulously spelled out the diamond-making recipe in his monograph *Le four électrique*, translated into English as *The Electric Furnace* in 1904. In that same year another Frenchman, Monsieur Lemoine, capitalized on Moissan's publicity and claimed to have made large diamond crystals in his own modified electric furnace. A diamond expert from Kimberley was dispatched to Paris, where he watched Lemoine "transform" ordinary charcoal into a diamond. Unfortunately, Lemoine's supposedly man-made stone had all of the unmistakable surface markings of a river-washed gem. The unscrupulous Lemoine was subsequently arrested and tried for fraud.

But not all of Moissan's followers were frauds. His widely acclaimed experiments served as the starting point for the work of many other respected scientists. One of the most ardent and unquestioning believers was Professor J. Willard Hershey, who conducted more than a decade of misguided diamond-making experiments as classroom exercises for his chemistry students at McPherson College in Kansas. Hershey even dedicated his own *Book of Diamonds* to "all my students who have had any part in helping to make synthetic diamonds under my instruction."

Also among the avid readers of Moissan's *The Electric Furnace* was Sir William Crookes, a towering figure in nineteenth-century British science, remembered as much for his baffling fascination with the occult as for his solid technical contributions. Crookes's impressive catalog of accomplishments includes discovery of the element thallium and invention of the radiometer. He also designed an improved vacuum pump, discovered new applications for spectroscopy, and made important advances in photography and in methods for extracting valuable metals from ore. He founded the influential journal *Chemical News* and was its sole editor for almost half a century. He served as president of the Royal Society and many other organizations and enjoyed a knighthood and numerous other public and professional honors. Yet his obsession with spiritual phenomena, his endorsement of certain well-known mediums, and his belief in a psychic force that could modify gravity and cause other physical manifestations complicate the portrait of a man who achieved so much in the "rational" world of science.

In a career so sweeping and vibrant, Crookes's few diamond-making experiments appear to rate little more than a footnote, but his novel experimental strategy foreshadowed the techniques of the twentieth-century diamond-making industry. In 1896, in his sixty-fourth year, Crookes spent nearly a month studying the mineralogy and geology of Kimberley. He saw diamond mines at first hand and investigated the natural chemical origins of the gems, grasping the key role of pressure in diamond synthesis. Then for almost a decade other research, particularly in the youthful field of radioactivity, distracted him, but the 1904 publication of Moissan's treatise and Crookes's second South African trip in 1905 persuaded him to try his hand. His attempts to duplicate Moissan's contracting-iron experiments seemed to work well, for Crookes reported the creation of "veritable diamonds" (probably silicon carbide) with all the distinctive attributes of the natural stone.

Part of the challenge of chemistry, however, is to find new paths to synthesis. Moissan's procedures were old news, and they were noncommercial to boot. Crookes knew that a cheap method of diamond synthesis would have great commercial applications, so rather than dwell on what had already worked, he elected to try a new approach, taking Hannay's sealed-tube method a step further. The highest temperatures and pressures available in Crookes's day had been obtained by Sir Andrew Noble, who studied the effects of explosives. Noble had packed steel tubes with gunpowder or cordite and heated them until they exploded with tremendous force, briefly attaining pressures of 8,000 atmospheres at more than 5,000°C. Crookes was given the chance to study the solid residues from these blasted tubes. He wrote, "After weeks of patient toil I removed the amorphous carbon, the graphite, the silicon, and other constituents." Subsequent treatment by heat, nitric acid, and sulfuric acid yielded a residue of tiny transparent crystals. "Chemists will agree with me that diamonds only could stand such an ordeal; on submitting them to skilled crystallographic authorities my opinion is confirmed . . . In these closed vessel experiments we have another method of producing the diamond artificially."

For a second time, Crookes believed he had produced diamond, although modern researchers are convinced otherwise. None of his synthetic material has been preserved, but we know that the explosive method could not possibly have produced sufficient temperatures and pressures. Chances are that silicon carbide was, once again, the impostor.

Most of the would-be diamond makers of a century ago dedicated their energies to one novel idea for a few years and then went on to tackle a completely different problem. Sir Charles Algernon Parsons, son of an Irish earl and privileged recipient of the best education money could buy, was different. Diamond making became his lifelong obsession, and he tried every scheme he could think of to get the job done.

Persistence was certainly one of Parsons's strong suits. Though shy and introspective by nature, he could be doggedly determined in his efforts to publicize and promote his work. His chief claim to fame was the 1884 invention of a steam turbine for ship propulsion. This new power source was both efficient and reliable, but its implementation was blocked for more than a decade by legal technicalities and a tradition-minded British Royal Navy. Parsons turned the tide in 1897 when he rocketed his own ship, the *Turbina*, at an incredible thirty-plus knots through the Diamond Jubilee fleet review while Queen Victoria and her wide-eyed admirals looked on. The dramatics paid off, for within a few years Parsons's steam turbines became standard equipment for most new British ships, including the mighty HMS *Dreadnought* and Cunard's magnificent *Lusitania*.

Experiments on steam turbines provided Parsons with firsthand experience in controlling high temperatures and pressures, and he applied that experience to diamond making as early as the mid-1880s. In his first series of experiments on pressurized carbon he subjected either wood charcoal or coke, a carbon-rich by-product of baked coal, to extreme electrical currents approaching 100,000 amperes and pressures to about 4,000 atmospheres—a force of about thirty tons per square inch. The yellowish crystal mass produced in these experiments suggested to Parsons the characteristics of diamond and inspired a long succession of similar attempts.

Parsons's diamond-making experiments, though never successful, captured the public's imagination and quickly entered American popular culture. Howard Garis, alias Victor Appleton, based *Tom Swift Among the Diamond Makers*, the seventh volume of his immensely popular series of boys' adventure tales, on Parsons's ideas. Published in about 1911, just a few years after Parsons described the results of hundreds of attempts to synthesize diamonds using electric current, the book invokes a clever modification of the electric arc method in which lightning is used to transform a carbon mixture into the precious gem.

Appleton's tale of adventure may be the most enduring consequence of Parsons's electric experiments, but after exhausting that procedure the scientist was by no means through. He attempted to modify Moissan's chilled-iron method by compressing a molten mass of carbon-saturated iron to 12,000 atmospheres. He tried melting graphite at extreme pressures and temperatures in the hope it would cool as diamond. He mixed carbon with other elements—including kimberlite rock—and even fired high-velocity bullets into carbon-rich material to attempt to make the gems by impact.

Charles Parsons was a careful and conscientious scientist who dutifully recorded the conditions and results of thousands upon thousands of diamond-making experiments, spanning thirty years of effort. He methodically isolated suspected diamond crystals and preserved them on glass slides for others to examine. For most of his career he was thoroughly convinced that he was making diamonds. But, sadly, as chemists analyzed and rejected sample after sample as merely carbides or simple oxides of aluminum and magnesium—all logical by-products of his experimental methods—Parsons came to realize that his dream had eluded him. After decades of fruitless labor, Parsons eventually admitted to friends and colleagues that he, and all others, had failed. At the time of his death in 1931, not one reproducible experiment by any of a century of wishful diamond makers had succeeded.

Hannay, Moissan, Crookes, and Parsons, along with many contemporaries, all evidently failed to make diamonds, but their research was neither flawed nor useless. All scientific progress is built on the hard-won knowledge of previous generations, and these scientists had taken the first steps in striving to achieve the pressures and temperatures that would eventually accomplish this elusive goal. They also proved beyond a doubt that making diamonds would not be easy.

With each failure by another distinguished researcher, the stakes in the diamond-making game rose higher.

While Hannay and others engaged in their futile attempts to synthesize diamond, other scientists were learning more about what made the crystal unique. Albert Einstein relied on diamond data to support his 1907 theory of specific heat, the energy associated with atomic vibrations. Every crystal stores two kinds of energy. First, there is the bond energy itself—the potential energy of atoms held together by the attraction between negatively charged electrons and positively charged atomic nuclei. Everything you touch—the air you breathe, the food you eat, the clothes you wear—exists because of this stored bonding energy. The second kind of energy stored in the crystal is the energy of atomic motion, or heat. Every atom is in constant motion, and in a physical world motion means energy—kinetic energy.

These two kinds of crystal energy—binding and heat energy—obey different kinds of rules. Binding energy changes only slightly with temperature: the carbon-to-carbon bond energy of a substance is almost exactly the same at freezing temperatures or at red-hot heat. Heat energy, on the other hand, is directly dependent on temperature: hot matter has a lot more heat energy than cold. Einstein and his contemporaries worried about the exact nature of the heat-temperature relationship, and that's where diamond entered the picture.

Some scientists believed that an atom's energy can assume any value. If this is true and energy varies smoothly and continuously, as in the classic theory of heat, then the graph of heat energy versus temperature has to have a distinctive curved shape. If, on the other hand, we live in a world where energy comes only in tiny discrete bundles—quanta—then the graph of heat versus temperature will show a rather different shape at low temperatures near absolute zero ($-273°C$). Einstein assumed the quantum model and predicted the distinctive shape this second curve would have. Diamond, because of its high heat conductivity, was the perfect test case: it holds so little heat energy that quantum effects persist at relatively high temperatures. Experiments showed that diamond matched Einstein's predicted behavior almost perfectly, buttressing the revolutionary quantum theory.

Energy is not the only feature of our physical world that is quantized; matter, too, comes in discrete bundles, called atoms. Before the discovery of x-rays, no one had seen direct evidence for these physical building blocks. No one knew their exact size or how they filled space to make the world around us. But with the invention of x-ray crystallography in 1912, chemistry entered the modern era. For the first time, scientists could determine the very architecture of our material world.

The principle of x-ray crystallography is simple enough. Every crystal is made of layer upon layer of atoms, repeating almost endlessly. X-rays striking a crystal will scatter off these layers, much as a beam of light will bounce in different directions off an irregular surface. But if the x-ray beam is directed at a certain angle and the atomic planes are carefully aligned, a sharp stream of x-rays—diffracting x-rays—flies from the crystal. By measuring the exact directions and intensities of these diffracted beams, crystallographers can calculate the size and arrangement of the atoms in the crystal.

In 1913 the father and son team of William and Lawrence Bragg employed these newly discovered principles of x-ray diffraction to deduce the elegant atomic structure of diamond, finding an arrangement in which every carbon atom is surrounded by a pyramid of four others. This dense interlocking network contrasts sharply with the layered arrangement of graphite, in which each carbon has only three close neighbors, all arrayed in a plane. Little wonder that graphite and diamond behave so differently. The carbon-to-carbon bonds within the layers of the graphite structure are quite strong, so the atomic sheets are tough and resilient, but the bonds between atomic layers are much weaker. Often atoms can exploit this weakness: they enter the interlayer regions and allow the sheets to slide across one another, making graphite an excellent, soft lubricant. Diamond, by contrast, has a rigid, three-dimensional structure, like cross-braced steel girders of a trestle bridge. Carbon atoms are densely packed in a

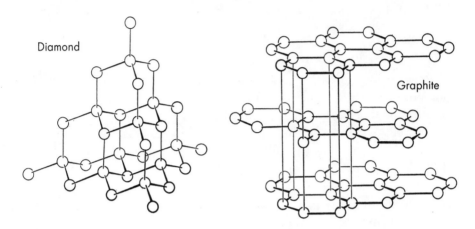

Diamond

Graphite

The contrasting properties of graphite and diamond originate from their very different atomic structures. In diamond (*left*), carbon atoms are each surrounded by a pyramid of four other carbons, creating a three-dimensional atomic network of unparalleled strength. In graphite, on the other hand, each carbon is strongly bonded to three neighbors in layers, while bonds between layers are relatively weak.

diamond; in fact, diamond has more atoms in a given volume than any other solid.

Scientists wondered what extremes of temperature and pressure were required to form diamond instead of graphite. The science of thermodynamics, which helps chemists relate a material's stability to the energy of its atomic arrangement, provided the answer. Chemists learned that atoms always try to arrange themselves in a way that minimizes their stored energy. Think of different substances as boulders strewn around a mountainous valley. Some rocks sit precariously on the mountain slopes, ready to tumble down at the slightest jostle. These stones have excess energy—called gravitational potential energy because it is so readily available and ready to be unleashed. Explosive chemicals behave in this way—a slight jiggle and the atoms can settle into a more stable arrangement, releasing lots of energy in the process. Other boulders, however, rest firmly on the valley floor and nothing much will move them. These stable boulders, like everyday stable chemicals, have lower potential energy and therefore do not change spontaneously.

At any given combination of temperature and pressure, the structure of a substance most likely to form will be the one with lowest energy. Very high pressure, as you might expect, favors densely packed arrangements of atoms, like diamond; very high temperature tends to stabilize more open structures, like graphite. Of course, it's not quite this simple. Other factors, like the size of the atoms or the way they vibrate, also play a role. But the basic idea holds true.

The science of thermodynamics took the guesswork out of predicting stable forms of a substance. If you know a few basic facts about the forms—their density, their atomic structure, and the energy tied up in their atomic bonds—you can often calculate which one will be most stable under a given set of conditions. Fortunately, the physical properties of diamond and graphite, the two competing forms of carbon, had been measured with great precision.

At very low temperatures and pressures the measurements were easy: scientists compared the amount of energy stored in graphite verses diamond by determining the heat released as a given weight of each substance burned. These experiments showed that the carbon-carbon bonds in diamond hold more energy than those in graphite. Like a boulder poised on the side of a steep valley, diamond at room conditions seemed ready to tumble down to the more stable graphite form. At low pressure, graphite is always the stable form.

The only reason diamond doesn't spontaneously convert to graphite is that carbon-carbon bonds are too strong to break without a large energy jolt. You can turn a diamond to graphite by burning it with a blowtorch, but that takes a lot of energy. It's as if a precariously perched boulder, though high above the valley floor, is sitting in a deep pit. You'd have to lift the boulder up over the lip of the pit before it could tumble down the slope to a more stable resting place.

At extremely high pressure, where atoms are forced together and atomic bonds are compressed, the story is quite different. The graphite structure collapses as weakly bonded layers of carbon atoms are forced uncomfortably close together. The internal energy of the squashed structure increases dramatically under such pressure. But diamond, with its dense atomic arrangement, stabilizes at high pressure; its bonds hardly change at all. At high enough pressure, diamond has the lower energy and is therefore the more stable form.

Thermodynamics allowed scientists to calculate whether diamond or graphite would be the more stable form for any combination of temperature and pressure. During the period between the two world wars, many scientists attempted to calculate the relative stabilities of graphite and diamond, and all agreed: at room temperature, up to a pressure of at least 10,000 atmospheres, graphite remains the stable form. At the higher temperatures needed to make carbon atoms sufficiently mobile to change structure, pressures must be much higher. These researchers produced a carbon phase diagram, a graph of temperature versus pressure that showed which conditions

The phase diagram of carbon shows whether diamond or graphite is the more stable form for any combination of pressure and temperature. In this early phase diagram, calculated by Frederick D. Rossini and Ralph S. Jessup in 1938, a line separates the high-pressure region where diamond is stable from the low-pressure graphite region. This figure guided the efforts of many would-be diamond makers.

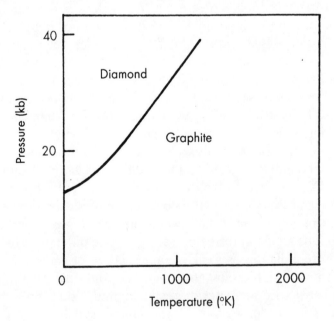

would produce which form. The diamond field revealed the high temperatures and pressures at which diamond's energy is lower; the graphite field corresponded to the stable lower energy state for that mineral.

The message was unambiguous. If diamond was to be made in a laboratory by high-pressure methods, a lot more pressure was needed. Percy Bridgman was the man for the job.

3

✧

The Legacy of
Percy Bridgman

If intensely hot carbon . . . were subjected to an enormous pressure might not diamonds be formed? . . . Would you send me a diamond so made?

— Miss Martin to Percy Bridgman, June 10, 1923

I have thought a good deal about the possibility of making diamonds by subjecting carbon to high pressures, and whenever I have had a new kind of apparatus made that presented features that I had not tried before, I have always surreptitiously put into it a little piece of carbon before applying the pressure. . . . I will certainly send you a diamond when I find how to make them—the second one—the first has been promised for a long time to Mrs. Bridgman.

— Percy Bridgman to Miss Martin, July 4, 1923

Armed with a vision of diamond's violent origins and a growing body of research testifying to the methods that wouldn't work, scientists were ready to tackle the synthesis problem with new intensity. By the first decades of this century virtually everyone in the diamond-making game agreed that pressure was the key to diamond synthesis.

No one was more fascinated by pressure's transforming power than Percy W. Bridgman, the Harvard physicist who ushered in the modern era of high-pressure research by squeezing just about everything he could get his hands on. He devised new ways to compress solids, liquids, and gases between steel vise jaws, and he used novel techniques to measure the properties of the compressed matter. Along the way, he produced some amazing phenomena. Bridgman found new kinds of ice by compressing ordinary water. He watched everyday gases like nitrogen and carbon dioxide turn to crystalline solids under pressure. He caused simple salts to become metals and observed minerals crushed to half their normal volumes. In a half-century of Nobel prize–winning research, Percy Bridgman studied almost a thousand different substances, yet no single problem occupied more of his career or posed more of a challenge than his attempts to change graphite into diamond.

What drives a scientist to study matter at high pressure? For some it's the massive steel tools of the trade—machines that harness thousands of tons of force and can crush rock to dust or flatten an automobile into a few cubic feet of scrap metal. Surely some scientists are captivated by pressure's awesome power.

But there is something more subtle in the allure of squeezing matter. In a scientific world that focuses ever more intently on the incomprehensibly small and unimaginably brief phenomena of the quantum world, in a century in which relativity has turned our perception of time, space, and physical reality on its head, it is comforting to do science on real stuff that you can see and hold in your hand. There is a concrete satisfaction in taking a chunk of matter, placing it in the jaws of a powerful vise, and turning the screw.

Percy Bridgman understood that allure. As an American boy growing up in the 1890s, he accepted the country's prevailing view that inventors Thomas Edison and Alexander Graham Bell were among the greatest living physicists, and he embraced those inventors' empirical philosophy. As twentieth-century physics gradually became more abstract, Bridgman retained the belief that models of the universe had no meaning if they could not be tested by direct observation. The only meaningful questions, he said, were those that could be answered by running real experiments in a real world. And that is what he did.

Percy Williams Bridgman was born in 1882 in Cambridge, Massachusetts, the college town that he called home for almost all his life. His father, a journalist and author of earnest books and poems on social issues, embraced the inflexible Puritan values of strict Congregationalism. Young Percy, captivated by the unambiguous empiricism of science, rebelled against such blind orthodoxy and ultimately rejected any organized religion, much to the sorrow of his father. Yet he retained the Protestant ethic of honesty, idealism, and hard work throughout his academic and professional life. He applied these traits as a diligent student, both in the public schools of Newton, Massachusetts, and at Harvard University, where he graduated summa cum laude in 1904.

Bridgman spent his entire professional career at Harvard, where he rose through the ranks from doctoral student and research fellow to professor emeritus. Friends and colleagues remember him as a man of reserved grace and quiet charm. In all of his passionate interests—chess, handball, gardening, photography, mountain climbing, and, most of all, high-pressure research—he found an outlet for his solitary kind of genius.

Bridgman was a loner. He had little patience with committee work, faculty politics, or teaching, and he successfully avoided routine university chores. He was described as a terse, even cryptic lecturer by undergraduates, and he was uncompromising in his demands on students, who rarely lived up to his standards. He was also disappointed in most graduate research students, even though he had the pick of the best young physicists in the country. In the early 1920s, John C. Slater, later a leading theoretician of quantum mechanics, and J. Robert Oppenheimer, who was to become the controversial head of the Manhattan Project, were among his trainees. Yet, given a choice, he rebuffed such bright students and worked alone or with his research assistant, Leonard Abbott.

Rain or shine, Bridgman arrived at his physics lab by bicycle. He often wore an old rumpled suit and slouched hat that looked as if they'd been slept in. Those who met him in later years, when the Nobel prize winner had to deflect a steady flow of gawkers and favor-seekers, remember a man fiercely protective of his time and privacy.

When Hatten S. Yoder, Jr., a distinguished high-pressure researcher in his own right, had his first, strange meeting with the legendary figure in the fall of 1946, he found that Bridgman budgeted his time to the minute, with high-pressure experiments dictating when and where he could be seen. As a graduate student in geology

Percy Bridgman lecturing on high-pressure research before the Cornell Section of the American Chemical Society in 1948. (Courtesy of Harvard University: Cruft Photo Lab.)

at MIT, a few miles downstream from Bridgman's Harvard lab, Yoder had called for an appointment to talk about the design of a high-pressure apparatus. Promptly at the appointed hour Bridgman came to his laboratory door, opened it a few inches, and said, "You have seven minutes."

Standing on opposite sides of the partially opened door, Yoder asked the master about pressure vessels, gaskets, and heating elements. Bridgman was cordial and generous with advice, but after seven minutes he abruptly ended the meeting; it was time for another experiment.

Yoder was granted several other interviews—on one memorable occasion he spent a full half hour in Bridgman's tiny cubicle office—but they were all no-nonsense meetings. Bridgman would talk only about science with a single-mindedness that many found to be off-putting; he had no time to waste on social niceties. Alvin Van Valkenburg, a high-pressure researcher at the National Bureau of Standards, remembered that, outside of a small circle of friends, "everybody was scared of him."

But whatever Percy Bridgman's shortcomings as a conversationalist or socializer, he more than made up for them by being one of the greatest experimentalists of his generation. He was a brilliant inventor with exceptional manual dexterity and a thorough practical knowledge of metalworking and machine tools. Much of his most significant work involved the design and construction of advanced pressure seals and gauges. In fact, Bridgman's research career actually began with a lucky discovery in the machine shop.

In 1905, while working on his doctoral thesis—a rather ordinary study on the effects of modest pressure on matter and light—a minor explosion destroyed a critical piece of glassware. Unfortunately, the replacement part would have to be shipped from Europe. Frustrated, Bridgman busied himself modifying an existing high-pressure apparatus he found elsewhere in the lab. In the process he stumbled upon a new design for high-pressure experiments that would become the cornerstone of his career.

Bridgman's extraordinary discovery involved a simple modification in the machinery used to generate high pressure. Every high-pressure experimental system incorporates three principal components: a press, an experimental device, and a sample. The press is simply a frame or support that generates force, usually along a central vertical axis. The press dominates a high-pressure laboratory, often standing taller than a man, and usually has cylindrical steel supports as thick as tree trunks to brace its massive metal and plates. Any of three different mechanisms—screws, weights, or hydraulics—can be employed to provide the compressive force. Presses are usually rated in tons—typically a few hundred tons in Bridgman's day—according to the force that can be exerted on a sample.

Bridgman's antiquated press at Harvard used a giant screw to apply force. It operated something like an antique printing press, a hand-operated wine press, or the vise in your workroom. Although Bridgman had to heft an awkward six-foot-long wrench to turn the central load-applying compressor screw, his apparatus was much less cumbersome than those with older screw drives. He recalled seeing "enormous capstan-like arrangements that required the force of one or two men to operate" in other high-pressure laboratories.

Heavy metal weights piled on top of a press provided an effective, though even more laborious, alternative means of applying pressure, and some presses were even fitted with giant overhead tanks of liquid mercury to provide continuous variation of the overhead weight. But all things considered, the most convenient presses employed a hydraulic ram to generate large forces along the vertical axis.

The experimental device, which rests between the flat steel plates of the press, is a carefully crafted metal machine that transfers the press's great force to a small sample. The design and construction of a device are complicated by the requirement that it constantly adapt to the size of the sample, which invariably becomes smaller when squeezed. Thus the sample chamber must have at least one movable wall, with the moving parts sealed against leakage. One of the most common devices in Bridgman's day was a kind of piston-in-cylinder arrangement in which the sample was placed in a closed cylinder resting on the bottom surface of the press. A snug-fitting metal rod, pressed into the sample chamber from above, applied the pressure. Other devices used a simple pair of circular anvils or a deformable casing of iron or copper to transfer pressure.

Perhaps the most challenging part of squeezing matter is keeping the sample from squirting out; the design of the sample chamber is thus critical to success. Physicists at the beginning of the twentieth century found that many samples were difficult, if not impossible, to confine at high pressure. A central problem was finding a suitable leakproof seal. Researchers experimented with new gasket materials, coated contact surfaces with sealing compounds made of thick oil or grease, machined metal parts with painstaking care, and plated parts to achieve a perfect fit. Even so, the samples—whether gases, liquids, or solids—often squirted out of the sample chambers. As a result, experimentalists at the turn of the century rarely achieved sustained pressures of more than 2,000 or 3,000 atmospheres before their sample chambers failed.

However, by some combination of luck, intuition, and keen observation, Bridgman stumbled upon both a wonderful new experimental design and the perfect material with which to execute it. He

Bridgman's unsupported-area packing represented a new kind of high-pressure connection between a pipe and pressure vessel. The area of the gasket seal is less than the area of the sample, so the pressure on the seal is always greater, preventing sample leaks. This figure, from Bridgman's treatise *The Physics of High Pressure*, provides an enlarged view of the connection.

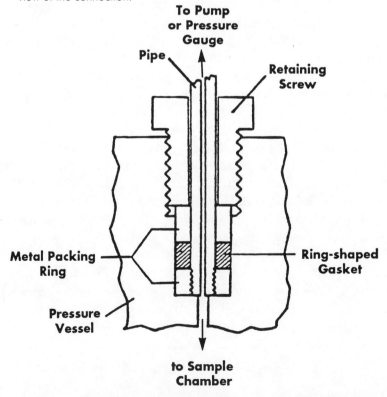

used a very soft solid as the pressure seal and kept this soft solid at a pressure always a bit *higher* than that of the sample. In this way, the pressurized sample could not possibly leak past the higher pressure of the seal.

To accomplish this feat, Bridgman substituted an easy-to-assemble two-piece piston for the traditional single metal piece. He inserted a short metal piston segment that looked something like an inverted mushroom with a flat disk-shaped head and short cylindrical stem into the cylinder, flat end first. Around the mushroom's stem Bridgman placed a ring of Sioux Indian pipestone, a soft, carvable rock. He then placed a second piston around the first. The second piston was a carefully machined cylinder with a central hole the same diameter as the mushroom stem; its shaft was slightly longer, to accommodate the stem with room to spare. The beauty of Bridgman's device lies in its exploitation of pressure as a force acting on an area. Regardless of the force applied to the piston, the ring-shaped pipestone gasket has less area and therefore is subjected to more pressure than the circular sample of identical diameter.

Bridgman later recalled the crucial discovery: "In the interval of waiting for the replacement [part for my thesis work] I tried to make other use of my apparatus for generating pressure. While designing a closure for a pressure vessel, so that it could be rapidly assembled or taken apart, I saw that the design hit upon did more than originally intended; the vessel automatically became tighter when pressure was increased, so that there was no reason why it should ever leak."

This discovery of an impervious, self-tightening seal transformed high-pressure research. "The whole high-pressure field opened up almost at once before me, like a vision of a promised land, with the discovery of the unsupported area principle of packing, by which the only limit to the pressures attainable was the strength of the metal parts of the apparatus." The original thesis project was abandoned, and Percy Bridgman took off on a lifetime of exploration in high pressure.

Within a couple of years he could routinely attain pressures of 7,000 atmospheres, or about 50 tons per square inch—considerably higher than that achieved in any other laboratory, even though Bridgman was hampered by his antiquated screw compressor. Rather than immediately strive for even higher pressures with a modified press, however, Bridgman focused his attention on a less exotic problem. He realized that attaining high pressures meant little without the means to measure those pressures. He therefore spent much of his graduate student years devising new ways to measure the unprecedented pressures he was now able to achieve.

Scientists have created a bewildering variety of units for pressure. Pressure is defined as a force applied to an area, such as pounds per square inch. One atmosphere (the unit used in most of this book) is produced by a 14.7-pound weight on an area of one square inch; one atmosphere is also approximately equivalent to the pressure generated when one kilogram pushes down on an area of a square centimeter. A bar, another common pressure unit, is defined as one million dynes (a unit of force) per square centimeter. Fortunately, that pressure is only slightly less than one atmosphere (1 bar = 0.987 atmosphere), so bars and atmospheres are more or less interchangeable.

Meteorologists, who often measure atmospheric pressure with a mercury-filled barometer, talk about inches of mercury; the weight of all the air above you is more or less equal to the weight of a liquid mercury column thirty inches high. To make matters even more complicated, physicists decided a few years ago that the official international unit of pressure should be pascals, defined as a newton (another unit of force) per square meter—about equal to the force of a feather resting on your finger. It takes exactly 10,000 pascals, or 10 kilopascals, to make a bar, which, as you remember, is close to an atmosphere. I could also tell you about torrs and slugs, but you don't really want to know.

Bridgman's first step was to establish a primary pressure scale, based only on direct measurement of force per area. In the nineteenth century, for pressures up to a few hundred atmospheres, scientists used tall open columns of mercury to do the trick. In France, for example, researchers used the Eiffel Tower to support a mercury column several hundred feet tall (one atmosphere is equal to about thirty inches of mercury), while even higher columns were constructed in a deep French coal mine. But at the pressures of Bridgman's new device, the open mercury column would have to be several miles tall. Obviously, another approach was required. Bridgman based his primary pressure measurement on an accurate set of metal weights (the force) pushing down on a precisely machined piston of known cross-sectional area. In such an assembly, the pressure—the force acting on the area—could be calculated directly from the weight pushing on the piston.

In principle, all of his experiments could have employed such a pressure-measuring system, but handling heavy weights and ensuring precise piston areas can be a tricky business. It proved much easier to use the primary weight scale in just one crucial set of measurements in order to calibrate a more convenient secondary scale based on the way an easily measured property varies with pressure, the same way we commonly use the volume of mercury as a measure of temperature in a thermometer. Many researchers had relied on a fluid's volume change—its compressibility—to measure pressure, while others calibrated pressure by observing the elastic deformation of a metal bar or spring. Bridgman used a different approach, based on the significant decrease of mercury's electrical resistance with pressure. His mercury resistance gauge would provide a fast and reliable way to measure pressure for decades of experiments to come.

The results of Bridgman's thesis, published as two papers in the 1909 *Proceedings of the American Academy of Arts and Sciences* under the collective title "The Measurement of High Hydrostatic Pressures," presented a comprehensive protocol for attaining and measuring unprecedented pressures in the laboratory. Yet, in spite of fifty pages of experimental details, Bridgman did not divulge the geometry of his double-piston apparatus or the identity of his new pipestone packing material. He knew he had the edge on the competition and, for a time at least, he alone would profit from his discovery.

Armed with new techniques to confine and calibrate pressure, Bridgman was ready to set a few world pressure records. As a research fellow in 1910, he replaced his antiquated screw compressor with a hydraulic ram press and immediately achieved more than 20,000 atmospheres, a pressure so high that he was almost apologetic about claiming it. "The magnitude of fluid pressure mentioned here requires brief comment, because without a word of explanation it may seem so large as to cast discredit on the accuracy of all the data."

Within a few short years Percy Bridgman had created a laboratory like none other in the world. He had at his disposal the apparatus to squeeze samples as they had never been squeezed before, and the logical research strategy was obvious to him. He decided "to use this new technique to the limit, attacking with it any problems in which the information to be expected from the behavior under high pressures seemed likely to be of significance."

He then engaged in an unabashed program of experimental prospecting, pressurizing almost anything he could lay his hands on, confident that a world of fascinating phenomena lay in wait. He acknowledged that "this is not the usual procedure in scientific work, in which the problem usually presents itself, and the suitable technique discovered." But he proceeded without apology, making wonderful discoveries and in the process serving as a model for countless thousands of researchers to follow—scientists who, in our age of exorbitantly expensive research apparatus, become tied for life to a piece of fancy hardware. When scientists spend a million dollars for an electron microscope, or a group invests several billion dollars for a superconducting supercollider, it becomes imperative for them to select experiments that require that piece of equipment.

That's not necessarily a bad situation, especially if you can make discoveries like Percy Bridgman's. After some fairly routine studies of metal compressibilities, he made his first high-pressure headlines by squeezing water to more than 20,000 atmospheres—five times more than any previous water investigation. At such pressures, Bridgman declared, "results for water are much more varied and richer . . . appearing in no less than five [solid] forms." In 120 pages of details, he described the temperatures and pressures at which the extraordinary and unexpected forms of high-pressure ice occur—each variety heralded by a sudden change in sample volume.

One of these varieties, Ice VI, stable to at least 95°C, or 200°F, was dubbed "hot ice" in the popular press and evoked a flurry of ill-founded interest in commercial applications. E. F. McPike, manager of an Illinois Central Railroad fruit-shipping concern, wrote to Bridgman, "I have read a brief note in the newspaper regarding your production of a solidified form of hot water. Might we inquire if in your opinion this process has commercial possibilities for use in transit in a manner similar to ice to protect fruits and vegetables . . . against cold instead of heat? Portable heaters have been used to some extent by carriers and if there is any prospect of a better process we would be glad to know about it." Bridgman had to inform Mr. McPike that Ice VI, like all the other high-pressure forms, can only exist under pressure and melts immediately upon its release.

Following his fascinating work with water in 1911, Bridgman tackled other liquids. In 1912 he studied a dozen common organic fluids, including alcohols, ether, and acetone; the next year he expanded his domain to include more and more materials—solids, liquids, and gases. In 1914 he squeezed a dozen common salts and several pure elements including sodium, potassium, phosphorus, and mercury.

For the next twenty years he studied the compressibility and electrical properties of hundreds of compounds at pressures up to 20,000 atmospheres. Every experiment was virgin territory, and time after time he uncovered new crystalline structures that can only form at high pressure—just like diamonds. But except for a few high-pressure electrical resistance measurements on graphite made in the early 1920s, Bridgman did not publish any data on the forms of carbon, nor did he record any concerted effort to make diamonds in those early days. But it would have been strange indeed if he had not, on occasion, placed a small disk of graphite in his mighty press, just to see what happened.

✧ ✧ ✧

For two decades Bridgman was content to study matter at pressures up to 20,000 atmospheres, but higher pressures beckoned. Fascinating physics waited to be explored, and throughout the later stages of his career, from the mid-1930s on, he concentrated on improving the design of his high-pressure gear.

Bridgman suspected that there were probably limits to the pressures humans could achieve in the laboratory. Even the best-built experimental apparatus had a limit to the amount of stress it could endure before exploding. In fact, high-pressure researchers often refer to their sealed cylinders, especially those pressurized with gas, as "bombs"—a term that is quite realistic in its bravado.

Every high-pressure experiment carries with it the danger of catastrophic failure, and rare is the worker in the field who does not duck flying metal at some point in his or her career. The most serious high-pressure accident at Harvard occurred on May 19, 1922, when engi-

Bridgman's high-pressure "bomb" (circa 1950) consisted of a vertical hydraulic piston that was pressed into a cylinder. (Courtesy of H. S. Yoder, Jr.)

neering research fellow Atherton K. Dunbar and assistant William Connell were killed while pressurizing a tank with oxygen. A terrible explosion ensued, as described in the following contemporary newspaper account: "The middle section of the basement was completely wrecked. Dunbar was blown to pieces, and the carpenter Mr. Connell was instantly killed. Eight students in the room above were injured, the floor being lifted bodily, and a heavy dynamo turned over onto some of them." Shortly thereafter, Harvard's high-pressure research was moved to a sturdy concrete-and-wood garage that had previously served the campus ROTC unit. The new research facility, a bit crude but eminently functional, was christened the Dunbar Laboratory. For almost forty years it was the site of Percy Bridgman's experimental triumphs.

Although Bridgman was not involved in the Dunbar tragedy, he braved more than his fair share of explosions and devoted an entire chapter of his 1931 book, *The Physics of High Pressure*, to the "variety of interesting ways" that a pressure vessel could rupture. Pressure systems, like chains, fail at their weakest point. Bridgman found that pistons made of tough file steels or ball-bearing steels were sufficiently strong as they compressed a sample, but the steel cylinders, which bulged out under tension, frequently cracked and exploded. Bridgman realized that this problem was not unique to pressure research. The same kind of failure concerned the military, whose cylinders discharged bullets and explosive shells. To solve this problem, Bridgman devised a clever method for shrink-fitting a thick steel girdle around the central cylinder to compress the tube and reduce the chance of high-pressure failure.

Nevertheless, laboratory explosions were inevitable. In experiments with sealed tubes, failure often occurred when one end of the pressure vessel sheared off. The resulting explosion could launch the contents, including the sample and metal rods used to pack the sample chamber, at the speed of a rifle bullet. Once one of Bridgman's Dunbar Laboratory bombs blew out and embedded a steel filler rod deep in the wall a few feet away. Bridgman felt it was a lucky miss, for he often walked by that very spot on the way to his cubbyhole office. After the incident, it is said, he would step carefully across the spot. By the 1950s, after decades of work, Bridgman's lab walls had quite a few impressive holes.

Harvard University's Dunbar Laboratory, circa 1950, home of Percy Bridgman's high-pressure lab, was converted from an ROTC garage. (Courtesy of H. S. Yoder, Jr.)

Every high-pressure experiment is limited by the strength of the materials used to build the apparatus; every material will break when stressed beyond its limits. Even the strongest steels—even diamonds —will break if pushed too far. Designers of high-pressure apparatus thus focused on two major concerns: selecting the strongest available materials and finding the most dependable way to build a device out of them. These problems were never far from Bridgman's mind, and he jumped at the chance to build better equipment as stronger, more advanced steels became available.

His simplest device, which is still used today in many laborato-

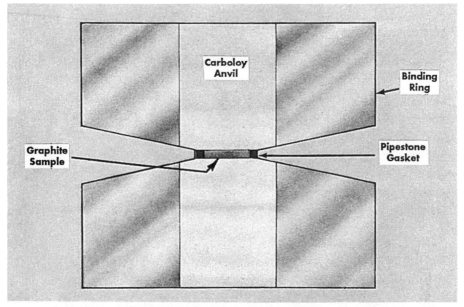

Bridgman's simple opposed-anvil device featured two tapered anvils that clamped together like a vise. A ring-shaped gasket confined a sample, which could be squeezed to more than 100,000 atmospheres. (Courtesy of F. R. Boyd.)

ries, was nothing more than a vise with opposed tapered anvils. The first model, introduced in 1935, employed anvils of hardened steel with flat round faces a quarter inch across. The opposed anvils could be rammed together to generate 50,000 atmospheres of pressure on the sample, which was surrounded and contained by a ring of pipestone. The device was relatively easy to use and was soon dubbed the "simple squeezer." Within a few years Bridgman had compressed more than one hundred elements and compounds to this extreme pressure. He reported his results in epic scientific papers with titles like "Polymorphic transitions of 35 substances to 50,000 kg/cm^2" (1937) and "The compression of 46 substances to 50,000 kg/cm^2" (1940)—titles that speak of his exhaustive research effort.

In the late 1930s Bridgman learned of a new material, a variety of tungsten carbide sold by General Electric's Carboloy Division. The new metal was much harder and stiffer than ordinary steels, and Bridgman lost no time constructing new carbide anvils. He supported the anvils with shrink-fit girdles of steel and placed them in his press.

Almost at once he achieved a useful pressure he believed to be in excess of 100,000 atmospheres. (We now know it was closer to 70,000 atmospheres—still a record for his time.) Armed with this extraordinary squeezing power, Bridgman commenced a period of incredible productivity. "Modest" pressures below 50,000 atmospheres were a cinch and led to mammoth surveys like "Rough compressions of 177 substances to 40,000 kg/cm^2," completed in 1948. During the 1947–48 academic year Percy Bridgman averaged almost one new sample a day, six days a week.

Part of Bridgman's astonishing productivity was the result of his machining skill, which allowed him to build and repair high-pressure devices himself. He often made his own steel pressure vessels even though he had a full-time machinist, Charles Chase, working with him. His prowess and patience with a lathe are legendary. In one publication he described the extraordinary efforts he made to drill his own high-pressure tubing, taking extreme care to start with high-grade metal, centering the drill, and rotating the tubing at high speed while keeping the growing hole clean. "It is easy, if all precautions are observed, to drill a hole $\frac{1}{16}$ of an inch in diameter 17 inches long in from seven to eight hours."

As the world's foremost authority on high pressure and master of the world's foremost array of high-pressure equipment, Percy Bridgman was no stranger to the idea of making diamonds. He reminisced about the quest to synthesize diamond in the November 1955 issue of *Scientific American:* "I suppose that over the last 25 years an average of two or three people a year have come into my office, offering to share the secret and the profit of making diamonds in return for my constructing the apparatus and reducing the idea to practice. The problem has got into the thriller literature, and I have often encountered the belief that the successful solver of this problem would be in danger of his life from the Diamond Syndicate."

The professor was hardly immune from the lure of transmuting graphite into diamond. David T. Griggs, among the only Ph.D. candidates to work directly under Bridgman, wrote, "It was my privilege to work in Bridgman's laboratory during the period when working pressures were increased from 20,000 to 100,000 [atmospheres]. As each new apparatus was readied for trial, I noticed that Bridgman would become secretive and brusque. During the first run, visitors were not welcome. I subsequently learned that in each case *graphite* was the first substance tried."

Bridgman's strategy for making diamonds was simple: he just squeezed a sample of graphite as hard as possible between two strong surfaces. The hardest steels crafted into his simple squeezer splintered at about 60,000 atmospheres without producing any change in the graphite, so Bridgman turned to his new superhard Carboloy anvils. By replacing steel components with Carboloy, he could subject graphite to much higher pressures. The opposed carbide anvils provided an estimated 150,000 atmospheres before they broke—still not enough to transform diamond. But Bridgman had not run out of ideas. Next he tried a single carbide anvil, less than a tenth of an inch across, which he crushed into a flat carbide surface. Bridgman reported pressures estimated at an incredible 425,000 atmospheres—about 3,000 tons per square inch—yet graphite persisted, bouncing right back to its original form when the pressure was released. Bridgman abandoned that effort to make diamond with the wry observation that in graphite he had discovered "nature's best spring."

Bridgman was not through with the diamond-making game, however. General Electric and its Carboloy Division, the principal suppliers of the carbide components, which could only be shaped with diamond-impregnated tools, and the Norton and Carborundum companies, the largest consumers of industrial diamonds, joined forces in January 1941 and persuaded Percy Bridgman to spearhead another diamond synthesis effort. They installed a brand-new thousand-ton hydraulic press at Harvard's Dunbar Lab, provided a staff of assistants to help build and operate experimental devices of Bridgman's design, and committed resources for a five-year research and development program.

It was well known that at room pressure and very high temperatures (above 1,500°C in the absence of oxygen), diamond reverts to graphite. Perhaps, Bridgman and others thought, the reverse would happen at high pressure and similar temperatures. The principal roadblock to this approach was that steel and carbide anvils soften at high temperature, thus greatly reducing the pressure they could apply. In one set of experiments, Bridgman subjected graphite mixed with tiny diamond seed crystals to red heat (perhaps 700°C) at 75,000 atmospheres. Nothing happened.

In a second series of experiments, Bridgman heated wafers of graphite to 2,800°C and quickly transferred them to the press. The seven-second operation proved too slow, the graphite cooled too quickly, and again no diamonds formed, although the experimenters did manage to destroy all traces of the original diamond seeds, which had converted to graphite. Unbeknownst to Bridgman, P. L. Gunther and his German colleagues had tried the exact same approach in the early 1940s. They too had been unsuccessful.

After those failures, Bridgman and his coworkers tried yet another procedure. This time they took a disk-shaped sample of graphite and diamond seed crystals and surrounded it with thermite, a chemical that burns at very high temperature. They pressurized the sample assembly between carbide anvils and then triggered a fire, thereby creating sustained conditions of 30,000 atmospheres and 3,000°C for a few moments. Once again, no diamonds formed, but for the first time the diamond seed crystals did not revert to graphite, suggesting that the investigators were on the right track.

The principal conclusion of the unsuccessful research was that sustained temperatures greater than 1,000°C at pressures above 50,000 atmospheres—conditions beyond the Harvard lab's capabilities—would be required to make diamonds. Bridgman had been trying to make diamonds for only two years when he was diverted by the demands of other World War II research. In one project he was called upon to measure the compressibilities of uranium and plutonium—data critical to the Manhattan Project. The diamond-making effort had to be abandoned.

In 1946, Percy Bridgman was honored with the Nobel prize in physics "for the invention of an apparatus to produce extremely high pressures, and for the discoveries he made therewith in the field of high-pressure physics." Four decades of achievements had placed him in the foremost rank of scientists. He had overcome obstacle after obstacle, broken record after record, and single-handedly transformed the science of pressure. Even so, the mystery of diamond making had eluded him.

✧ ✧ ✧

In the spring of 1959 scientists at the National Bureau of Standards approached Harvard University Press and proposed that the experimental papers of Percy Bridgman be collected in one set of volumes. Many of his more than two hundred papers, including classic descriptions of high-pressure apparatus and studies of hundreds of materials, were scattered among dozens of different periodicals, many of which were unavailable in smaller libraries. Bridgman agreed to collate and edit the volumes himself, while the National Science Foundation supported the project with a grant in July 1961.

Bridgman selected 198 papers for inclusion in the seven-volume set and prepared a preface, annotations, and indexes for the work. It was to be his last scientific effort. In the spring of 1961 he was increasingly troubled by what was at first thought to be muscular rheumatism. The correct diagnosis, an inoperable bone cancer known as Paget's disease, was made in midsummer. Suffering from ever-increasing pain and loss of muscle control, Bridgman worked on the collected papers to the very last day, when the indexes to his life's work were completed and sent to the publisher. Then, determined to control his own destiny, Percy Bridgman went to the pumphouse behind his summer home, sawed off the barrel of a shotgun, placed it in his mouth, and pulled the trigger. Like the careful experimenter he was, he left nothing to chance.

Though he gave no formal classes and taught few students, Bridgman left an incalculable legacy to solid-state physicists and high-pressure researchers. His colleagues mourned the loss not only of a friend and associate, but also of his tremendous knowledge, much of it gained through years in the laboratory and never written down, knowledge that died with him.

Some saw in Percy Bridgman's last violent act a final affirmation of his intellectual honesty and integrity—an effort to spare friends and family the pain and expense of a protracted decline. Others condemned the suicide as a thoughtless cruelty to his wife and children. Who can imagine what passed through his mind or what his pain must have been as he wrote his last words: "It isn't decent for Society to make a man do this thing himself. Probably this is the last day I will be able to do it myself."

4

✧

Baltzar von Platen and the Incredible Diamond Machine

As I passed the School of Botany, I saw that one wall was covered with Virginia Creeper. Its leaves were a beautiful red. Every autumn brought the change from green to red, and passers-by would pause at the display of colour in sudden admiration. I was one of these passers-by, and had no idea that my pleasure in this seasonal beauty would later play an important role in my life. . . . I had no suspicion that later this sight would show me the way to construct a machine which makes diamonds.

—Baltzar von Platen, *Modern Very High Pressure Techniques,* 1962

Of all the many attempts to create diamonds in a laboratory, none was more outrageously impractical and shamelessly extravagant than the effort of ASEA, Sweden's major electrical company. Then again, the Swedish company's diamond project was conceived and constructed by Baltzar von Platen, a scientist who was, by some accounts, quite mad.

In the early 1940s two rival companies had taken up the diamond-making challenge. It was no coincidence that both groups were principally concerned with electrical power, appliances, and light. Both companies relied on diamond tools to machine great dynamos and other electrical devices. Both had considerable expertise in using electricity to generate the high temperatures critical to diamond-making success. And both expected to win the race. The two companies were Sweden's Allmänna Svenska Elektriska Aktiebolaget, or ASEA

Baltzar von Platen (Left) and Erik Lundblad, circa 1955. (Courtesy of Erik Lundblad.)

(roughly translated, Swedish General Electric Company), and America's General Electric Company. Of the two, ASEA always seemed to be one step ahead.

The ASEA effort started with the dreams of one man. Baltzar von Platen—called "a genius maniac" by some—was the kind of half-crazy inventor stereotyped in popular movies and dime-store novels. Tracy Hall, a key player in the General Electric diamond-making effort, first met von Platen in 1957 during a visit to Stockholm. "He drove an ancient car," Hall recalls. "When he stopped at a red light he'd turn the engine off. Then he'd restart it when the light turned green." Longtime associate Erik Lundblad was well acquainted with von Platen's quirks. "He carried a name well known in Sweden since the eighteenth century, when his namesake built a great canal from the Baltic Sea to the North Sea and was raised by the king to the nobility. Everyone believed that our Baltzar was [a descendant] of the old man, and he himself spared no pain in letting people believe they were right—which they were not."

Some colleagues speculated that his idiosyncrasies may have arisen, in part, from a facial deformity—a large disfiguring birthmark on the left side of his chin that embarrassed him greatly. But whatever the cause, he marched to a very different drummer. Baltzar von Platen's most famous invention, a portable thermal refrigerator that produced ice with a gas flame, epitomized his quirky brilliance. He used an ammonia refrigerant that was vaporized by a blue-hot gas flame at one end of his contraption; the ammonia gas flowed through the system to condense in refrigeration coils at the other end. Before the universal availability of electricity, von Platen's thermal refrigerators, manufactured and marketed by Electrolux, were a godsend that transformed rural life in many parts of Europe and America.

This paradoxical appliance was the height of sanity compared to von Platen's other efforts. With his reputation as an inventor assured, he went on to play the role with gusto. "His imagination was unlimited," Lundblad recalls. "His destiny was to solve the world energy problem by designing a perpetual motion system. To make the idea more reliable he declared the second law of thermodynamics . . . invalid." Evidently, a lot of people believed him. Major corporations, including Volvo, sponsored his research at considerable expense. "Once they realized they had been swindled they often felt so embarrassed they never opened any lawsuits."

He began thinking about synthetic diamonds as early as 1930, when he read an article describing the extreme conditions required to convert graphite to diamond. He knew that the tremendous temperatures and pressures necessary were too much for any device made of steel. He concluded that to make diamonds you had to accept as inevitable the destruction of your machine in the process. But, he emphasized, if you accept the fact that your machine's destruction is inevitable, that knowledge allows you to approach the design in a radical new way: to build the device as if it were already broken.

Many years after the ASEA effort, Baltzar von Platen contributed a strange, rambling chapter on his diamond-making machine to the 1962 monograph *Modern Very High Pressure Techniques*, which is for the most part a rather dry, technical book. However, in prose atypical of scientific exposition, von Platen revealed the mystical source of his inspiration, which was found in a bit of ancient mythology regarding the origin of brilliantly colored autumnal foliage. According to the myth, the spirit-philosopher Demiurge convinced leaves to begin the inevitable process of death and disintegration while still attached to their tree, rather than succumb to death by falling to the ground in a fresh and green state. By beginning the irreversible process of decay before falling from the branches, leaves provide some beauty and benefit for others and, in the process, cheat death out of two or three weeks.

This quaint story evidently came forcefully to mind as Baltzar von Platen contemplated the diamond problem. "All at once a thought struck me and an association sprang to life. It was utterly unexpected, for up to then I had done no work at all on the diamond problem, though I had often been tempted to get to grips with it. Suddenly I saw how Demiurge's principle for prolonging the life of the leaves could be applied to a machine for making diamonds. One had merely to convert botanical facts into mechanical ones, and the parallel between the corresponding details seemed to me quite complete."

In von Platen's extraordinary mind, the myth contained the philosophy around which to build an experiment: if destruction is inevitable, then turn that destruction to your advantage. "You know your machine must fall to pieces when it is destroyed—when it is killed—by the enormous pressure. And the form of these pieces will be wrong, since the dead steel has not been invested with . . . wit and knowledge. . . . You must let your machine go to meet Death by dividing it up into pieces, but you must give these pieces the shape that the machine itself would have wished, had it been a living organism like the leaves. Then it will stand much higher pressures, and live longer. And then you will be able to make diamonds."

This is not typical experimental protocol, and von Platen's metaphors do not speak persuasively or hold any relevance to most working scientists. Nevertheless, although it is difficult to see how a high-pressure invention could follow from Demiurge's principle, von Platen's apparatus successfully generated extraordinary temperatures and pressures, and his idea continues to serve as the basis for many of today's most successful high-pressure machines.

Von Platen, who enjoyed a steady royalty income from Electrolux for the thermal refrigerator, established his research laboratory in downtown Stockholm in a magnificent early-seventeenth-century hunting palace built by King Gustav Adolf II for his mistress, Ebba Brahe. The structure had largely fallen into disrepair, but it provided ample room for research and living quarters. It was here that he began to construct his diamond-making machine in the late 1930s. The task soon proved too big—both physically and financially—for his personal resources, so he approached ASEA for funds in 1941. His seductive proposal called for nothing less than the synthesis of gem-quality diamonds several centimeters across and dozens of carats in size. According to Erik Lundblad, von Platen planned to make "home made 'Koh-i-noors,' nothing less would do."

Von Platen's diamond-making strategy was more than a little odd, but given his previous spectacular success, people were reluctant to dismiss his new ideas. ASEA believed the considerable risk of failure was more than offset by the potential bonanza if he proved successful. By mid-1942, a contract for joint research and development was signed, and designs for new equipment were begun almost at once. Von Platen was to provide whatever high-pressure apparatus he had already built and prepare schematic drawings for additional components of his elaborate experimental device—a pressure vessel built as if it were already broken into pieces. Once the blueprints were finished, the inventor advised ASEA on the construction and use of his machine, but his primary attention shifted to other projects.

The hard work of assembling and running the equipment was left in the able hands of ASEA engineers, led by Ragner Liljeblad, head of the company's research and development effort. In 1945, just after World War II, ASEA moved von Platen's pressure equipment to the main corporate laboratory in Västerås, about one hundred kilometers west of Stockholm, where engineers had facilities for heavy-duty machining.

The initial stages of the project required ASEA to build a massive press, or "yoke," capable of achieving and sustaining 12,000 tons of force. Into the jaws of the powerful ASEA yoke the team of engineers and technicians inserted the most costly and cumbersome de-

A copper-jacketed cube-shaped sample assembly, approximately three inches along each edge, formed the center of the ASEA device. Inside the deformable metal cube was a carbon-rich sample, surrounded by a tennis-ball-sized sphere of thermite. (Courtesy of Erik Lundblad.)

vice ever built for high-pressure research. Von Platen had designed a massive and complex contraption to compress a carbon-rich sample the size of a marble. The ASEA workers surrounded the sample with a sphere of thermite, an unstable, sometimes explosive chemical mixture of barium peroxide and magnesium metal; once ignited by an electric current, thermite burns at more than 4,000°F. The tennis-ball-sized thermite mass was cautiously packed in a shell of soapstone insulation, which in turn was encased in a cube-shaped cover of soft metal, usually copper or iron. The final sample-holding cube measured about three inches across and weighed a few pounds.

Six steel and carbide anvils, each a segment of a sphere, compressed the ASEA cube sample. (Courtesy of Erik Lundblad.)

Von Platen's experimental device was designed to apply the same kind of pressure that formed diamond in nature. Deep within the earth, pressure is generated by gravity, which causes rock to squeeze together from all sides at once, much the way a diver is squeezed from all sides by water. This kind of pressure—hydrostatic pressure—is distinct from the uniaxial action of a vise, which only compresses along one axis. Von Platen achieved hydrostatic pressure by surrounding his sample with six pyramid-shaped anvils that came together to form a solid sphere. By pushing simultaneously on all six anvils, each of which pressed on a different face of the sample, tremendous uniform pressure could be achieved at the sample core.

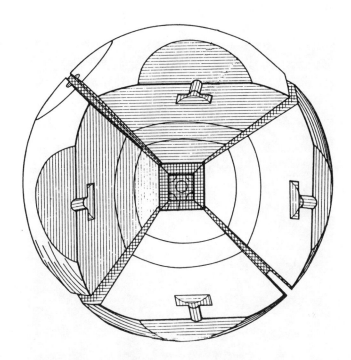

Baltzar von Platen's split-sphere apparatus incorporated six wedge-shaped anvils, each directed at a face of a cube-shaped sample. This figure illustrates the assembly, with one of the anvils removed. The entire split-sphere assembly was jacketed in copper and immersed in a high-pressure water tank. (Courtesy of Erik Lundblad.)

When properly positioned, the six anvils and sample assembly formed an iron ball almost two feet across. The Swedish workers enclosed this entire sphere in a strong copper jacket, creating a high-pressure chamber that weighed in at almost half a ton. Yet this extraordinarily complex arrangement, constructed from more than two dozen separate pieces, did absolutely nothing by itself. Somehow, the entire device had to be pressurized.

ASEA technicians sealed the spherical chamber in a water-filled cylindrical tank that could be pressurized to about 6,000 atmospheres —a pressure several times greater than that at the bottom of the ocean's deepest trench. The principal technical challenge was to confine a large volume of water at such high pressures; the tiniest leak

A watertight copper jacket surrounded the ASEA split-sphere device, which was almost two feet in diameter. (Courtesy of Erik Lundblad.)

could create a high-velocity water jet capable of drilling through a technician's hand.

The researchers wrapped the body of the cylindrical tank with hundreds of loops of taut piano wire to prevent the sides of the pressurized tank from bursting. Then they reinforced the tank's top and bottom by placing it inside the nine-foot-tall steel yoke. The yoke itself was constructed from thick steel plates, welded together and wrapped with even more piano wire. The tank and yoke were hulking, massive chunks of metal, difficult and expensive to assemble. Even so, each experiment placed such tremendous stresses on these components that metal fatigue often ruined new tank and yoke assemblies —in some cases after only two or three runs.

Von Platen's experimental hardware was extraordinarily difficult to build, but its operational strategy was simple. Since pressure equals force divided by area, the 6,000 atmospheres of water pressure applied to the split sphere's very large surface would become focused and concentrated to tremendous pressures—greater than 50,000 atmospheres, it was hoped—on the relatively small area of the central cube-shaped sample assembly. As water pressure crushed the sphere and forced the six anvils against the sample assembly, researchers would ignite the thermite, thereby providing a few minutes of intense simultaneous temperature and pressure.

As soon as all the hardware was in place, ASEA's first order of business was to calibrate the beast. It was no easy task to determine the pressure and temperature at the center of such a device, and precise measurements of pressure and temperature were never obtained, although it now appears that pressures exceeding 60,000 atmospheres were generated in some experiments. The tedious and largely futile calibration process was followed by several abortive diamond-making runs. These experiments failed to produce much of anything except broken anvils and deformed copper jackets. ASEA workers had to labor for as long as three or four months to assemble each experiment because so many of the components had to be replaced after each run. With no sign of success and years of seemingly wasted effort, ASEA considered abandoning the project.

Von Platen's apparatus—the reinforced tank, the massive yoke, the six mighty anvils, and all the other bits and pieces of exotic high-pressure machinery—were shipped back to the old Stockholm palace in 1948, and for a year or more very little was done. For a brief time the world's efforts to make diamonds seemed to have ceased altogether.

But for some reason the corporate powers that be changed their mind, and near the end of 1949 ASEA resolved to try again with twice the financial resources and a new team of five scientists and engineers. This time all the work took place at the Stockholm palace, where von Platen could be consulted on a regular basis, though the inventor played almost no direct role in the experiments. The top-secret diamond-making project was code-named QUINTUS, and the research facility was dubbed the Quintuslaboratorium.

The actual experiments took place in one of the most historic outhouses in the city. The giant yoke, weighing in at fourteen tons, was much too heavy for the floors of the main palace, so the high-pressure laboratory had to be located in one of two elaborate bathrooms in the palace courtyard. The toilets were removed from one building, and it was outfitted with heavy-duty pumps, gauges, and other machinery. The adjacent outhouse retained its original function, and at least one summertime visitor recalled an unpleasant odor in the lab, perhaps unique in the annals of high-pressure science.

A senior ASEA research director, Halvard Liander, oversaw the project, while the energetic young scientist Erik Lundblad took over the hands-on aspects of the work. Lundblad is remembered as providing a striking contrast to the reserved von Platen. He was a big, bullish extrovert with an appetite for large meals, strong drink, good cigars, and (so the stories go) blondes. Erik Lundblad made friends easily and struck colleagues as more like a politician than a scientist. Some may have seen him as simply the front man for von Platen's genius, but his expertise and enthusiasm would prove essential to ASEA's success.

It would be hard to overstate the drama surrounding each experiment of the QUINTUS project during the attempts of the early 1950s. The team first repeated the procedures used in earlier runs. Months of painstaking machining of new parts, dangerous shaping and packing of thermite, meticulous assembly of the six anvils, and difficult copper jacketing preceded each run. Each step had to be perfect or the entire effort would fail. Once the spherical high-pressure assembly was ready, it had to be tightly sealed in the potentially explosive water tank. Once the maximum pressure was obtained and stabilized, the experimenters held their breath, waiting to see if the deeply encased thermite would ignite properly. If that crucial step failed, the whole apparatus had to be dismantled and assembled anew. This process was made more exciting by the added danger of extracting the unstable thermite, which could burst into sunlike flame at any moment.

Lundblad recalled that the dismantling process "could be completed in one day unless everything exploded. . . . This happened

Erik Lundblad tests electrical connections before an experiment with ASEA's diamond-making apparatus. (Courtesy of Erik Lundblad.)

quite frequently and I can understand the feelings which Hannay so graphically described. . . . The situation became especially critical when we went over to [thermite-type] chemicals for heating. These were both explosive and toxic. Fortunately, no safety inspectors knew what we were up to."

Even if everything went exactly as hoped and high pressures and temperatures were achieved, there was still no guarantee of success. Many nervous hours must have passed as the water pressure was released, the tank removed, and the sphere disassembled. It would take days before all the run products could be carefully tested—dissolved in acid, examined by microscope, and x-rayed for telltale signs of diamond. The months and years slipped away. Every ASEA run failed.

When one experiment doesn't work, the obvious strategy is to do something different, and the QUINTUS scientists tried everything they could think of. In 1951 they focused on direct conversion of graphite to diamond. In some experiments the flat graphite crystals were carefully stacked, in others the orientation was varied. In 1952 they experimented with mixtures of carbon and metals in the sample assembly, but the sample appeared to react chemically with the thermite, and no diamonds were found. It was about this time that von Platen sold all rights to his high-pressure designs to ASEA and discontinued his consulting relationship with the firm.

Early in 1953 Lundblad and coworkers changed their strategy again and tried an iron carbide and graphite sample mixture that contained a single small transparent diamond crystal and fine diamond powder. The reasoning behind this effort followed directly from the experiments of Moissan and others, who had showed that carbon dissolves in molten iron at high temperature and will crystallize out in its stable form when cooled at high pressure. Iron carbide provided the densest, most concentrated form of iron and carbon available to Lundblad and his colleagues. The scientists wrapped the central carbon-rich sample in a foil shell of platinum and tantalum to prevent chemical reaction with the thermite.

On February 16, 1953, the experiment was run under a pressure later estimated to be 83,000 atmospheres sustained for a full hour. Upon releasing the pressure, Lundblad and his coworkers disassembled the split sphere and recovered the sample; the foil-wrapped core was still intact. With exquisite care they unwrapped the foil, and quickly found the original single diamond crystal. It had emerged from the ordeal opaque, the result of surface cracks, but was otherwise intact—proof that the pressure and temperature achieved in the experiment were close to that at which diamond is the stable form of carbon. The scientists subjected the rest of the black sample to the closest scrutiny. The tedious process of repeated acid baths and microscopic analysis eventually revealed forty or fifty crystals, the largest no bigger than a grain of sand. These crystals hadn't been in the starting materials, and subsequent x-ray analysis confirmed the men's hopes. The new material was diamond.

For millennia humans had held the gem in awe, and for centuries they had sought a way to make it. On February 16, 1953, that quest was ended.

The moment of discovery is remembered as one of unrestrained joy for ASEA's QUINTUS team, though it was a joy that could not be widely shared. The synthetic origin of the sample was still top secret—no one outside a small group of employees knew the source of the crystals. "The fellow who performed the x-ray analysis could not understand why I became so excited when he reported that my sample indicated only the presence of diamond," Lundblad recalled. "My God, I still get headaches thinking of how this was celebrated."

The historic success was repeated twice in 1953, first on May 24, when they synthesized diamond from a starting mix containing no seed diamonds, and again on November 25, when the experimental products were independently identified by an expert not associated with the project. Each experiment is said to have yielded a trove of tiny synthetic diamonds.

But ASEA's success was bittersweet. The unwieldy technique was difficult to reproduce and much too slow and costly to have commercial applications. While ASEA researchers struggled in secrecy to perfect their process, credit for achieving diamond synthesis went to a rival team of American diamond makers.

The most inexplicable aspect of ASEA's diamond-making victory was their absolute, absurd silence. After hundreds of years of concerted effort in which brilliant scientists from Hannay to Bridgman had failed, ASEA had triumphed. The first chapter of the diamond-making saga might have ended—should have ended—in 1953, if only ASEA and its researchers had followed normal scientific protocol. If they had announced and published their historic results, if they had filed a patent application, even sent a sealed document describing the breakthrough to a neutral party, their contribution would have been endorsed throughout the world. But they did none of these things. Instead, they waited and said nothing.

Two years later, after rival diamond makers in America had announced their own successful synthesis, ASEA made a brief and relatively uninformative mention of their diamond-making activities in the *ASEA Journal*. A formal description of the synthesis procedures did not appear until 1960, seven years after the event. Indeed, so much of the ASEA story was told only in retrospect—some of it decades after the original work—that many details of the experimental results, and even the motivations for the experiments, are difficult to document.

Why ASEA hesitated to report the breakthrough has remained a mystery. Part of the reason must have been their disappointment in making only diamond grit instead of magnificent gemstones. The cumbersome split-sphere process devised by von Platen could hardly have become economical unless each experiment produced a large, valuable diamond. But in a year of successful synthesis, employing five researchers and millions of dollars of hardware, ASEA had grown only a fraction of a carat of tiny diamonds. Their first successful experiments held little promise of commercial viability.

Erik Lundblad's explanation for ASEA's silence seems plausible. "We at ASEA made no public announcement in 1953, mainly because we wanted to improve on the size and quality of the diamonds and also to gain more detailed knowledge of the conditions of diamond formation," he said. The thermite technique was dangerous, destructive, and far from being perfected. Any premature announcement would have just given rival companies a chance to catch up, and safety inspectors reason to shut them down. Furthermore, based on their conversations with Percy Bridgman in 1951, the ASEA group believed that no one else had joined the diamond-making game. "There we were apparently misled," Lundblad lamented. Rather than publish their results right away, they tried to incorporate a more accurate electrical heater in the design and to adopt a simpler piston-in-cylinder-type mechanism for generating pressure. "We thought we had time," he said.

A rather different account is advanced by publicists of the De Beers company, who joined with ASEA to form the Scandiamant diamond-making company in 1965. De Beers took full control of this firm in 1975 and since then has more or less assumed the role of partisan historian for ASEA's efforts. In a 1990 issue of *INDIAQUA*, a De Beers public-relations magazine, the company presented what, at best, seems a revisionist view of history. "What, then, was the motive?" the article asks. "Hardly commercial, nor due to an actual need of the product. Despite the fact that diamond is rare, there was no actual shortage of diamonds. No, the interest as far as [corporations] were concerned lay in the challenge of being able to do something which no one else could do, and thereby gaining an even greater reputation for their respective companies." But if reputation was the key, and if ASEA had spent millions to make diamonds, confirmed the synthesis with x-ray diffraction, and then duplicated the feat in 1953, surely they would have announced their triumph immediately. Furthermore, in 1953, at the height of the Korean War, there *was* a diamond shortage, and a new potential source would have had tremendous significance. Why did ASEA wait for years after General Electric scooped them to make an announcement? The De Beers corporate explanation doesn't ring true.

Skeptics, particularly those associated with General Electric, who admittedly have their own historical agenda, have proposed another version of events. Might the ASEA workers have failed to identify the tiny 1953 synthetic diamond crystals until *after* the 1955 GE announcement? Perhaps ASEA scientists were the first to make diamonds but didn't realize it until two years later.

Whatever the reason for ASEA's silence—caution, secrecy, or ignorance—the delay of their announcement negated any claim they might have made for priority of discovery. Scientists have established certain rules for deciding who accomplishes something first. Most important, an experimental result must be fully described by the discoverer and then duplicated by independent researchers before it can be accepted. Full public disclosure is not required when proprietary procedures and equipment, like the ASEA diamond machine, are involved, but complete details of the process can still be written down, deposited in a sealed document, and placed in the custody of a neutral party. These actions must be taken prior to disclosure by a rival group.

Although they are not officially credited with the discovery, Erik Lundblad and his ASEA coworkers are often mentioned as possibly the first to synthesize diamonds. Baltzar von Platen's bizarre split-sphere device—expensive, ungainly, dangerous, and self-destructive

—probably succeeded where earlier attempts had failed. But ASEA's failure to publicize the feat until after General Electric's announcement has relegated the Swedish success to little more than a historical footnote.

Years after the event, von Platen regretted ASEA's failure to announce the creation of diamonds. "I write now as I should have written perhaps twenty years ago. Then, it was the high pressure and the great volume of the high pressure chamber which were prime considerations. They were the goal which had for so long slipped away like a mirage into the seemingly impossible. Yet when these things were finally achieved one found that there were new difficulties to be overcome." By failing to share his secrets with the world, Baltzar von Platen lost his greatest opportunity for fame.

5

The Crystals of
Loring Coes

Using new techniques, it was found possible to synthesize most of the
well-known high-pressure minerals. . . . The main motive in this work was
to study the conditions attendant on the formation of natural diamond.
　　　　　　　　—Loring Coes, "High-Pressure Minerals," 1955

By the late 1940s American efforts
to synthesize diamonds had acquired a new urgency as cold war tensions gripped the nation. Only diamond could machine and polish
the carbide tools needed to cut and shape the critical components of
aircraft engines, gun barrels, vehicle armor, and other military hardware. Except for an emergency stockpile of industrial diamond in
Canada, North America was completely dependent on South Africa,
a vulnerable target easily cut off from the West, to satisfy the growing
demand for diamonds. The nation turned its hopes to the diamond
makers.

　　Percy Bridgman had taken up the challenge of diamond synthesis
in 1941 at the behest of the Norton-GE-Carborundum consortium,
but he abandoned the effort for other research during World War II
and was disinclined to return to the problem afterward. Bridgman
must have realized that his experimental skills did not extend to the
high-temperature technology necessary for diamond making. Rather
than give up on high-pressure research altogether, the Norton Company decided to continue the project on its own. They moved Bridgman's thousand-ton press to their Worcester, Massachusetts, re-

search laboratory and began to think about new ways to make diamond.

From 1945 to 1955 Norton employees ran a variety of high-pressure experiments, but the work of chemist Loring Coes, Jr., yielded the most important discoveries. Bridgman's work had almost always relied on pressure alone, and he spent little effort designing furnaces or electric heaters, but Coes took a different approach. Taking his cue from the way diamonds formed in nature, Coes started with rather ordinary mixtures of chemicals, heated them to more than a thousand degrees, squeezed them to tens of thousands of atmospheres, and, as often as not, came up with something no one had ever made before.

Coes was small and unassuming, remembered by his friends as a taciturn man, difficult to get to know. He was inclined to smoke too much and drink too much, but he proved to be an intense and creative scientific researcher. After graduating with bachelor's and master's degrees in chemistry from Worcester Polytechnic Institute, he became a researcher for the Worcester-based Norton Company, a high-tech firm with a strong interest in superhard materials. Coes's triumphs in high-pressure research represented a high point in a life ultimately marked by personal failures and disappointments.

Coes was a meticulous, dedicated scientist who worked long hours in his Worcester lab and at home. For four decades he remained a loyal employee at Norton, where he impressed colleagues with his innovative thinking and unusual technical skills. An outstanding chemist, Coes brought an intimate knowledge of chemical reactions, synthesis techniques, and properties of materials to his research. He was an accomplished glassblower who fabricated all of his own experimental glassware as well as glass vessels for the Norton analytical laboratory. He also had an extraordinary memory and a gift as a precise and articulate public speaker.

Coes's career at Norton encompassed many research projects, from work on organically bonded ceramics to the development of the theory of grinding, but he is remembered today almost entirely for Project A-39, a brilliant six-year foray into the high-pressure synthesis of minerals. This diamond-making project was the brainchild of Samuel Kistler, Norton's imposing, inspiring associate director of research. Standing six-four, with thick-lensed glasses and a professorial air, Kistler was a walking encyclopedia, a lively personality with an abundance of ideas and enthusiasm—the perfect foil for Milton Beecher, Norton's conservative vice president of research. It was Kistler who pointed Loring Coes toward high-pressure science.

Coes was joined by a small team of coworkers. Max Wieldon, a gregarious and athletic forty-year-old mechanical engineer with a degree from Middlebury College, focused on designing and building high-pressure apparatus. George Comstock, recently graduated from Worcester Tech, searched for the strongest pressure-vessel materials and studied ways to calibrate pressure and temperature. Chinese-born research assistant Wing Moy assisted Coes in the laboratory, while Peter Jensen, a Danish tool and die maker, was also critical to the effort.

Coes was well aware of the earlier attempts to make diamonds—except, perhaps, for the secret ASEA project—and he knew about the difficulty of generating sufficient simultaneous high temperature and pressure. So rather than tackle diamond synthesis immediately, he decided to creep up on the conditions necessary for the gem's formation by making some of the other forty or so known dense, deep-earth minerals that had never been produced in the laboratory. Not only was this research of great scientific interest, but it also seemed to provide the most promising avenue for finding tough new abrasives—and for uncovering the secrets of diamond synthesis.

Percy Bridgman's work had provided one clear message to would-be makers of diamond and other deep-earth minerals: pressure alone is not enough. You must heat while you squeeze. Unfortunately, high temperature weakens steel or carbide. Coes had to devise a mechanism strong enough to support unprecedented pressures at extreme temperatures. Most pressure devices failed because all the force was directed along just two opposed pistons. Failure occurred when the pressure first deformed the metal ring surrounding the samples, which then blew out sideways, just like a grape bursting in a wine press. The key was to find a way to confine all sides of a sample at once. Von Platen and his ASEA followers had gotten around the problem by using six anvils, each pressing on a side of a cube, but that device was top-secret, and expensive and ungainly to boot. Coes's team had to find their own way.

Most high-pressure scientists with access to a huge press like the

Norton thousand-ton machine would have been seduced into working on a large scale with bulky devices and big samples, but Coes and his colleagues thought differently. Pressure is force per area, and you can create a lot of pressure by subjecting a large surface to a huge force, but you can do it much more easily by subjecting a very small area to a modest force. Furthermore, as a chemist, Coes knew that sustained high temperatures are often a lot easier to achieve with smaller samples. So the Norton team got rid of the big press (it was modified for routine manufacturing chores) and turned their attention to building a smaller, beautifully crafted piston-in-cylinder machine.

Coes, Kistler, and Wieldon built their simple device from two high-tech materials. The first material, tungsten carbide, was well known to high-pressure workers thanks to Percy Bridgman's experiments, but the ultratough compound was not generally available to researchers. Only a handful of U.S. companies controlled its distribution; fortunately, Norton was one of them. Two tungsten carbide pistons, each one-quarter inch in diameter, applied force on the sample from either end of a cylindrical steel sample chamber with a quarter-inch central hole.

To make the sample cylinder, another extraordinary high-tech material was used—a hard and rigid ceramic dubbed Alundum, available as a specialty product from Norton. Ceramics are wonderfully useful materials. They make up substances like china, bricks, and most rocks, all of which are composed primarily of microscopic interlocking crystals. Ceramics can be found almost everywhere, from coffee cups and bathroom tiles to high-voltage electronic components and the space shuttle's exterior insulation. They are typically very hard, usually act as good electrical insulators, can resist extremely high temperatures, and have a tendency to shatter when dropped.

Norton had developed a variety of ceramics under the trade name Alundum, a reference to the material's principal constituent, aluminum oxide or, in its natural form, the hard mineral corundum. The gemstones ruby and sapphire are nothing more than exceptionally rare colored forms of this common, normally colorless compound. Coes might have contemplated using cylinders of single-crystal corundum in his press, but large single crystals are rare in nature, difficult to grow in the laboratory, almost impossible to machine, and tend to break along the lines and planes of crystal weakness. Single crystals of corundum, even if available, would make poor high-pressure components.

Alundum, on the other hand, could be easily made by compressing and heating powdered corundum in a precisely machined mold. This process, known as hot pressing, causes the tiny powdered grains to recrystallize and cement together to form a polycrystalline mass with virtually no pores or directions of weakness. Coes selected an Alundum recipe using the purest aluminum oxide available and had the Norton technicians make him a steady supply of perfect cylinders with an inner diameter of exactly one-quarter inch to match the tungsten carbide pistons. Alundum was the perfect choice for the job.

The Norton workers pressed the finished ceramic cylinder into a thick, tightly fitting outer ring of steel with a slightly tapered hole. This metal binding ring reinforced the rigid ceramic cylinder, preventing the sample from bursting through the cylinder walls. A larger cylindrical water-cooling jacket fit around the entire piston-cylinder mechanism to complete the simple assembly. Coes's press took full advantage of the materials expertise of the Norton Company—one of the few companies in the world that could have supported his high-pressure effort.

Perhaps the most brilliant and elegant feature of Coes's device was its heating capability. Aluminum oxide, which formed the cylindrical walls of the sample chamber, is an excellent electrical insulator, while the tungsten carbide pistons that formed the chamber's top and bottom surfaces are good electrical conductors. To produce extreme temperatures, all Coes needed was an electrical heater between the two carbide pistons. For this task he turned to an old standby: graphite. By attaching electrical leads to the two carbide pistons, bridging the gap between the pistons with a graphite cylinder, and turning on the juice, Coes could heat samples to more than 1,000°C by exploiting graphite's electrical resistance. Furthermore, because a graphite heater would be present at the heart of every run, no matter what mineral was being studied, Coes had an excellent opportunity to make diamond as well. Simple fifty- and hundred-ton hydraulic presses, a half-dozen in all, would be all that Coes and his team needed to squeeze a steady stream of samples.

At the extreme pressures and temperatures of Coes's experiments, almost every run broke the aluminum oxide cylinder. The tungsten carbide rods, which were hard but brittle, and the deformable graphite cylinder heaters also needed frequent replacement. Yet unlike the cumbersome ASEA device, which took months to repair after each experimental run, Coes's simple system took only an hour or so to ready for the next experiment. None of the parts was large or difficult to make, and Norton technicians kept Coes supplied with all the pistons, cylinders, and graphite heaters he needed to keep the operation running efficiently.

The research agenda was almost as simple as home cooking. Measure out samples of common chemicals like magnesium oxide, silicon carbide, and aluminum hydroxide. Thoroughly mix and grind the powders and enclose the mix in a copper or iron foil capsule. Heat and squeeze for an hour or two. Open the capsule and, voilà, look at the beautiful crystals.

Although this procedure was relatively simple, Coes had a few secrets to ensure success. All of the dense minerals that he attempted to make were silicates—compounds of silicon and oxygen, usually with one or two other elements. The most logical approach would be to mix these elements together as powders, and the simplest powders to use were oxides—mixtures of oxygen and a second element. If you wanted to make the high-pressure garnet pyrope—a silicate composed of magnesium, aluminum, silicon, and oxygen—the normal, reasonable procedure would be to weigh and mix the correct proportions of magnesium oxide, aluminum oxide, and silicon oxide; seal these oxides tightly in a capsule so nothing could escape; and then heat and squeeze. Unfortunately, this procedure won't make pyrope.

Coes defied conventional logic. To make pyrope he mixed magnesium nitrate, aluminum hydroxide, and silicon carbide, a combination many earth scientists found absurd. Then, instead of sealing his starting materials tightly inside metal capsules, he simply crimped the ends of the capsules closed, purposely allowing impurities to spoil his experiments. And Coes made beautiful crystals of pyrope, nearly every time he tried.

What at first appeared to be sloppy procedure was in fact good chemistry. It turned out that Coes's "secret" ingredients made the atoms in his samples much more mobile and reactive than the atoms in simple oxides. The slightly open capsule allowed the undesirable volatile material produced by Coes's mix—water, nitrogen, carbon dioxide, and hydrogen—to escape, leaving behind perfect crystals of garnet. Time after time he grew silicates from unlikely starting materials—nitrates, sulfates, carbides, even chlorates. His crystals were tiny but exquisite, with perfect geometric faces, and his technique was so simple that a single worker could complete three or four experiments in a single day.

Coes hit paydirt almost immediately using his innovative process, producing an extraordinary range of mineral-like phases that normally only occur miles deep within the earth. In his first experiments Coes focused on the minerals found in eclogite, a beautiful deep-earth rock, occasionally diamond-bearing, that displays deep red garnets and stunning green pyroxenes. Garnets, pyroxenes, and other eclogite minerals grew in abundance in his laboratory. Coes also synthesized several common metamorphic minerals—crystals like staurolite and kyanite that form when ordinary mud, silt, and other sediments are buried and baked many miles deep within the earth. Geologists had long known about these minerals from metamorphic rocks in the Appalachians, the Alps, the Urals, and other ancient mountain ranges, wherever thick piles of cooked sediment have been brought back to the surface. But Loring Coes was the first to synthesize these minerals in the laboratory.

Coes also produced semiprecious gemstones with ease. In his press he grew crystals of zircon, idocrase, tourmaline, beryl, sphene, and topaz—dozens of different minerals were created in hundreds of runs. Coes used an old brass petrographic microscope, which had special optical attachments favored by geologists, to identify and describe his growing cache of experimental products.

Coes's most stunning discovery occurred when he squeezed one of the simplest, most common minerals of all, ordinary quartz beach sand, or silica. Before this work on quartz sand, his experiments had always produced well-known minerals. But when Coes squeezed quartz to 35,000 atmospheres at 800°C he found a new dense silica, a crystal substance never before seen. This unexpected find had two profound implications. First, the new form of silica was very dense and hard, perhaps not a commercially viable abrasive, but better by far than most known minerals. Coes thus proved what many had suspected—that previously unknown superhard materials could be found at high pressure. More importantly, however, Coes had produced astonishing direct evidence that less than fifty miles below the earth's surface there might be other dense minerals that had never been seen before. If a mineral as common as quartz could have an alternate form, what other strange and wonderful minerals might exist beneath our feet?

From 1947 until 1953 Loring Coes worked in obscurity, his extraordinary results completely unknown to the outside world. Because he served an industrial laboratory where discoveries counted as important corporate assets, sharing those discoveries was seldom a high priority. Furthermore, Coes was by nature a quiet and introspective man who hesitated to trumpet his own accomplishments. But upon discovering the transformation of quartz, he was given permission to publish a brief technical note, "A New Dense Crystalline Silica," which appeared in the July 31, 1953, issue of the prestigious weekly journal *Science*. That short abstract—a condensation of several years' work—sent a shock wave through the earth science community. "The possibility exists," he wrote, "that the existence of this form of silica in nature may have been overlooked." In form, color, and optical behavior the new dense silica could easily be mistaken for other common minerals, he suggested. Coes, completely unknown to his audience, tantalized readers with the promise that "a subsequent paper on the synthesis of several naturally occurring minerals will greatly amplify this information."

The mineralogy of the earth's interior—almost all of the earth's volume—was literally terra incognita in the 1950s, and the geological community eagerly sought any new technique that might open up the earth to laboratory investigation. Within a few weeks of the *Science* report, Hatten S. Yoder, Jr., a dynamic young high-pressure researcher at the Carnegie Institution of Washington's Geophysical Laboratory, invited Coes to come to the nation's capital. Yoder had been trying for years to make high-pressure minerals. He had accomplished much in a device that used extremely high gas pressure, but synthesis of minerals like pyrope garnet and kyanite from pure oxides had eluded him. He received the news of Coes's success with a combination of excitement and skepticism.

Coes made the trip to Washington on Monday, September 21, 1953, and provided Hat Yoder with a brief outline of what he had accomplished in the Norton lab. Much of the research was proprietary, and many details could not be discussed at that time, but what Coes did reveal—the new minerals synthesized in his lab and the new materials used to construct his high-pressure and high-temperature device—was more than enough to whet the appetite of the lab's high-pressure scientists. Yoder knew he had to visit Worcester to see Coes's work for himself.

After receiving Norton's official okay, Yoder contacted Harvard geophysicist Francis Birch, who assembled a contingent from Cambridge, Massachusetts, to meet Yoder at Norton. He also invited Alvin Van Valkenburg of the Washington-based National Bureau of Standards to join the expedition.

The December 4, 1953, meeting at the Norton Company in Worcester, Massachusetts, brought together many leaders in high-pressure research. At the meeting Loring Coes demonstrated his novel method for synthesizing high-pressure minerals. Seated, from left to right: Loring Coes, Jr., Cornelius Hurlbut, Francis Birch, Hatten S. Yoder, Jr., Alvin Van Valkenburg. Standing: Rustum Roy, Francis R. Boyd, James Thompson, Gordon MacDonald, Eugene Robertson. (Courtesy of H. S. Yoder, Jr.)

The memorable Friday-afternoon meeting took place at 2:00 P.M. on December 4, 1953. Many of the nine scientists present would become key players in the high-pressure game. The Washington contingent included Van Valkenburg, Yoder, and Francis Boyd. Francis Birch, postdoctoral fellows Eugene Robertson, Gordon MacDonald, and Jim Thompson, and the distinguished mineralogist Cornelius Hurlbut rounded out the Harvard group. Birch and Robertson were particularly intrigued by Coes's revelations because they had been struggling for almost two years on a contract with the Office of Naval Research (ONR) to study the properties of materials at high pressures and temperatures, a project whose unspoken ultimate goal was to make diamonds.

The scientists from Harvard and Washington were also joined that day by Rustum Roy, a high-pressure expert from Penn State and a remarkable figure in high-pressure history. Roy graduated with a bachelor's degree from India's Patne University and in 1946 arrived at Penn State as a graduate student interested in micas, one of India's major mineral exports. As he was finishing his Ph.D. thesis in 1948, Roy was asked to stay on as a postdoctoral fellow by E. F. Osborn, who had just received an ONR contract to make high-pressure rocks in the lab.

In a short, immensely productive period in late 1948 Osborn and Roy designed apparatus and techniques for what they called routine hydrothermal synthesis of samples at pressures up to a few thousand atmospheres. They encapsulated water-bearing mixes of elements in gold and transformed the contents with pressure and heat. By late 1953 the Penn State group had studied numerous mineral systems but had repeatedly failed to make the high-pressure metamorphic mineral kyanite. Roy was alerted to the special December fourth meeting by a friend who worked at Norton; he decided he had to be there to see it for himself.

"We arrived as a bunch of doubting Thomases," remembers Alvin Van Valkenburg, whose high-pressure work at the National Bureau of Standards focused on the optical behavior of minerals. "No one believed he could have made the things he claimed."

"We were all skeptics," Rustum Roy echoes. Some scientists believed that the formation of deep-earth minerals depended on complex stress patterns and the control of the rocks' water content—

factors not easily reproduced in the laboratory. They felt that the only rocks you could hope to mimic in the laboratory were those found in near-surface deposits. After all, a lot of researchers had tried and failed in the quest for deep-earth minerals.

It didn't take Coes long to change everyone's mind. When they handled the sophisticated tungsten carbide and hot-pressed Alundum equipment, when they saw the crystal specimens—many large enough to pick up with tweezers—when they looked in the microscope and read the unambiguous x-ray diffraction patterns that identified each high-pressure mineral, there could be no doubt. Gene Robertson remembers the meeting as an extraordinary learning experience. "It was clear right from the start he knew what he was doing." Not only had he created numerous synthetic minerals in novel ways, from combinations of materials that no one had thought of before, but he accomplished this feat in an elegant apparatus made from materials that the visiting researchers had never seen before.

"He made all the really high-pressure [minerals], which were like holy grails at the time," recalls Roy. Norton Company policy prohibited the visitors from taking photographs or writing notes, so the eager scientists had to rely on their memories to retain the information that Coes offered. Hat Yoder remembers visiting a men's-room stall at one point and furiously writing everything he could recall on the back of the only usable scrap of paper at his disposal, a blank check from his wallet. That check, still preserved in his notes, is crammed with tiny formulas involving strange starting materials and extreme conditions of synthesis.

Coes later bent the rules a bit, giving Yoder a Polaroid black-and-white photograph of the neatly arranged pieces of the device. Coes labeled each piece in crisp printing—"hot pressed alumina mold liner," "WC [tungsten carbide] pistons," "steel mold retainer," and all the rest.

"It was a powerful stimulant," Joe Boyd recalls of the visit. "It really shook people up." Overnight, Coes's pioneering syntheses changed the way scientists thought about investigating the earth. The nine scientists left Norton amazed; none of them would ever see the world in quite the same way again.

✧ ✧ ✧

Upon his return to the Geophysical Laboratory, Hat Yoder wrote to Coes with the thanks of all the participants. "We all greatly appreciate the fine tour of your laboratory and the opportunity to see some of the details of your apparatus. You probably do not realize what a tremendous contribution you have made to the field of mineral synthesis and to geology in general. The impetus you have given our work is very great."

Yoder's words were no exaggeration. In one way or another, the December fourth meeting profoundly influenced all the participants. Hat Yoder began to construct a copy of the Norton device almost immediately upon returning to the Geophysical Laboratory. He lacked access to the sophisticated tungsten carbide and hot-pressed alumina components, but he substituted the highest grade steels available. For the dramatic first run he invited the lab's newly appointed director, Philip Abelson, to watch. The experiment had barely gotten under way when a sickening crack was heard. The pistons had broken and become hopelessly, permanently jammed in the cylinder. Tungsten carbide pistons and hot-pressed alumina cylinders, items not yet commercially available from Norton, were evidently critical to success. Yoder went back to work making high-pressure history with his own invention, a 10,000-atmosphere gas-pressure apparatus that could accurately reproduce the full range of temperature and pressure conditions found in the earth's crust.

Joe Boyd, then a Geophysical Lab postdoc fresh out of graduate school at Harvard, had already resolved to study minerals in the new high-pressure, high-temperature regime typical of Coes's work. After the historic Norton meeting he designed and built a piston-cylinder device of his own and proceeded to study the behavior of silicate minerals under deep-earth conditions. One of his first studies at the Geophysical Lab, made in collaboration with longtime colleague Joe England, was the careful measurement of the exact pressures and temperatures at which quartz becomes the new form of silica discovered by Coes.

The Norton meeting was also pivotal for Harvard professor Francis Birch and his postdoctoral fellow, Gene Robertson. Perhaps more than anyone else, Birch had carried on Percy Bridgman's legacy at Harvard. After studying with Bridgman as a Harvard physics graduate student in the early 1930s and spending World War II at Los Alamos working on the Manhattan Project, he continued pressure research at Harvard's Department of Geological Sciences. Birch and Robertson had labored to produce diamond for ONR, with little success. The project, begun in 1952, relied on a Bridgman-type device to attain sufficient pressure, but the researchers lacked the tough new anvil materials necessary to make significant progress. Coes graciously offered to help by supplying hot-pressed alumina components. Birch and Robertson never did make diamonds, but the Norton expedition did point them in promising directions, and they went on to make critical measurements on jadeite, kyanite, and pyrope—all minerals first synthesized by Coes.

Rustum Roy and his Penn State colleagues were also inspired to try something new. In collaboration with colleague O. F. Tuttle, Roy spent a year or so engaged in what he describes as an "amateurish look" for diamonds. The project was underwritten by the Carborundum Company, but they were never able to achieve sufficient pressures. In subsequent years Roy and his associates moved on to use a Bridgman-style opposed-anvil device that could generate pressures up to 100,000 atmospheres at 550°C. With it they produced more than a hundred new compounds, including novel forms of phosphates, fluorides, oxides, and metals. Roy credits Coes for pointing him on his way.

The December 1953 visit had one final consequence. The revelations that came from the Norton meeting, coupled with his widely lauded discovery of the new dense form of silica, made Loring Coes a living legend in the earth science community. Less than a year after Coes published his discovery of the synthetic silica, Robert Sosman, an earth scientist at Rutgers, wrote a letter to *Science* advocating an appropriate name for the new compound. "Fearing that the discoverer might be too modest to name the phase after himself," Sosman proposed the name coesite for the high-pressure form. Sosman apologized to mineralogical purists, who might object to giving an official mineral name to a synthetic material. "As an alternative for the benefit of any reader who wishes to stand firmly on the mineralogist's principle, I suggest that he call Coes' new phase of silica *silica C*." Everyone called it coesite.

Inevitably, just a few years after Coes's announcement of the synthetic silica, the same substance was found in nature. Edward Chao, a geologist with the U.S. Geological Survey, was studying the effects of shock waves on quartz by examining sandstone blasted by the Canyon Diablo meteorite at Meteor Crater, Arizona. Scrutinizing the material under his microscope, Chao noticed tiny crystals quite distinct from quartz. On a single day, an exhilarating Monday early in 1960, Chao isolated the material and identified it as Coes's silica compound. The extreme shock of the meteor's impact had converted everyday quartz to its dense high-pressure form.

For a short time Chao wanted to exercise his right as discoverer to name the mineral boydite, in recognition of Joe Boyd's ongoing research in the high-pressure mineralogy of silica, but the unauthorized name coesite had gained a strong, and deserved, foothold. The International Commission on New Minerals, ultimate arbiter of such matters, officially approved the name coesite in 1960, in honor of the man who first synthesized it.

Loring Coes gave scientists new hope in their quest for diamond. If so many different deep-earth phases could be reproduced in the laboratory, why not diamond? But Coes never became a central figure in that adventure. In 1952 he was appointed Norton's assistant director of research and development, a job that diluted his effectiveness as a researcher. Alan G. King, a researcher under Coes at that time, remembers Coes's unique directorial style: he left his people alone. "I've never been under so much pressure in my life," King recalls. "You really try to excel when you're thrown into something like that."

The year 1962 was tragically pivotal for Loring Coes. As the scientifically better qualified of two candidates for the prestigious job as director of research at Norton, he looked forward to moving up the corporate ladder. But management found Coes's introspective manner and scientific inclination incompatible with the top management job. On more than one occasion he had bluntly refused to pursue what he perceived as impractical research directions, in opposition to his superiors' wishes. The Norton CEO passed him over, a blow from which he never fully recovered.

In November 1962 Coes was given a new and ostensibly prestigious research position as consultant in research and development, but it was little more than a consolation prize. Depressed and subject to bouts of alcoholism, Coes saw his life begin to fall apart. He was arrested for drunk driving and lost his license. His marriage failed, and his wife took all their possessions, leaving him with little more than a cot in his large house. Though he remained a researcher with Norton for another sixteen years, he never repeated his extraordinary research success of the early 1950s.

Lung cancer, the consequence of a lifetime of heavy smoking, killed Loring Coes in 1978 at age sixty-three. He died in relative obscurity, with little more than a local obituary to mark the passing of the man who had transformed high-pressure science.

The search for high-pressure minerals was always cited as the principal scientific motivation for the Norton research. But Norton's research head, Sam Kistler, had actually begun Project A-39 in the hope of making diamonds, and almost from the start rumors circulated that traces of the precious material had been recovered from experimental runs. It appears that these samples were never subjected to rigorous testing, and it seems doubtful given the relatively low pressures involved that diamonds were ever made, though Coes fervently believed that in several experiments with diamond seed crystals he had succeeded in adding a thin layer of diamond to the original stones.

Although Coes abandoned his high-pressure synthesis studies in 1953, his assistant, Paul Keat, took over the project and for two years focused his efforts on creating diamonds. Realizing that higher pressures were essential for success, Keat obtained a larger press and concentrated on building a bigger device with opposed, tapered tungsten carbide anvils and a strong girdle to confine the sample. The project was well conceived and, had there been no competition, it stood every chance of success. But Norton's effort proved to be too little and too late; others had gotten there first.

In 1950, after three years of high-pressure studies, Coes and the Norton management had come to the conclusion that they were not going to make diamond, at least not with the double-piston device. They had enjoyed tremendous success creating high-pressure minerals, but diamond making would clearly take something more. In what may have been their most significant contribution to the history of diamond making, the Norton Company approached General Electric about a possible joint effort. Norton hinted that they had a "sniff of diamond" in some of Coes's synthetic runs and described the unprecedented synthetic products they had already created. On that basis, without revealing any information about the key experiments or the techniques employed, Norton asked GE to become their collaborator.

It must have been a tempting offer, and General Electric officials and lawyers tried to draft a cooperative arrangement. But a satisfactory agreement was slow in coming, and after considerable thought, General Electric management declined Norton's proposal. Instead, they decided to do it themselves.

6

✧

Project Superpressure

The history of attempts at diamond synthesis probably started in 1797, almost at the moment diamond was first shown to be a form of carbon.
—C. Guy Suits, *The Synthesis of Diamond*, 1960

Baby boomers remember the 1950s as a time of unbridled, can-do optimism. Americans had built the bomb and had won the war. We were the richest, strongest nation on earth; there was nothing we could not do. It was a time when almost everyone shared in the benefits of wonderful new technologies—jet planes, sleek cars, and colorful plastic. People's lives were transformed by television, the pill, and credit cards. Medical miracles from the polio vaccine to open-heart surgery raised average life expectancy above sixty-five for the first time in human history. The time was right to make diamonds.

In earlier days the problem of diamond synthesis had been tackled by individuals. Clever, dedicated scientists such as Hannay and Moissan had taken on the challenge like solitary knights on a quest. But time after time, these men had failed in their mission.

By the postwar years, high-tech research had changed forever. The awesome new technologies spawned by war—developments like radar, guided missiles, and, of course, the atom bomb—were the products of large group efforts. World War II hammered home the lesson that teamwork was the answer to achieving big goals, a concept not lost on the postwar diamond makers.

No one person could pull off the diamond-making trick, for no one person could muster all the necessary expertise. Steel devices didn't work, so you had to have a materials expert with access to the best quality carbide components, as well as machinists skilled enough to craft that carbide into anvils or pistons of precise dimensions. Chemical heating with thermite was dangerously impractical, so you needed an expert electrician with the knowledge to heat a sample by electric current and the ability to do it in a cumbersome high-pressure system. Direct conversion of graphite to diamond didn't work, so you had to have a master chemist to discover the right recipe of minerals to squeeze.

Trying to make the diamonds was only part of the battle. You also had to isolate and identify the experimental products, a process complicated by the crystals' minute size. Many researchers had been fooled by tiny diamond-like grains of other hard materials—spinel, corundum, chromite, silica, and carbide were all found to grow in a high-pressure environment and all formed hard crystals with triangular facets, just like diamonds. As a result, your team had to have an expert in analytical chemistry and x-ray crystallography just to prove that you had made the real stuff. And, finally, you had to have deep pockets and a lot of time.

Diamond synthesis required so many different specialists that bitter controversies over proper credit were perhaps inevitable. Decades of contentious debate between volatile personalities, coupled with a well-oiled corporate publicity campaign, have distorted and confused this dramatic history. What remains clear is that by 1950 all the easy approaches to diamond making had been tried and had failed. Without the financial backing and long-term commitment of a determined corporation, the chances of making diamonds were slim.

The General Electric Company was born a century ago, the brainchild of Thomas Edison, whose revolutionary innovations in electrical power, lighting, and transportation transformed the world. From the earliest days, GE corporate research and development carried on the Edison tradition, securing the company's fame and fortune. Invention after invention poured from the labs. They pioneered improved lighting, developing long-life tungsten filaments, soft-white frosted glass, and fluorescent bulbs. They transformed domestic life with countless new appliances, from refrigerators and air conditioners to toasters and electric blankets. They introduced mobile radio systems, modern x-ray tubes, and advanced propulsion systems for jet planes, electric trains, and ocean-going ships. By the first decades of the twentieth century, Edison's company had changed the way Americans used energy, and the GE logo was recognized throughout the world as a symbol of American excellence and know-how.

The diamond game was serious business to GE, which depended entirely on expensive supplies of foreign diamonds to cut and shape their carbide products and to draw out the fine tungsten filament wire required for light bulbs. For that reason, the management of GE's wholly owned Carboloy subsidiary had approached Percy Bridgman about making diamonds by substituting carbide anvils for his weaker steel ones, and General Electric had assumed a leading role in the 1941 consortium that commissioned Bridgman's diamond studies. In 1950, with the research efforts of other companies showing no significant progress, GE committed its own considerable resources to diamond making.

The diamond-making effort, code-named Project Superpressure, was undertaken at the General Electric Research Laboratory in Schenectady, New York, a bustling city of 100,000. Located on the scenic Mohawk River a dozen miles northwest of Albany, Schenectady is a town of industry, with sprawling factories and vast rail yards. It is a city with a clear purpose—a city that makes useful products and ships them off for Americans to buy. While not the first place you'd think of when talking about diamonds, Schenectady was a place where they knew how to get things done.

General Electric's first step was to find an experienced project manager, to keep the team running smoothly. They turned to Anthony J. Nerad, a man remembered with tremendous respect and affection by his former colleagues. His was an American success story. His parents emigrated from Czechoslovakia and settled in Milwaukee, and Tony took advantage of his opportunities by earning a degree in engineering from the University of Wisconsin. He gained renown at General Electric for a number of innovations, most notably his development of a critical jet engine combustion chamber that is still in use today. He was also respected as a man who knew how to energize his research team, to get everyone to contribute and keep them happy.

Longtime associate Bob Wentorf remembers Nerad's unique style. "He knew that a man could not do his best if he was pestered with red tape or disturbed by rumors. He shielded us from such distractions. He knew that a man could do better work if someone else took an interest in his progress. He would visit each of us at least twice a week, often more, and sit down and talk about what we were trying to do." And finally, Wentorf recalls, "He argued that if you weren't having fun, no matter what the circumstances, it was your own fault. Don't go around complaining—it's a sign of incompetence."

Tony Nerad jumped at the opportunity to direct GE's diamond-making effort, and he began to assemble his research team. First on board were Francis Bundy and Herbert Strong, two eager and experienced scientists with much in common. Both men were in their early forties, both had received their Ph.D.s in physics from Ohio State, and both were five-year veterans of GE's research and development department, where they fostered a fierce corporate loyalty that persists to this day. A close friendship developed between the Bundy and Strong families, who spent many vacations hiking and camping together and shared in the excitement and occasional danger of their favorite hobby, gliding.

For several years Bundy and Strong shared a top-floor office in General Electric's historic Building 37, the neat redbrick office building with the famous bold fluorescent GENERAL ELECTRIC sign and circular GE logo (their office was just below the "EL"). As members of Nerad's Mechanical Investigation Section, Bundy and Strong had been trying to improve the efficiency of the insulation used in GE refrigerators. Heat is relentlessly opportunistic, and it seeks out cold places, flowing along every available pathway to even out the temperature. It is a law of physics that no matter how hard you try, you can never remove all heat from an object, and that the colder you want to make something, the more energy you must expend. That's why you have to plug in your refrigerator and pay electric bills.

Bundy and Strong knew that heat flows best along solid pathways, so they reasoned that the best insulation would have the fewest solid pathways. Their simple and elegant solution, vacuum-encased fiberglass in which randomly crisscrossing glass strands fill space while having only minuscule contacts, provided one of the best insulations ever seen. The only drawback was the need to encase the insulation in a vacuum-tight enclosure. Reliable vacuum-tight metal panels proved too heavy for a domestic appliance. Plastic panels might have provided a good alternative, but no one had yet developed a reliable vacuum-tight plastic. Their superinsulation has been used in a few specialized applications, such as vacuum bottles for holding liquefied air, but so far that is about it.

Bundy's and Strong's commitment to Tony Nerad and the diamond-making project involved more than just a change of research. Their lab would be located in a completely new General Electric research facility, The Knolls, which had opened in 1948. The grand property overlooking the Mohawk River had been built by the Hanson family, who had made their fortune from "Pink pills for pale people." Francis Bundy, for one, was delighted with the change. His home was just a short drive from the new laboratory, but he had another commuting option. On days when the weather was favorable, he would canoe the two miles down the Mohawk River and simply walk up the hill to work.

GE situated the high-pressure laboratory near a loading dock on the new building's ground floor, right next to the sophisticated machine shop, a fortunate circumstance considering how many parts would be smashed and broken in the coming years. The new facility quickly began to take on a character all its own, thanks in part to an executive assistant, Dudley Chambers, who selected a truly awful shade of institutional green to coat just about everything. "Chambers green" became a trademark of The Knolls, and the color persists to this day.

How do you begin making diamonds? All scientific progress builds on the past, so Bundy and Strong did what all good researchers do first: they went to the library and read everything they could get their hands on. They scoured the literature, tracking down classic papers by Hannay, Moissan, and others. But mostly what they found were stacks of articles by Percy Bridgman.

Any new project at GE required at least a little paperwork—in the form of a research proposal—to define objectives and methods.

In June 1951, Bundy, Strong, and Nerad accordingly prepared a short document in which they briefly spelled out the two major problems they needed to overcome to synthesize diamond. First, the GE team had to devise a method to sustain the high temperatures and pressures at which diamond might form. Bridgman's designs seemed a good starting point. Then they had to find a chemical in which graphite would dissolve and out of which diamond would crystallize. From the beginning they placed considerable emphasis on iron, which was known to dissolve carbon easily.

You can't do high-pressure research without a press, so Bundy and Strong scrounged up a four-hundred-ton hydraulic press that dated from the turn of the century, when General Electric was still a fledgling concern. The press was evidently used in GE's earliest experiments on extruding tungsten filaments for light bulbs. These days when people talk about hydraulics, they are usually referring to devices that use a sophisticated synthetic oil in the pressure lines. But this old wreck was a true *hydraulic* press that ran on water pressure. "It leaked so badly," one of the team members recalls, "that rubber footwear, mop, and bucket were standard accessory equipment, and the press's hydraulic lines were wrapped with rags to reduce the overhead water spray." Even so, four hundred tons was better than nothing.

Bridgman's flat anvil apparatus, in which the sample is squeezed between two tough Carboloy surfaces, held all the high-pressure records in 1950, so Bundy and Strong quickly decided to start there. Bundy traveled to Cambridge, Massachusetts, where he was cordially received by the grand old man and given a comprehensive tour of his laboratory, advice on building and operating high-pressure devices, and sets of plans for his homegrown apparatus. Following Bridgman's blueprints, the GE team constructed carbide anvils with supporting steel rings, and they copied Bridgman's technique of using a ring of Indian pipestone as a gasket to confine the sample. The trouble was that only Percy Bridgman seemed to have a reliable supply of the exotic material.

Bridgman's career succeeded for many reasons, creative designs and hard work chief among them. But Bridgman also gave more than a little credit to lucky breaks. Indian pipestone—a natural gasketing material that provided both the necessary deformation and strength

—was one of those breaks. In 1950, the only satisfactory high-pressure gasketing material was high-grade Indian pipestone from quarries in Minnesota located on a Native American reservation.

In desperation, Bundy and Strong wrote to Bridgman. Bridgman's answer was typically blunt. He told them, "If you want pipestone, you have to know an Indian." Being of generous disposition, he supplied them with a name—but not that of his own carefully guarded source.

The General Electric Company wrote a detailed letter to this man, requesting his help in acquiring a reliable supply. In due course a four-page hand-scrawled letter came back, in which the correspondent complained about the government, the weather, and his mother-in-law. Finally, in the last two sentences, he wrote, "Have pipestone. Send $80."

GE sent the money. The pipestone never came.

For their first experiments Bundy and Strong were forced to use an inferior grade of pipestone, and their results in November 1951 were hardly encouraging. In their naïveté they tried to grow diamond simply and directly by passing high electric current pulses through compressed graphite disks. Bundy's lab notebook of November 23, 1951, captured a typical effort: "The test was run between 9:30 and 11:00 A.M.—the sample was loaded to 150,000 atmospheres and 20 bursts of heating current were passed through it. The calculated temperature was 1,400°C.

"Then the load on the press was gradually decreased. The Carboloy anvils snapped and spalled [fragmented] as the load was diminished. When the upper anvil was lifted clear, the pipestone was scattered around with many flaky fragments of Carboloy, and the top surface of the anvil fell away completely. . . . But the graphite sample remained unchanged."

There was not the slightest hint of transformation in the sample. It was time to get serious.

✧ ✧ ✧

Tony Nerad asked GE for better equipment and more manpower. First, they urgently needed a better press. A rough calculation suggested that a 5,000-ton press would be optimal, but such a machine would be huge and prohibitively expensive. After much debate, they settled on a 1,000-ton design, weighing 55 tons and standing two stories tall. Blueprints of the beast were drafted and sent out for competitive bids. The Birdsboro Company of Pennsylvania made the best offer—about $125,000. A purchase of that magnitude required corporate-level approval, so a second internal proposal—titled "Exploratory Project in High-Pressure and High-Temperature Processes"—was submitted to management. Diamond was certainly the prime goal of the project, but scientists can't always promise results. Guy Suits, GE vice president of research, took the view that discovering a way to make diamond would be the ideal outcome, but something good was bound to turn up in any case. The expenditure was approved.

With the failure of their Indian contact, the diamond-making team needed to locate a reliable source of gasketing material. They took this problem to a General Electric ceramics expert, Louis Navias, who suggested the mineral pyrophyllite, a soft, machinable rock sold commercially as wonderstone. Wonderstone, with its extreme uniformity and stability at high temperatures, was perfect (it's still used by high-pressure workers around the world), and it saved the day. The irony, not lost on GE workers, was that the best source of wonderstone for diamond making is South Africa.

New presses and better materials were important, but Tony Nerad knew that the real key to success was the right personnel. In late 1951 he added a much-needed technician, James E. Cheney, who had recently graduated from Siena College with a degree in biology. Carrying the official title of engineer, Jim Cheney's job was to assist the others, especially Herb Strong, in the innumerable tasks associated with the complex experimental program.

Also on board in 1951 was Harold P. Bovenkerk, who was to become a central player in the commercialization of synthetic diamond. Bovenkerk, a graduate of the University of Michigan, went to GE as an engineer in 1947 right after serving the better part of four years in the air force. Bright, affable, eager, and devoted to his company, Bovenkerk knew he wanted to be an engineer from the day at age twelve when he took apart a friend's car and put it back together without his ever knowing. Most junior GE employees were bounced around from project to project, three months at a time, but Francis

Bundy and Herb Strong knew a good man when they saw him, and Hal Bovenkerk was too good to let go. The partners convinced Tony Nerad to keep the young engineer on as a member of their team. Bovenkerk had originally joined Bundy and Strong to work on insulation; he continued that work after Bundy and Strong began their high-pressure studies, but he found himself increasingly drawn into the fascinating challenge of making diamonds. In the process, the young bachelor became almost another son in the Bundy and Strong households.

About the same time, Tony Nerad, who recognized the critical role of chemistry in the project, gathered twenty members of the General Electric Chemistry Division together and asked if anyone wanted to join Project Superpressure. Only one young scientist, H. Tracy Hall, accepted the invitation; he went on to become a key player in the diamond-making team.

Hall stands out as different from the rest of the GE diamond makers. He was intense, brilliant, driven, and more than a little egocentric, and it's easy to see how frictions might have arisen between him and his coworkers. Eventually Hall came to feel betrayed by an ungrateful company. His distress was all the more difficult for him to bear because, for as long as he could remember, Hall had wanted to work for General Electric.

As a boy, Hall was fascinated by the company that grew out of Thomas Edison's inventions and transformed America with electric power. Once a week his parents would go into town, dropping Tracy at the Ogden, Utah, library. He would devour books on science and technology; Thomas Edison and Henry Ford were his heroes. When his fourth-grade teacher asked students what they wanted to do when they grew up, Hall answered, "I want to be a scientist at GE."

The dream was not easy to fulfill, for Hall's family was poor and he had to work his way through college and graduate school. But in 1948, Ph.D. in hand, he applied for a job at General Electric's research laboratories. "I found this company to be disinterested in acquiring my services," he later wrote. "I was persistent in seeking employment, however, and was hired—reluctantly—by the G.E. Research Laboratory in the fall of 1948."

Hall joined General Electric's Chemistry Division and was assigned to work on new plastic-like materials. Du Pont's remarkable

Teflon had just come on the market, and GE worked feverishly to develop materials with similar properties. Hall's first exposure to high-pressure research came at this time. General Electric had designed a promising new plastic, but it wouldn't dissolve in any known liquid (plastic is only useful if it can be dissolved and poured into molds). Hall knew that high pressure increased the dissolving power of many chemicals, and he found a number of solvents that worked effectively at twenty or thirty atmospheres pressure. Management had little interest in Hall's discoveries, however, and he was not entirely sanguine about his prospects as a GE chemist.

It was in this uncertain frame of mind that Tracy Hall heard Tony Nerad's call for volunteers. Hall had dabbled in the diamond problem at the University of Utah, where he had studied the effects of strong electric fields on carbon crystallization. He jumped at the chance to participate in the expanded GE venture.

Shortly after Tracy Hall joined Project Superpressure, the final member of the original diamond-making team came on board. On the last day of 1951, Robert H. Wentorf, Jr., twenty-five years old and fresh out of graduate school, arrived at General Electric.

Bob Wentorf was a natural-born experimenter. When he was four years old he had delighted at watching sparks fly and fuses blow as he hooked up a string of metal objects and plugged both ends into a wall socket. "My father had to lock up the tool chest to keep me out of trouble," he recalls with a smile.

Wentorf enrolled in the chemical engineering department at the University of Wisconsin in 1944, but he found that his interests lay in the more theoretical aspects of chemistry, so he switched to physical chemistry in 1948 for his Ph.D. studies. Upon graduating in late 1951 he went straight to GE. Having inherited a considerable fortune, he didn't need to work for a living; apparently, he did it just for fun. The only obvious sign of Wentorf's wealth was his sleek black Porsche. Tracy Hall recalls one wild eighty-mile-per-hour ride on the newly opened, virtually deserted New York Thruway. In those days you had to buy a twelve-dollar permit to drive on it, and Wentorf was one of the privileged few who could afford one.

Wentorf was immediately perceived by his colleagues to be very bright, able, soft-spoken, and the kind of guy you liked to be around —traits he retains to this day. He is a tall, wiry man, with twinkling eyes and a hint of a smile. His large, strong hand envelops yours as he greets you, and with his easygoing manner he has always made friends quickly. He shared an office with Tracy Hall and remembers with pleasure their daily conversations about diamonds and life.

When scientists attempt to do something that no one has done before, they have to be willing to try lots of new ideas, most of which prove to be wrong. "You make mistakes as fast as possible," Bob Wentorf quips, "but try not to make the same mistake twice." There was no way for Tony Nerad to legislate success, but there had to be progress on two broad fronts if there was any hope of making diamonds. First, they needed a better device for obtaining and sustaining high pressure and temperature—preferably one that didn't break every time it was used. They also had to solve the complex chemical problem of diamond synthesis, because direct conversion of graphite didn't seem to work. All of the team members—Bovenkerk, Bundy, Hall, Strong, and Wentorf—were free to take off on their own, to try their hunches and take chances. At the same time, they were encouraged to interact and share ideas.

Tony Nerad decided that it was important to have a supply of diamonds to test and use as seed crystals to induce diamond growth. On May 16, 1952, Tracy Hall spent a day in New York City at the Acme Diamond Tool Company, where he was shown the bewildering variety of diamonds used by industry: gem-like crystals with perfect facets for coarse grinding; tiny shard-like chips, called points, obtained from rough shaping of gems; and black masses of microscopic diamonds. Hall was authorized to purchase up to $1,000 worth of industrial diamonds; his actual bill totaled $994.72, almost half of which was for nineteen carats (about a tenth of an ounce) of diamond points—specimens that would later play a central role in the intense controversy over who made the first diamonds.

Francis Bundy came up with the group's first new high-pressure device, a modification of Bridgman's anvils dubbed "the flying saucer" because of the distinctive shape of pressurized samples. Bridgman's anvils had failed because high temperatures softened and eroded the Carboloy surfaces. Bundy circumvented the problem by altering the anvil shape and using protective inserts of magnesium oxide for insu-

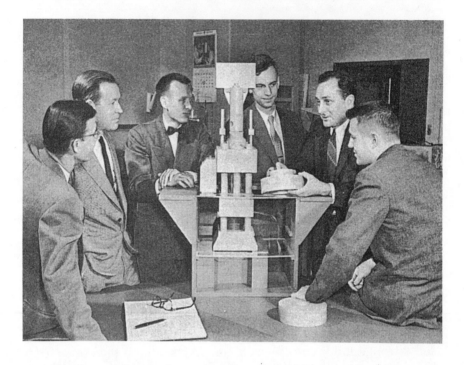

The General Electric diamond makers, circa 1955. From left to right: Francis Bundy, Herbert Strong, Tracy Hall, Robert Wentorf, Anthony Nerad, and James Cheney. (Courtesy of F. R. Boyd.)

lation. The flying saucer could repeatedly withstand much higher temperatures, up to 2,700°C, and it became the lab's workhorse during the experiments of 1952.

Unfortunately, the saucer device could not reach pressures high enough to make diamonds. Achieving high pressure requires squeezing a sample into a smaller and smaller volume, but no matter how the GE workers arranged their gaskets and samples, the two carbide anvils came into contact with each other at relatively low pressures. Once contact was made, no further sample compression, and thus no increase in pressure, was possible. At the time, Bundy believed that the flying saucer's highest possible pressure was only about 35,000 atmospheres—adequate for learning the high-pressure ropes, but not enough to make diamonds. The team was able to convert diamond partially to graphite at high pressure—a process that hinted at the

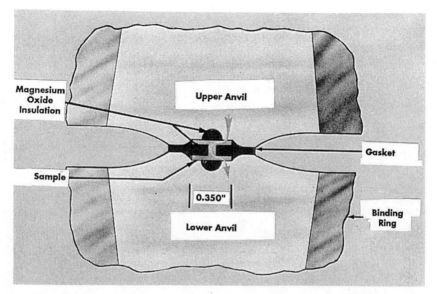

Francis Bundy's "flying saucer" device, a modification of Percy Bridgman's opposed anvil apparatus, got its name from the distinctive shape
of the sample chamber. (Courtesy of F. R. Boyd.)

conditions needed to trigger the reverse process—but they were still
a long way from their goal.

There were new devices to design and complex chemical experiments to try. It was a free-for-all, with the scientists involved in countless brainstorming sessions, each member of the team following up
on his own hunches.

While this approach would ultimately produce success, it also
sowed the seeds of an enduring and bitter controversy.

7

✧

The Breakthrough

The evidence at hand confirms that the birthday of diamond synthesis was during the night of December 8th–9th, 1954. Very shortly afterwards, diamond synthesis became a routine procedure.
—Herbert M. Strong, "Early Diamond Making at General Electric," 1989

On December 16, 1954, I discovered how to make diamonds. Others have claimed prior discovery . . . but there was something unique about mine. My method could be reproduced by others.
—H. Tracy Hall, "Personal Experiences in High Pressure," 1970

In the four decades since GE scientists first made diamonds, two contradictory interpretations of the dramatic historic events of 1953 and 1954 have persisted. These rival descriptions, each passionately argued by the central parties and each endorsed by a loyal following, differ hardly at all in the framework of facts. But the central question—who was the first to make diamonds —remains a point of contention.

One version of the history, endorsed by General Electric management as well as by Francis Bundy, Herb Strong, and Bob Wentorf, emphasizes the years of teamwork and corporate support. Guy Suits, vice president and director of research at GE, was responsible for the most extensive telling of this tale. He based his corporate history on a detailed review of laboratory notebooks and published his interpretation in 1960 as a pamphlet entitled *The Synthesis of Diamond—A Case History in Modern Science.*

Suits provides a straightforward, upbeat narrative that underscores the crucial importance of collaborative research in GE's inexorable drive to success. "I find it difficult to imagine that a single investigator could have carried the work through to a successful conclusion," he wrote. There were too many false leads, too many technical subspecialties required, and too much basic data for any one person to collect. Furthermore, he argues, "Joint effort is an almost indispensable ingredient of morale and courage." Even if one person makes a key finding, everyone in the team must share the credit equally, he argued, because "negative results contribute heavily to the final positive success." Suits recognized that this corporate policy carried with it "some penalties." In particular, "credit for progress is shared, and individual identification is partly subordinate to group achievement. But if aggregate achievement is great enough, as in this case, there is credit enough for everyone." Suits's research philosophy affected his policy for recognizing employees' discoveries. Individual creativity was viewed as secondary to group effort and all members of a team shared in the credit and financial reward.

Suits's corporate history is echoed and amplified by Herb Strong's two recent articles, "Early Diamond Making at General Electric" and "Early Diamond Making Revisited," which closely examine the critical events of November and December 1954. Strong, too, speaks proudly of the GE project as a paradigm of cooperative research and unselfish collaboration. Over the years the story has become a kind of company gospel, retold in countless brochures and even cast in bronze at the entryway of the main diamond-making plant in Worthington, Ohio.

However, a very different version of the history comes from the pen of Tracy Hall, who argues for his own unique and pivotal role in the synthesis of diamond. Hall publicized his interpretation in several short, bitter articles, including the outspoken "Personal Experiences in High Pressure" that appeared in *The Chemist* in July 1970. Hall dismisses the importance of collaborative research at GE and promotes his own central role. Though hampered by a bureaucratic management and unsympathetic coworkers, his story goes, Hall solved the key problems of device design and chemistry almost entirely himself. Many in the scientific community, impressed with Hall's brilliant subsequent innovations in high pressure, have tended to accept this version as closer to the truth. Tracy Hall is unequivocally cited as the first to make diamonds in several authoritative histories, and it was he alone who received the American Chemical Society's gold medal for creative invention in 1972.

As Hall's narrative implies, the history of diamond making at GE is actually several, intertwined stories. Bovenkerk, Bundy, Hall, Strong, and Wentorf were all gifted men; each had his own ideas and ambitions, and each followed his own hunches. The General Electric history is the story of a team, constantly brainstorming. The extent to which ideas were developed collectively or independently is unrecorded, but there was certainly a great deal of interaction. Nerad held group meetings at least twice a week to hash out ideas and discuss priorities, and there were incessant informal conversations as well. Still, by everyone's account, Tracy Hall was the odd man out.

In Hall's opinion, the reason for his isolation boiled down to one simple fact—he was a Mormon, and that didn't sit well with the others. His social life revolved around the church and his large family. Weekend camping trips, skiing vacations, and socializing after work with the other guys were out of the question. "My problem was that the others were a club," he laments. But the isolation seemed to go beyond that. Hall is convinced that he was the victim of religious discrimination. General Electric promotions and raises were based in part on peer review; Hall believes that he was penalized for spending too much time with his church. He also recalls the jokes—vicious, distasteful jokes about Mormons and polygamy. How much of this is true (the others strongly deny any prejudice), and how much was in the imagination of an embittered employee, is impossible to say, but the rift was real.

Money represented another bone of contention. For Francis Bundy, Herb Strong, and Bob Wentorf, promotions and raises and bonuses never seemed a central concern. Bundy and Strong lived simply, had small families, and were content to spend vacations camping; Wentorf inherited a small fortune from his parents and was unconcerned about salaries and retirement. But Hall had a large family to support and a church that expected sizable contributions as well. He desperately wanted to improve his family's lot, and he expected much more from General Electric than he ever got. "I went five years without a raise," he laments. When he made diamonds he

was finally given a paltry salary increase, from $10,000 to $11,000—
"much less than what Bundy and Strong were making. I loved GE,
and they didn't love me back." Hall speaks passionately about his role:
"I hit the home runs, but they took the credit. It was worth a Nobel."
Tracy Hall has found many reasons to be resentful.

Who was the first to synthesize diamond? The answer lies not so
much in what any one person did on a particular day, but rather in
the nature of scientific discovery itself. What does it mean to make a
discovery? What does it mean to be the first?

Early in 1953 the GE diamond
makers faced a major dilemma. Bundy's flying saucer device could
sustain high temperatures and so was a distinct improvement over
Bridgman's simple opposed anvils, but the saucer couldn't squeeze
samples into the minute volume needed to generate really high pressures. Everyone was pushed to think about new devices.

Piston-in-cylinder designs provided a promising alternative. A
simple piston-in-cylinder arrangement can, at least in principle,
achieve any desired pressure by squeezing a sample into a smaller and
smaller volume. The piston-cylinder design is limited, however, by
the difficulty of supporting the piston, which tends to break under the
stress of high temperature and pressure. The GE team had to find a
compromise, combining the durability and temperature capabilities
of the flying saucer with the ease and pressure capabilities of a piston-
cylinder device.

Strong, Wentorf, and Hall all designed and tested modifications
of the basic piston-cylinder apparatus. Each scientist waited impa-
tiently for the machine shop to build his design, and waited again for
time on the press to try it out. The men came up with all sorts of
intriguing possibilities like the stubby piston and cylinder, the collared
piston and cylinder, and more. Wentorf was especially prolific,
though none of his devices was very successful. "I have more high-
pressure apparatus patents than Herb and Francis put together, and
none of them ever worked," Wentorf laughs.

But attaining high pressure was only part of the challenge. The
samples also had to be heated to temperatures approaching 1,500°C.

Strong and Bundy favored the tried-and-true technique of passing electricity through a coil of platinum wire, which glowed intensely hot around the sample. The technique produced the desired high temperature, but replacing the platinum coil after every experiment was expensive and time-consuming.

The GE team also tried heating samples by passing electric current through a graphite heater, much as Loring Coes had done. This simple and elegant solution to the high-temperature problem used a short graphite cylinder to surround the sample. The cylinder not only functioned as a heater, it also provided more carbon for potential conversion to diamond.

As competition intensified and the queue for machining and press time lengthened, the first real signs of conflict began to disrupt the group. During 1953, Herb Strong and Tracy Hall each perfected a device that combined many of the best features of the saucer and the piston-cylinder designs. Strong's cone apparatus, the more conservative of the two machines, featured two simple beveled anvils with flat surfaces, much like Bridgman's, but also incorporated a thick-walled cylinder of steel or carbide to provide a larger sample chamber. The upper anvil drove a Carboloy piston into the sample chamber.

Rather than use a single gasket of soft wonderstone, Strong's device relied on a clever sandwich of alternating layers of wonderstone and steel. This arrangement could accommodate larger samples and sustain higher pressures. Tracy Hall claims that he suggested this improvement, which set pressure records at the GE lab. Hall recalls that his idea of a sandwich gasket was rejected when first proposed at a group meeting but was adopted by Strong a short time later, without credit. Hal Bovenkerk believes that *he* was the first to suggest the gasket modification, while Herb Strong insists that the sandwich gasket was an obvious way to increase pressure; such composite seals had been used in high-pressure work for more than half a century. Whatever the truth, Strong's cone apparatus was far more successful than previous GE devices. It easily achieved 40,000 atmospheres at temperatures up to 2,000°C.

Hall's rival device, known as the semi-piston-and-cylinder or half-belt, displayed many of the same features as Strong's cone apparatus, but it represented a much more radical departure from traditional high-pressure design. The upper anvil had an unprecedented graceful

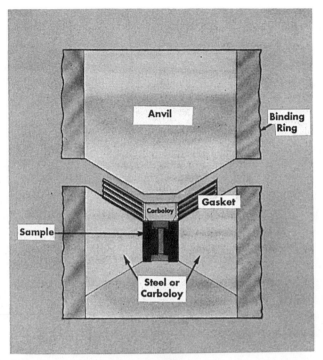

Herb Strong's cone apparatus featured a strong binding ring and a layered gasket of alternating steel and pyrophyllite cones that helped to confine the sample laterally as it was compressed by the massive piston. (Courtesy of F. R. Boyd.)

concave surface that fit into a well in the lower anvil, which had a slightly steeper curve. This complex geometry reduced piston break-age, helped to control gasket failure, and provided a greater sample volume than the saucer, while maintaining the saucer's heating ca-pabilities. Hall was able to push his half-belt repeatedly to 40,000 atmospheres and more than 2,000°C—the temperature at which the device itself melted.

With three working devices—Bundy's flying saucer, Strong's cone apparatus, and Hall's half-belt—and only one press (the new thousand-ton press was not expected until early 1954), there were bound to be conflicts. Hall was convinced that his half-belt idea was best, and Strong was equally determined to promote his cone apparatus. These tensions were exacerbated when Tracy Hall asked to build an even more radical device—the full-belt. Hall complained:

> The Half-Belt gave higher steady-state pressures and temperatures than had ever been achieved simultaneously. But because my colleagues felt negatively about it, when I proposed to build an improved version, the "Full-Belt" or just plain "Belt," the proposal was rejected, although the cost was less than a thousand dollars. I fretted about this for a time and then decided on a sub-rosa solution. Friends in the machine shop agreed to build the Belt, unofficially, on slack time. This took several months. Ordinarily, it would have taken only a week.

Tracy Hall's half-belt apparatus incorporated features of both the flying saucer and the cone. However, the gradually tapered piston and curved pyrophyllite gasket was original to this design. (Courtesy of F. R. Boyd.)

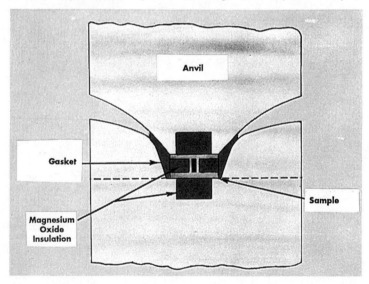

The completed belt apparatus was a thing of beauty—sleek and shiny with curves of elegant function and form. Hall had relied on the traditional opposed piston geometry, but he tapered and curved his anvils and drove them into the rounded openings of a steel doughnut he called the belt. As the two tapered anvils compress the ends of the disk-shaped sample with increasing force, the belt provides more support around the circumference of the sample, allowing the device to achieve higher pressures. Hall also relied on clever wonderstone and steel gaskets—called flowerpots because of their distinctive tapered form—to hold the sample in place.

Hall's simple, elegant belt apparatus worked wonderfully well, though the tapered anvils had an annoying habit of breaking after every few runs. The belt was easy to use with a graphite heater, and extreme temperatures and pressures could be maintained for long periods without difficulty. "It operated so successfully, in my view,

Hall's full-belt apparatus employed two tapered pistons and a doughnut-shaped binding ring. This design greatly increased the stroke—the total travel distance of the pistons—and thus allowed for higher pressures. (Courtesy of F. R. Boyd.)

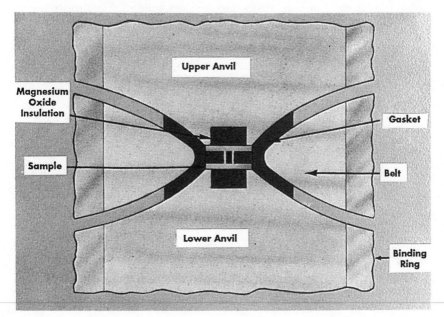

that I desired to have the critical components constructed of [Carbo-loy]. This would allow much higher pressures to be generated. Man-agement, however, would not approve the purchase of the carbide."

In spite of General Electric's expertise in making carbide com-ponents, the Superpressure group did not have free access to the material. Carbide pieces were expensive and time-consuming to pro-duce. Bundy's flying saucer and Strong's cone apparatus had first been built from hardened steel, and it seems to have been standard policy to test the steel version fully before going to carbide. Neverthe-less, Hall saw the denial as another slight, another cause for resent-ment, and once again he looked elsewhere for support. "Having been stopped by the Superpressure people, I appealed to my former super-visor [chemist Herman Liebhafsky] and spoke at a seminar of his group concerning the Belt. He and his group were impressed and shortly thereafter permission was received to buy the carbide compo-nents."

By early 1954 the General Electric team had its devices in place. Herb Strong placed his cone apparatus in the new two-story, thou-sand-ton Birdsboro press, which had just arrived at the lab. Tracy Hall's improved belt apparatus was assigned—relegated, Hall would say—to the antique four-hundred-ton hydraulic press, where Hall and Wentorf were able to sustain experiments at 70,000 atmospheres, with shorter excursions to pressure estimated as high as 100,000 at-mospheres. The race to make diamonds began in earnest.

Achieving high pressures and tem-peratures was only one arena for the fierce competition between sci-entists. The men were also in a race to discover the chemistry of diamond synthesis. Hundreds of promising avenues had to be tried, and each of the scientists was encouraged to pursue his own ideas. Chemist Bob Wentorf decided to run a series of experiments on so-dium carbide and lithium carbide, and he was the first to smell dia-mond. In the fall of 1953 he found that lithium carbide decomposed at high pressure and temperature, producing tiny crystals that might have been diamonds. Herb Strong recorded the apparent success in his notebook: "From many tests on scratching glass, and [x-ray evi-

Francis Bundy, Herb Strong, and Jim Cheney operate the thousand-ton, two-story-tall Birdsboro press, while Tracy Hall (left center) uses the antiquated four-hundred-ton hydraulic press, circa 1954. (Courtesy of H. T. Hall.)

dence], we now feel quite certain that diamonds were made," though later he backed off this claim.

In spite of these initial indications, repeated attempts failed to improve the yield or clarify the x-ray results, and that tack was finally abandoned. Unfortunately, all the samples, which sat in a drawer for years, were thrown away a decade ago without ever being reanalyzed. Modern analytical techniques could easily have revealed any traces of synthetic diamond.

Wentorf also experimented with mixtures of aluminum oxide and carbon. When heated and squeezed, the mixture produced hard, brilliant crystals less than a thousandth of an inch across, with diamond's familiar octahedral shape. But Wentorf's hopes were dashed when further analysis showed the crystals to be corundum, the common abrasive form of aluminum oxide.

Tracy Hall concentrated on pressurizing chemicals containing carbon and oxygen. He too produced tiny diamond-like crystals, though they were too small to positively identify as diamonds. Hall also tackled the challenge of direct conversion of graphite to diamond using the new high-pressure capabilities of his belt apparatus, but even at sustained conditions approaching 100,000 atmospheres and 4,000°C, no diamonds were found.

Intervals between these groundbreaking experiments were punctuated by more routine lab exercises. During the crucial late autumn weeks of 1954, Hall devoted much of his energy to establishing a reliable way to measure temperatures in the belt. He also attempted to duplicate several of Loring Coes's experiments on high-pressure minerals, and had time to muse about some rather unorthodox experiments: on December 3, 1954, he wrote in his lab notebook, "I should measure the effect of ultra-hi-P and hi-T on bacteria. . . . Perhaps they will stand much higher temperature at a high pressure."

Meanwhile, Herb Strong was putting his cone apparatus through its paces. In his first experiments he tried to induce growth on a diamond seed crystal. Before being squeezed, the seed crystal displayed sharp angular features, but afterward "the edges were rounded and the faces had the appearance of a contour map as though rapid growth had occurred." In retrospect, however, it seems unlikely that the cone apparatus achieved conditions for diamond growth.

Strong also began thinking about a more pivotal set of experiments, inspired by the discovery of diamonds in some iron meteorites. In the tradition of Moissan and Parsons, he suggested dissolving carbon into iron and other metals. His lab notebook entry of November 22, 1954, records this key idea: "[Iron and other metals] should be investigated at high pressure as a solvent for carbon. . . . I think the work will have an important bearing on diamond growth."

Although the would-be diamond makers didn't realize it at the time, late November 1954 marked a crisis in the General Electric effort. All of the original research funds allocated to Project Superpressure had been exhausted a year before. Twice Tony Nerad had gone to GE's vice president and director of research, Guy Suits, and asked for additional funds; twice the money had been provided and used up. For a third time Nerad went to Suits, hat in hand. This time Suits brought the matter up before the November meeting of GE research managers. Nerad sensed trouble.

Project Superpressure was approaching its fourth anniversary— four years of GE investment in research that, to many, seemed rather abstract at best. Diamond making was a nice dream, but no one had forgotten the failures of Percy Bridgman and the Norton Company. When asked to discuss the benefits of continuing the high-pressure program, Nerad had nothing concrete to offer. When the question of continuing the project was put to a vote, the other research managers almost unanimously voted thumbs down. Fortunately for the diamond makers, General Electric was not a democracy; Guy Suits decided, for a short while longer at least, to let the high-pressure group proceed.

Time was running out. Nerad knew that his team couldn't meet a deadline, but he hinted to team members that some kind of breakthrough was needed, and needed soon. Strong took the warning to heart and decided to go all out with the cone apparatus and an iron solvent.

Strong began the critical run, experiment 151, on the evening of Wednesday, December 8, 1954. He selected two small diamond seed crystals, embedded them in black carbon powder, and surrounded the sample with iron foil. Strong loaded the sample into the cone apparatus and raised the pressure to an estimated 50,000 atmospheres pressure at 1,250°C. While most previous experiments had been relatively quick, taking just a few minutes, Strong had always had a nagging suspicion that time might be a critical factor—after all, nature seemed to take millions of years to grow diamonds. So Strong planned this overnight attempt for an unusually long sixteen hours. The run was monitored by a night watchman, who every so often recorded the heater power settings displayed on a large meter. Except for some annoying fluctuations in current that raised temperatures above the preset conditions, the run seemed completely ordinary.

Strong removed the specimen on the morning of December 9 and examined the products. The two seed crystals tumbled free; they hadn't changed at all. No sign of diamond growth was found, and he chalked it up as just another failed experiment. However, he did notice that a portion of the iron foil had melted into a blob at one end of his sample chamber. One of his principal motivations for the experiment was to determine how much carbon could be dissolved in molten iron. He wanted to know if any reaction had taken place among the starting materials, so he sent the sample to the metallurgy division to be polished (and prepared for light microscopy) whenever they had a few free moments.

Herb Strong was totally unprepared for the message that came back from metallurgy a week later, on December fifteenth.

"I'm terribly sorry, but I can't polish your sample. It's gouging my polishing wheel," the technician complained. Strong rushed to the metallurgy labs to have a look. A distinctive octahedral point protruded from the hard metal mass of his sample.

Strong wrote his own account of the subsequent dramatic events. "The entire group gathered around to inspect that hard point. Initially there was a moment of stunned silence. Could it possibly be diamond? Finally, Tracy Hall spoke the verdict: 'It must be a diamond!' " Eventually, two shard-like diamonds, one-sixteenth of an inch in the longest dimension, were separated from the sample. X-ray analysis proved beyond doubt the identity of Strong's historic crystals.

✧ ✧ ✧

In the subsequent weeks, months, and years the members of the General Electric diamond-making team —Tracy Hall and Herb Strong, in particular—devoted an inordinate amount of time and energy debating the origin of those two tiny crystals. What is beyond debate, however, is that the very next day, on December 16, 1954, Tracy Hall performed a similar experiment in the belt. He added two diamond seed crystals to iron sulfide (a mineral associated with diamonds in meteorites) and placed this material in a cylindrical graphite heater. The experiment, performed at an estimated 100,000 atmospheres and 1,600°C, took only thirty-eight minutes.

Hall described what he found in vivid detail. "I broke open a sample cell after removing it from the Belt. . . . Instantly, my hands began to tremble. My heart beat wildly. My knees weakened and no longer gave support. Indescribable emotion overcame me and I had to find a place to sit down!

"My eyes had caught the flashing light from dozens of triangular faces of octahedral crystals that were stuck to the tantalum and I knew that diamonds had finally been made by man."

Weeks of feverish activity followed Strong and Hall's exciting discoveries. Reproducibility is critical to the confirmation of any scientific advance, and Bundy and Strong tried numerous times to duplicate Strong's feat. Tony Nerad also assigned Hal Bovenkerk the task of repeating Strong's run independently with the steel cone apparatus in the thousand-ton press.

They couldn't do it. "We wasted weeks," Bovenkerk complains. Pressures were never quite high enough, and iron carbide always appeared instead of diamond, thus effectively blocking the path to diamond growth. It was not until more than a month later, with the installation of carbide anvil components, that the cone apparatus routinely attained the pressures required for diamond synthesis.

Tracy Hall and Bob Wentorf, on the other hand, repeated their synthesis with ease. Armed with the belt apparatus mounted in the old four-hundred-ton press they made diamonds over and over again —twenty times in the next two weeks. Under Hall's supervision, GE physicist Hugh Woodbury became the first person outside the Superpressure group to confirm the synthesis claim, making a successful run on December 31, 1954.

The race to make diamonds was over.

✧ ✧ ✧

For years historians and the principal players have debated who was the first to synthesize diamonds. From the very beginning there were serious misgivings about the origin of Strong's two tiny crystals that he supposedly created on the night of December 8. Tracy Hall admits to having said, "It must be a diamond," when he saw a crystal embedded in Strong's experiment. But he is quick to add, "I never said it was a *synthetic* diamond. No one believed that."

Strong's inability to duplicate his diamond-making feat without substituting carbide parts for the cone apparatus's steel anvils cast great doubt on the validity of the December eighth experiment. In two detailed, complexly argued articles, Strong suggests that temperature fluctuations during the night of the eighth were just sufficient to create the extreme conditions necessary for diamond growth. Hal Bovenkerk, who struggled for weeks to duplicate Strong's experiment and subsequently spent four decades making diamonds for GE, isn't convinced. That frustrating, wasted month, while others enjoyed the thrill of making diamonds on Hall's belt, "made me a disbeliever," he says.

Of the two small diamonds from Strong's run, only the larger survives. It has become a piece of GE history, lovingly protected on a special wooden plaque with a built-in magnifier and engraved plate proclaiming it to be the "First Diamond Made in GE Research Laboratory." The plaque was presented in 1955 to General Electric's CEO, Ralph Cordiner, to display in his office, and there was some talk of transferring the display to the Smithsonian Institution. The souvenir lost some of its appeal, however, when Tracy Hall wrote a sharp letter to Cordiner and the Smithsonian discrediting the crystal and claiming priority for his own synthesis. Cordiner, not wishing to become involved in the controversy, returned the display to Herb Strong, who for a time kept it in his office. Eventually, the crystal was placed in General Electric's historical display in Schenectady, where it can still be seen.

Ironically, that sole surviving crystal, enshrined as a piece of history, now provides compelling proof that no diamonds were made on that December night four decades ago. General Electric experts now acknowledge that Herb Strong's crystal could not possibly be a synthetic diamond. GE insiders cite a litany of anomalies. The crystal is unusually large—perhaps ten times the size of any other crystal produced during those first weeks. The elongated shape is odd, too, for most of the early crystals were more or less round. Strong's diamond is water clear, while typical synthetic diamonds are yellowish; it displays atypical surface markings; its x-ray pattern lacks the distinctive "satellite" spots from growth defects characteristic of most man-made diamond. And, most damning, its infrared spectra, first measured in the spring of 1992, show distinctive features found only in natural diamond. In fact, Strong's diamond looks for all the world like one of the natural diamond points that Tracy Hall brought back by the hundreds from New York City.

The "first diamond" is nothing more than a shard from a natural stone. But, in a sense, the nature and origin of that one crystal is unimportant. Whether or not Strong's experiment was easily duplicated, whether or not the diamond crystal was grown by man or was natural and inadvertently slipped into the experiment, there can be no doubt that Strong's experiment pointed Tracy Hall in the right direction. The very day after Strong's "discovery," Hall did in fact make diamonds.

Without question Tracy Hall conducted the first experimental diamond synthesis that was easily and independently reproduced. Hall was the inventor of the belt apparatus and was able to make diamonds over and over again with it. But Hall's experiment of December 16 was the culmination of almost four years of focused research and was influenced directly by Herb Strong's announcement of the previous day claiming success with a sample of mixed iron and carbon.

Tracy Hall never worked in a vacuum, and it is unlikely that he could have learned to make diamonds without his Superpressure colleagues and the company that brought them together. By the same token, Tracy Hall, perhaps by virtue of being the lone wolf of the team, played a unique and pivotal role. His belt apparatus—virtually unchanged in its basic features to this day—was a brilliant advance and a key to GE's success. By ignoring the critical nature of his contributions, General Electric and its spokesmen have polarized and distorted the historical record.

It is sad, in a way. For more than a century diamond synthesis stood as one of science's most glamorous, intractable problems. Some of the world's foremost scientists, Nobelists Moissan and Bridgman among them, devoted years to the quest. General Electric's effort to synthesize diamond produced major advances in attaining extreme temperature and pressure, as well as the discovery of the appropriate chemical environment for diamond growth. The team's solution to the problem was the kind of breakthrough that deserved a Nobel prize and could have easily commanded it with the right kind of publicity. But General Electric's original team featured a half-dozen diamond makers, and Nobels can be shared by only three people. If GE had highlighted Tracy Hall's special role and promoted his nomination for the prize, General Electric could have heaped glory on top of their extraordinary commercial success. With such a magnificent discovery, there was plenty of credit to go around.

So much history has been lost. The exhaustive laboratory notebooks—except for the critical pages from late 1954—are unavailable for study and may have been discarded. All of the original high-pressure samples made from 1951 to 1954 were stored in a drawer and eventually thrown away. As a result, some key questions will never be answered. Did the General Electric team make diamond before December 1954? Were there tiny diamonds embedded in those tantalizing runs of 1953? Possibly, but we will never know for sure.

Nevertheless, it is clear that General Electric ultimately won the race to synthesize diamond because, in the words of Percy Bridgman, they "found out how to apply more pressure at a higher temperature and for a longer time than ever achieved before." They learned a quick, easy, reproducible way to do something no one had done before. But for the GE diamond makers, the adventure had just begun.

8

✧

Secrets

In February of 1955 I must confess that an ill-timed sneeze in the wrong
place would have wiped out the entire world supply of Man-Made diamonds.

—C. Guy Suits, "Scientific Competition," 1963

If anything frightened the General
Electric team more than failure, it was the prospect of proclaiming
success and then being proven wrong. The history of diamond research is littered with mistaken claims of synthesis, if not outright
fraud, and General Electric wanted no part of the embarrassment of
a premature announcement. Guy Suits insisted that Tony Nerad's
group redouble its efforts and take every possible step to confirm the
discovery.

Confirmation depended on a threefold strategy. First, make as
much diamond as possible with Tracy Hall's proven technique. Second, subject those samples to every test in the book to confirm their
identity and test their grinding properties. Third, discover as many
ways as possible to make diamonds at the high pressures and temperatures available with the belt and cone apparatus.

Tracy Hall was on a roll, synthesizing diamond in run after run
in the carbide-tipped belt. Each of his fifteen- or twenty-minute experiments produced up to a quarter of a carat of tiny diamond crystals. Hall's first diamond-making experiment used an iron sulfide, but
GE workers soon discovered that iron metal worked even better.

The group subjected their newly grown diamonds to every possible chemical and physical test. The crystals withstood immersion in the strongest acids and burned to yield only carbon dioxide; taken together, the tests provided convincing evidence that the crystals were pure carbon. X-ray diffraction studies revealed the characteristic pattern of natural diamond's atomic structure. The synthetic crystals' density (3.53 grams per cubic centimeter), distinctive optical properties, and extreme hardness also matched South African gems. There was no doubt whatsoever that the GE team had made diamond.

Even with such definitive proof, there was still one crucial step left to be taken. A completely independent group of scientists—men who could not possibly have conspired with the Superpressure team —were brought in to duplicate the experiment. On January 18 and 19, 1955, General Electric scientists Hugh Woodbury and Richard Oriani obtained their own independent sources of iron and graphite, and each made three runs with the belt apparatus on the four-hundred-ton hydraulic press. Hall and the other team members were not allowed to be present for this independent test, but Woodbury had completed one run under Hall's supervision and Hall had given him additional detailed instructions. Novice operators Woodbury and Oriani shaped wonderstone gaskets, packed metal and graphite samples, ran the experiments, and analyzed their products. They produced diamonds in all six experiments.

General Electric announced the creation of "Man-Made" diamonds, the new trade name for their product, at a well-orchestrated press conference on February 15, 1955, two years to the day after ASEA's isolated, unpublicized success. Curious reporters were allowed to view a small pile of undistinguished-looking blackish grains under the microscope. The original research group posed for photographs but was then sent away with strict instructions not to talk to anyone about the diamond-making process until the publicity died down. Bundy, Strong, Bovenkerk, and Wentorf went on a cross-country ski trip on frozen Lake George.

In spite of GE's promotional efforts, not everyone was impressed by the display. Some reporters wondered why a company would invest a million dollars to produce what looked like a thimbleful of grit. Of what possible use could these tiny crystals be? But the diamond world was stunned by the news, and the world's diamond market was thrown into turmoil. At the time General Electric made its announcement, diamond trading, both for gemstones and industrial-grade material, was controlled almost exclusively by the De Beers cartel. De Beers Consolidated Mines of Kimberley, South Africa, had a virtual monopoly, selling what it wanted, to whom it wanted, at whatever price it wanted. It had long been rumored that De Beers had stockpiled vast hoards of diamonds; some suggested that for every diamond sold, one was put away for the future, and still their profit margin exceeded 50 percent. News of a potentially unlimited source of synthetic diamonds did not please the cartel.

De Beers stock dropped precipitously, while the total value of General Electric stock jumped overnight by more than $300 million. Some jewelers with sizable diamond investments panicked, and bushels of mail arrived at Schenectady from around the world. Distraught gem merchants wanted to know if they had been ruined, outraged jewelers called GE's act unnatural, and would-be investors tried all sorts of ploys to obtain a piece of the pie. The value of stock and gemstone inventories returned to normal after a few days, but the diamond world had been changed forever.

Francis Bundy remembers his favorite letter from that turbulent time, one with a delightfully pragmatic approach to the GE announcement. Eight-year-old Chucky Singer of Peabody, Massachusetts, sent them a chunk of coal with a simple request. "I am sending you a piece of coal I found for you to make into a diamond in your machine. Please send it back to me." A few weeks later Chucky Singer received a small synthetic diamond in the mail.

Other correspondents were less optimistic. An anonymous California critic wrote, "You can't make real diamonds for they are nature grown. You can't make gold; no one can. They dig gold out of the ground and also diamonds. But no one can make them with a machine. That is just a lot of bull."

General Electric was happy to publicize its triumph, but the world wouldn't find out how they made diamonds for several years. The original diamond-making team was given strict instructions about what to say and how to act. Bundy, Hall, Strong, and Wentorf were allowed to publish an article entitled "Man-Made Diamonds" in the prestigious weekly journal *Nature*, but except for mentioning high temperature and pressure, the piece gave no details about the process, which infuriated some readers. Scientific papers, the disgruntled subscribers argued, should include enough information for any reader to duplicate the results; the General Electric article was nothing more than a free advertisement.

GE rushed to submit several patents—one for the belt apparatus under Hall's name, others for aspects of the diamond-making process signed by various combinations of the five principal team members. But when the documents reached the U.S. Patent Office they were immediately placed under a secrecy order; officials at the Commerce Department had not forgotten the fear of a diamond shortage during World War II. As a result of their ruling, no one else could see the patents or learn their secrets.

General Electric management accepted this news with mixed feelings. Without international patent protection other companies might discover how to do it, too. But GE administrators also knew that as soon as the patents were made public, other researchers could take that hard-won information and attempt to improve the process. The government-imposed secrecy gave the GE team years to perfect their procedures without other researchers breathing down their necks.

One vital question remained for General Electric engineers to answer: would synthetic diamonds work as an effective abrasive? For several feverish weeks, from early January to mid-February 1955, that question became the all-consuming passion of Hal Bovenkerk, who was to become a key player in the commercialization of synthetic diamonds. In early 1955 Hal Bovenkerk and Jim Cheney worked around the clock, completing dozens of fifteen-minute runs with the belt apparatus, sleeping near the presses. Hall's original belt had been refitted into a brand-new tabletop two-hundred-ton press, while the cumbersome thousand-ton monster stood idly by. The machine shop was kept busy with orders for a steady stream of wonderstone "flowerpots" and replacements for the belt components that broke with annoying frequency.

Each run produced a tough cylindrical plug of metal, graphite,

Harold Bovenkerk adjusting a belt apparatus, mounted in a thousand-ton press. (Courtesy of F. R. Boyd.)

and diamond somewhat smaller than a pencil's eraser. When cleaned in concentrated acids, each plug yielded a fraction of a carat of diamond. Finally, after more than a hundred synthesis runs, they had what they needed—a precious stockpile of twenty-three carats of tiny black synthetic diamond crystals. Bovenkerk hand-carried the supply to GE's Carboloy plant in Detroit, where the grit was fabricated into a test grinding wheel.

The synthetic crystals worked better than the scientists had hoped. Their sharp, tiny crystal faces proved ideal for grinding. And because the GE diamond makers were able to control the precise size of their crystals, they could produce diamond grit of unprecedented uniformity. A billion-dollar industry had been born.

✧ ✧ ✧

The GE project was an unqualified success, but the scientists on the Superpressure team would not share in the spoils. In exchange for their salary, researchers at General Electric sign away any rights to their patents, as is the case at most corporations. The diamond makers each received the standard company bonus, a twenty-five-dollar savings bond for each patent. There were no instant promotions or extravagant increases in salary. In the view of management, the Superpressure scientists were just doing their job.

But with his key contribution so poorly recognized, and with such small financial reward for his years of work, Tracy Hall had had enough. "Saddened and hurt, I left General Electric, a company I had admired and aspired to work for since the age of nine," he wrote. As news of diamond synthesis and Hall's special role in designing the belt spread, he became a hot property, and he had no trouble finding employment elsewhere. Philip Abelson, president of the Carnegie Institution of Washington, tried to get him to join the Geophysical Laboratory, where Joe Boyd and Hat Yoder had an active high-pressure program, but Hall wanted to return to his roots. In September 1955 he eagerly accepted the position as professor of chemistry and director of research at Brigham Young University in Provo, Utah. Though his starting salary was only $7,500, significantly less than he had been earning at GE, he was treated well and given a large Quonset hut for his high-pressure laboratory and enough money to fill it with equipment.

Ironically, Tracy Hall was forbidden by company and government strictures to build or publish details of his own pioneering belt apparatus design. He made several trips to the U.S. Department of Commerce in Washington in an effort to alter the secrecy ruling, but to no avail. "The solution to my problem dawned one day when a man from the Commerce Department said, 'Hall, why don't you invent another apparatus?' " In a brilliant display of defiance and determination, Tracy Hall proceeded to design a completely different kind of high-pressure device of breathtaking novelty. With it, he duplicated his diamond-making feat.

With the help of a $10,000 grant from the Carnegie Institution of Washington, courtesy of Phil Abelson, and additional funding from the National Science Foundation, Hall invented a remarkable press, different from anything seen before. With the exception of von Platen's split-sphere device, all previous designs applied pressure by squeezing a sample between two flat surfaces—an action as familiar and logical as squashing a bug. Hall, in his second device, resorted to a completely different geometry—a pyramid of four pistons, one pointing straight down, the other three angling upward to meet at the faces of a tetrahedral sample assembly.

The first tetrahedral-anvil press, completed by Hall in 1957, was unlike any other high-pressure device ever conceived. Even so, Hall

Tracy Hall's tetrahedral-anvil press incorporated four pistons tipped with carbide anvils, each piston directed toward one face of a tetrahedral sample chamber. This device was Hall's second novel diamond-making design. (Courtesy of A. A. Giardini.)

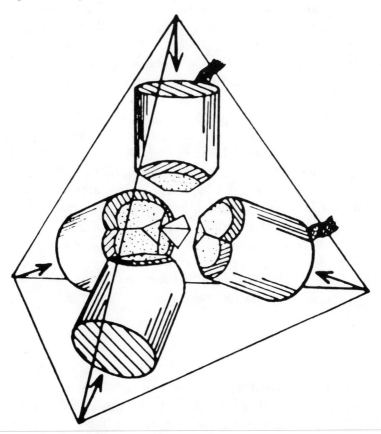

could not be sure that the government would treat it as a new invention; if in their opinion he had violated the secrecy agreement by building the machine, he would be subject to two years in jail and a $10,000 fine. "Never had I had so much anxiety and so many sleepless nights," he recalls. After much deliberation, he decided that his invention was original and accordingly filed for a patent, submitted a descriptive article to *The Review of Scientific Instruments*, and gave a triumphant talk at the spring 1958 meeting of the American Chemical Society. He also sent out reprints of the article to dozens of scientists around the world.

The triumph turned to farce shortly thereafter when the same Commerce Department official who had encouraged Hall to try something new and promised to waive any restrictions slapped a secrecy order on the tetrahedral press. It was too late to stop publication or retrieve all the reprints, but Hall was instructed to notify everyone who knew of the device that it was a secret and "conveyance of this secret to another was an act subject to the 2-year prison sentence and $10,000 fine." The fact that the experimental details were known to hundreds of scientists and that the design had been published in an international journal did not seem to matter to government bureaucrats. Commerce officials decided that Hall would have to notify the hundred or so individuals who had either seen the press in person or had asked for reprints of the article.

Fortunately the secrecy order was soon lifted, and by 1959 Hall was finally free to conduct high-pressure research and publicize his results without fear of reprisal. He received his patent and built and sold his tetrahedral apparatus to more than a dozen high-pressure laboratories. The invention of the tetrahedral press placed Hall at the leading edge of high-pressure research and, perhaps more than any other factor, convinced many of his central contribution to General Electric's diamond-making success.

✧ ✧ ✧

Of all the world's scientists who heard GE's diamond-making news, none was more intrigued than Percy Bridgman. After more than forty years of failed attempts, he wanted to see the feat accomplished at first hand. In the summer of

1955, just a few months after the GE announcement, Bridgman was asked by *Scientific American* to write a story on the historic breakthrough, so he paid a visit to The Knolls and had his chance. Bovenkerk, Bundy, Hall, Strong, and Wentorf stood aside, partly in pride and partly in reverence, as the old master assembled an experiment himself and, at last, made diamonds. Francis Bundy described the scene: "He put the cell together, put it in the high-pressure apparatus, did all the operations following our directions, and had a successful run. We gave him the diamonds he had made—and he treasured them." Of course, Bridgman wasn't allowed to reveal any proprietary details in the *Scientific American* article, but his endorsement was a great advertisement for GE.

General Electric was happy to take advantage of the Nobel prize–winner's interest and in late 1955 asked him to become a consultant

Percy Bridgman finally made diamonds during a visit to the General Electric Schenectady facility in March 1955. Bridgman (left) sits with fellow Nobelist Irving Langmuir, while (left to right) Bob Wentorf, Herb Strong, and Francis Bundy look on. (Courtesy of H. M. Strong.)

to help with improvements in the process. After just two visits, however, Bridgman offered his resignation, noting that the GE diamond makers knew far more than he did about their work. "Don't waste your money on me," he said.

By mid-1955 GE executives knew it was time to turn their years of research into a profitable business, but learning how to synthesize diamond grit was only the first step on the road to commercialization. Successful marketing depended on production of an abrasive that was uniform in size, shape, and grinding ability. Rather than rush mediocre material to market, General Electric decided to wait until the process had been thoroughly tested and perfected. After hundreds of synthesis runs at various temperatures and pressures, diamond makers in Schenectady and at the newly formed Diamond Section of the Detroit-based Carboloy division discovered that they could control crystal shape with great precision.

Every crystal, diamond included, has a variety of possible forms. Natural diamonds are found as tiny cubes with six square faces, as octahedrens with eight triangular faces, and as crystals containing combinations of those and other more complicated forms.

Each surface in a diamond crystal has a different atomic structure; as the crystal grows carbon atoms will attach to some surfaces more readily than to others. What may at first seem odd is that the flat face that grows fastest is the one that you *don't* see. It's something like trying to pile up marbles: it's easiest to add marbles to a layer parallel to the ground. You might start with a large flat area of marbles, but as you stack them higher and higher, that original plane—the likeliest growth surface—disappears and the stack ends up in a pyramid with a point.

In exactly the same way, carbon atoms stack to build a diamond crystal. If the six cube faces grow fastest, the crystal will end up with six corners and the eight-faced octahedral shape appears. Just the opposite happens if the eight octahedral faces grow fastest—you wind up with a cube with eight pointed corners and six faces.

Scientists don't know how to predict which form will occur, but methodical research revealed that perfect octahedrons form most easily at higher temperatures, about 1,600°C at 60,000 atmospheres, while cube-shaped crystals predominate at lower temperatures, perhaps 1,400°C at 60,000 atmospheres. At intermediate temperatures, combinations of the cube and octahedron result.

The diamond team in Detroit, to which Hal Bovenkerk had been transferred, found that slow growth conditions produced crystals of remarkably uniform shape, excellent for rock sawing. Fast growth, on the other hand, created a mass of more irregular crystals, ideal for grinding and polishing carbide parts. The team also learned to grow needle-shaped diamonds, which are particularly useful in grinding wheels, because they can be embedded deep in the tool's surface.

In November 1957, just a month after the Soviet Union launched its first Sputnik and shocked a technologically complacent United States to its core, General Electric began to sell Man-Made diamonds, its trademarked synthetic diamond abrasive. Francis Bundy reflects the pride of the GE employees: "We like to think that we, by being first with Man-Made diamonds, took a little of the sting out of the Soviets being the first to put a satellite into earth orbit." At the time of the announcement, General Electric's first diamond-making plant in Detroit had manufactured just seven pints of diamond grit.

The GE sales force hoped to be swamped with orders for the new product, but with a limited range of abrasive products and a severe recession under way, the initial response was lackluster. Some buyers expressed reservations about patronizing GE, fearing a retaliation by the De Beers diamond cartel if the synthesis venture failed. It took General Electric several years and a lot of persuasive demonstrations to convince industry that Man-Made diamonds performed as well as or better than natural material.

Ultimately, the balance was tipped by research, which provided General Electric's synthetic diamond with one clear advantage over De Beers's natural product. By carefully controlling the temperature, pressure, time, and starting materials of their runs, GE found it could produce a variety of diamond crystals with remarkably uniform properties. Synthetic diamonds could be tailor-made for specific applications: rock sawing and polishing, machining hard steels and carbides, gem cutting and polishing, and many other tasks.

Armed with an unparalleled array of diamond abrasives, General Electric undertook a massive publicity campaign to convince the machining industry to try their new products. Applications engineers in Detroit published numerous articles, complete with reams of statistics and dramatic photomicrographs of controlled grinding and cutting experiments, in trade journals like *Carbide Engineering*, *Machinery*, *Grinding and Finishing*, and *American Machinist*. They produced spiffy brochures loaded with graphs and tables, all designed to convince potential buyers that Man-Made diamonds were superior to natural ones for manufacturing automobiles, power tools, carbide components, and military hardware.

It was a tough sell, but gradually the message got through. As early as mid-1959 *The Wall Street Journal* could report that "GE already has weakened De Beers' hold on the U.S. industrial diamond market and forced the Johannesburg-headquartered company to offer special concessions to customers. . . . GE's rise marks one of the more serious competitive threats to De Beers in its long history." In 1959 GE sold approximately three quarters of a million carats of synthetic diamonds, capturing roughly 10 percent of the U.S. market, and they projected an increase in production to 3.5 million carats (about 1,500 pounds) the following year.

In 1957 the price of GE industrial-grade synthetic diamond was twice that of De Beers mined diamond ($5.30 per carat, compared to $2.87 for the natural material), but the Norton Company, which had spent the better part of a decade trying to synthesize diamond itself, willingly paid for the more expensive synthetic diamond to encourage the development of a domestic supply. As production increased, costs dropped rapidly, and GE soon matched the price for natural industrial diamond abrasive—from less than $3.00 per carat in 1959 to about $2.00 per carat by the mid-1960s.

The commercial applications of synthetic diamonds were, understandably, foremost in the minds of GE management, but Francis Bundy, Herb Strong, and Bob Wentorf were focusing on the years of fascinating science in front of them. Two spanking-new thousand-ton presses were added to the Schenectady research operation. Each was outfitted with a carbide belt apparatus—the device that had proven to be most efficient for diamond making.

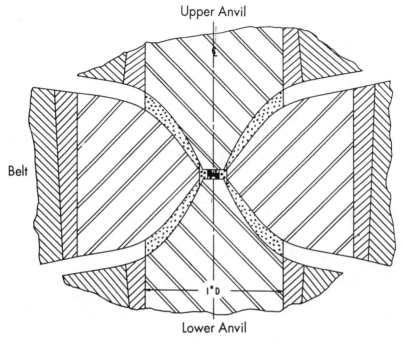

The highly tapered pistons of the superbelt enabled Francis Bundy to reach the extreme temperatures and pressures at which graphite could finally be converted directly to diamond without a metal solvent. (Courtesy of F. R. Bundy.)

After hundreds of experiments, the scientists discovered that virtually any combination of iron, nickel, chromium, cobalt, or a half-dozen other metals could be used to induce diamond growth. The key, it turned out, was to reach temperature and pressure conditions at which diamond was the stable form of carbon at the same time that the solvent metal was in a liquid state.

Given their unique diamond-making ability, the General Electric researchers were in an ideal position to study long-lasting scientific questions about carbon. They were especially eager to learn the range of pressure and temperature under which diamond could form, but they needed a device that would extend well beyond the belt's maximum of 60,000 atmospheres and 2,000°C, and they needed a way to calibrate temperatures and pressures at those conditions. Francis Bundy and coworkers developed a modified superbelt apparatus with thinner, more pointed anvils that allowed them to reach 150,000 atmospheres and attempt brief temperature excursions up to 5,000°C—conditions intense enough to actually melt carbon.

Bundy undertook a detailed study of graphite, diamond, and carbon liquid. Using the superbelt Bundy established the range of conditions under which graphite converted to diamond, and he discovered the carbon triple point—the unique combination of temperature and pressure (about 4,100°C at 125,000 atmospheres) at which graphite, diamond, and liquid carbon coexist. The extreme conditions produced in the superbelt apparatus also enabled Bundy to convert graphite directly into diamond without using a metal solvent or catalyst. Graphite, which Percy Bridgman had dubbed "nature's best spring," had at last been pushed to its breaking point.

Francis Bundy determined the carbon triple point—the unique combination of pressure and temperature at which graphite, diamond, and liquid carbon coexist—to be approximately 4,100°C and 125,000 atmospheres. (Courtesy of R. DeVries.)

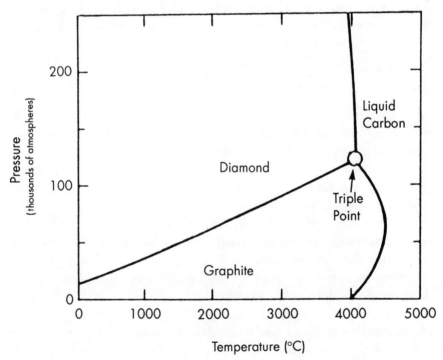

The years following the 1955 breakthrough were a heady time for GE's diamond team. With their unique technical capabilities, they enjoyed unrivaled opportunities for high-pressure research, but they were also under pressure to fend off the competition. In particular, they had to be sure that all the original diamond patents were indisputably correct. The first General Electric patent claimed that any carbon-rich material, not just graphite, could be converted to diamond with the GE process. That was a tall claim, open to challenge by other companies unless diamond had actually been made from a variety of substances containing carbon. So Bob Wentorf went to work on one of the most bizarre and amusing series of experiments in the history of high-pressure science.

Carbon-rich materials are everywhere. Plastics, sugar, wood, paper, glue, and all living things are loaded with carbon. Most scientists might have run diamond-making experiments on fancy-sounding carbon-based chemicals like polyethylene or pentanedione, but Wentorf, true to his whimsical nature, turned to more familiar substances. In high-pressure runs of remarkable flamboyance he squeezed Black Diamond roofing tar, aged maple wood, moth flakes, and his favorite brand of crunchy peanut butter. "The peanut butter turned into tiny green diamond crystals," Wentorf explains. "It was because of all the nitrogen." The novel peanut-butter experiments got Wentorf more press than almost anything else the GE diamond makers did, and they did prove that GE *could* turn nearly any carbon-rich material into diamond.

Wentorf's studies on graphite and diamond led him to study other compounds as well. One of the greatest lures of high-pressure research is the prospect of discovering entirely new materials with unusual properties. In 1956 Bob Wentorf made such an extraordinary discovery—a completely new abrasive that in some ways works even better than diamond. Wentorf studied the compound boron nitride, a soft white powder that normally has a layered atomic structure just like graphite. Wentorf suspected that, like graphite, it might have a hard, abrasive high-pressure form. His successful synthesis of cubic boron nitride provided the world with another industrial superabrasive.

Cubic boron nitride turned out to be almost as hard as diamond and every bit as resistant to attack by acids and other chemicals.

Unlike diamond, it persists to more than 1,500°C in air, a temperature at which diamond has long since burned away. While diamond, when heated by the grinding process, reacts chemically with iron-bearing alloys and becomes ineffective, cubic boron nitride can cut through iron-bearing alloys quickly and easily. Percy Bridgman and many other scientists were delighted to hear of this new and useful high-pressure material, but Eric Lundblad and his ASEA colleagues were chagrined by the news. They went back to earlier high-pressure experiments they had conducted on the same compound; sure enough, they had made cubic boron nitride themselves without knowing it.

The year 1959 was pivotal in the commercialization of synthetic diamond. Four years earlier GE had grudgingly accepted the government's secrecy order, knowing that it granted them extra time to study the process and an opportunity to develop a system that could monopolize the manufacturing of synthetic diamond. But they were constantly aware that all their efforts could be easily undercut by foreign rivals. If another group—especially De Beers—discovered how to make diamond before GE was allowed to file for patent protection abroad, then the American company would lose its foreign proprietary right over the process.

General Electric began selling its synthetic diamonds in 1957, and U.S. industry was at last assured of a secure diamond supply. But commercialization carried certain risks: every synthetic diamond contained telltale traces of the metal solvent used to create it, and by 1958 everyone in the business knew that iron and nickel had something to do with GE's secret process. Foreign research groups were rumored to be close to cracking the diamond-making riddle, and with the U.S. prohibition against filing for foreign patents still in place, General Electric stood to lose its potentially lucrative world market.

The sense of urgency was heightened when an American group headed by Armando A. Giardini at the U.S. Army's Electronics Research and Development Laboratory at Fort Monmouth, New Jersey, independently accomplished the diamond-making feat. Giardini and his coworker, Lieutenant John E. Tydings, spent a year and a half essentially reinventing the wheel. Their supported stepped piston-

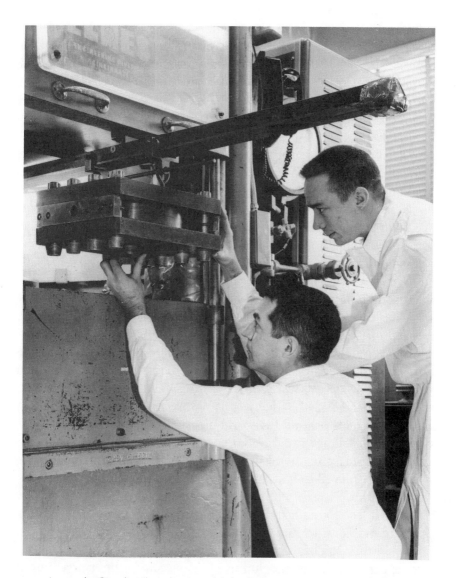

Armando Giardini (kneeling) and John Tydings, circa 1959, at the U.S. Army laboratory at Fort Monmouth, New Jersey, where they synthesized diamonds prior to the patent disclosures of General Electric. (Courtesy of A. A. Giardini.)

cylinder apparatus was similar to Hall's belt, and it enabled the two researchers to go straight to work on the chemistry of making diamond. The traces of nickel in some of GE's commercial synthetic diamond provided a critical clue; Giardini and Tydings took the hint and squeezed graphite with nickel. "We couldn't seem to do it. We had noticed everything from fused graphite spheres to lumpy masses of metal units in our reaction products"—but no diamonds. The simple solution to their problem came at the suggestion of Alvin Van Valkenburg, the high-pressure scientist from the National Bureau of Standards, who was visiting the New Jersey facility. "He asked if we had determined what was the cause of the lumps in the metallic stubs. We hadn't, not once. . . . While he was there we placed the metal in some [acid], and there before our eyes were revealed beautiful crystals of diamonds. I've never spoken much of this; I still feel foolish, and still feel grateful to Van." Giardini and Tydings quickly prepared a manuscript and submitted it to *The American Mineralogist*.

As early as June 1959, rumors circulated among high-pressure researchers regarding the imminent declassification of GE patents. The government asked expert witnesses, including Alvin Van Valkenburg, who had seen Giardini's diamonds, to examine the original GE patents, as well as GE's strongly worded petition for the lifting of secrecy. By the end of September 1959, the order was lifted. The very next day lawyers around the world filed patents in behalf of General Electric. The filings came none too soon, for a week later De Beers submitted its own diamond-making patents. The South African company was dismayed to find they were just days too late.

After four years of waiting, the original team of diamond makers was at last free to publish details of their breakthrough. "Preparation of Diamond" by Bovenkerk, Bundy, Hall, Strong, and Wentorf appeared in the October 10, 1959, issue of *Nature*, and the information was repeated in the news columns of *Science* and other magazines. A few months later *The Review of Scientific Instruments* for February 1960 contained Tracy Hall's detailed description of the belt apparatus.

At last the world had learned the secret. Now anyone with a press could become a diamond maker.

9

$\diamond$

Risky Business

Superman's challenge is to save Lois Lane and Jimmy Olsen from revenge-hungry tribesmen, who have lost the gemstone eye of their idol-god. Unscrupulous men have stolen and then misplaced the enormous jewel, but ever-resourceful Superman spies a lump of coal, squeezes it with his super powers while baking it with his x-ray vision, and produces a sparkling diamond replica of the lost eye. The warriors, poised to dispatch Lois and Jimmy, are suddenly appeased and all is well.

It seems extraordinary that when this TV episode first aired in 1957, just a couple of years after General Electric's diamond-making breakthrough, the process had already become a part of popular culture. So great was the publicity surrounding the technological breakthrough that most Americans knew you could make diamonds by heating and squeezing coal.

In 1959, when the world learned the details of how to synthesize diamonds, the process went beyond popular culture—it became part of the scientific record. General Electric scientists had told their peers exactly what to do to make diamonds, and anyone with a decent high-pressure laboratory could repeat the process. Naturally, a lot of them tried, and by Hal Bovenkerk's estimate more than two dozen groups did it within the year.

Armando Giardini and John Tydings, the scientists whose diamond-making efforts at Fort Monmouth, New Jersey, had succeeded in mid-1959 just prior to GE's revelations, were in the best position to duplicate the General Electric recipe. It was a straightforward matter for Giardini and Tydings to crank their device up to 85,000 atmospheres and 1,460°C with a graphite and nickel sample, and they produced diamonds on their first try.

Francis R. Boyd, a high-pressure specialist at the Carnegie Institution of Washington's Geophysical Lab, tackled diamond making as soon as he heard about the GE process. Boyd, in collaboration with Joe England, had been routinely using his own large press to study deep-earth minerals, and he repeated the diamond-making feat with ease, heating and squeezing graphite and nickel to 1,400°C and 75,000 atmospheres.

"We did it for sport," Boyd recalls of the diamond-making runs completed just a month or so after the GE announcement. "It was really an exciting experiment to make." The Carnegie Institution thought so too, and they issued their own press release on January 22, 1960, describing the tiny, faceted black crystals. Their one-page statement emphasized the role of the nickel catalyst and concluded with an intriguing idea: "Since rocks containing diamonds do not contain an uncombined metal, natural diamonds cannot have formed by [the GE] process." Boyd heard a few questioning remarks from Carnegie Institution trustees, who wondered why the Geophysical Lab hadn't tried to make diamonds first, but that wasn't why he did high-pressure research, and the Carnegie Institution wasn't in the patent business.

After diamond making had become routine for the GE research team, they set their sights on larger crystals. Was it possible to grow one-carat gem-quality stones? The resulting research program produced not only spectacular diamonds, but also one of the most spectacular accidents in the history of diamond making.

Explosions are a fact of life in high-pressure research; the bigger the press, the bigger the blowout. The catastrophic GE blowout occurred as the result of what is known as a Langmuir experiment.

In the 1920s Irving Langmuir, a Nobel prize–winning General Electric research scientist, had taken on the challenge of creating a

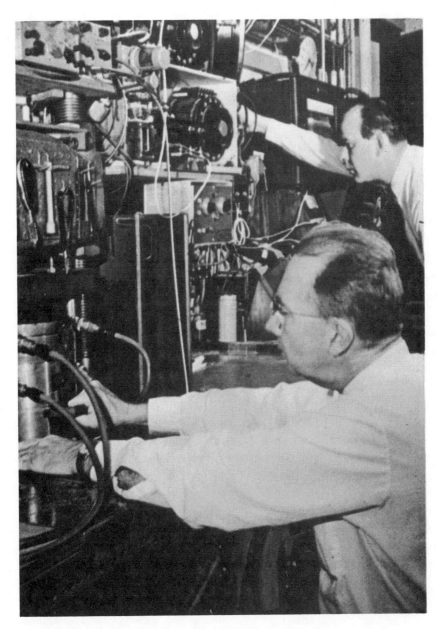

Joe England (foreground) and F. R. Boyd made diamonds at the Carnegie Institution of Washington's Geophysical Laboratory in January 1960, shortly after General Electric released details of the process. (Courtesy of F. R. Boyd.)

longer-lasting light bulb. At that time, light bulbs failed frequently, because air would leak into the bulb, burning up the hot filament. Langmuir wondered whether the problem could be avoided by getting rid of the vacuum and using a small amount of an inert gas like argon in the bulb instead. Conventional wisdom scoffed at the idea: scientists argued that heat from the glowing tungsten filament would flow right to the glass via the argon atoms, making an impossibly hot and inefficient bulb. Langmuir tried the experiment, but he started the easy way. Instead of constructing a vacuum bulb with just a little argon, he used a full atmosphere of argon—a full 14.7 pounds per square inch. If a little argon caused too much heating, he reasoned, then a lot of argon would exaggerate the effect and make it easier to measure. The result surprised everyone—even with a full atmosphere of argon the bulb worked fine, with a minimum of heating. Since that time, GE scientists referred to any experiment that exaggerates the variable of interest as a Langmuir experiment.

The diamond team's ill-fated Langmuir experiment was born when Herb Strong wondered why synthetic diamond crystals were always so small—usually no more than a few hundredths of an inch across. Would the addition of another element stimulate crystal growth? Following a suggestion by UCLA high-pressure expert George Kennedy, Strong decided to study the effects of hydrogen on diamond growth. Strong decided to add not just a little hydrogen but a huge amount in the form of a chunk of polyethylene plastic, which averages two hydrogen atoms for every carbon. At conditions of diamond formation, Strong was to learn, polyethylene breaks down to form carbon and hydrogen—lots of hydrogen. The trouble is that hydrogen at high pressure is one of the world's best wedges, exploiting every possible crack and defect in metal and gasket components. The hydrogen atoms can penetrate deeply, weakening the structure as they go. To make matters worse, hydrogen is chemically reactive, combining with iron to form weak, brittle iron hydride, which is highly susceptible to failure at high pressure.

The belt apparatus blew up during Strong's very first attempt. With a deafening detonation and impact that shook the entire research compound, the hydrogen gas escaped and then ignited in a miniature reenactment of the *Hindenburg* disaster. Shrapnel sprayed out across the room and ricocheted off the walls and ceiling. Luckily, no one was injured in the explosion, and thereafter, anyone at GE who tried to study polyethylene at high pressure and temperature proceeded with great care. The team would have to find another way to make large synthetic gems.

✧ ✧ ✧

After a decade of sporadic effort and much trial and error, Bob Wentorf and Herb Strong learned how to grow exceptional diamond crystals, more perfect than any in nature, at the rate of about one carat a week. Most GE diamond making relied on producing very uniform temperatures at high pressure, but Wentorf and Strong found that the key to making large single crystals was subjecting the carbon to a gradient of temperature. Wentorf found that if he put diamond powder at the hotter end of the sample chamber and a diamond seed crystal at the cooler end, the seed diamond would grow at the expense of the diamond powder. By 1970 the GE team could produce magnificent single-crystal diamonds approaching two carats in size. Under normal circumstances the GE crystals were yellow, the result of ubiquitous nitrogen impurities, but the addition of a nitrogen-binding element like aluminum or titanium facilitated production of purer, colorless gems. The General Electric scientists also used boron-rich starting materials to grow remarkable blue diamonds, which are extremely rare in nature.

Experts doubt that large synthetic diamond crystals will ever make a dent in the gem market; they take too much time to grow, the giant presses are too expensive to run, and synthetic gems lack the glamour of stones formed a hundred miles deep in the earth. But scientists and engineers covet these glorious synthetic stones for another reason: in one respect they are even better than natural diamonds. All carbon atoms contain exactly six protons in their nucleus, but the number of neutrons—the other heavy nuclear particle—varies from atom to atom. The commonest carbon isotope, carbon 12, has six neutrons, but about one out of every hundred carbon atoms has seven neutrons, to make carbon 13. Natural diamonds incorporate this variety, but GE scientists learned to synthesize isotopically pure carbon-12 crystals.

Using nuclear-age technology that separates atoms according to

Flawless diamond crystals more than one carat in weight were grown by GE scientists in the late 1960s. Herbert Strong (left) and Robert Wentorf, Jr., (right) show a collection of synthetic gems to GE vice president of research and development Arthur M. Bueche in May 1970. (Courtesy of H. M. Strong.)

their individual isotopes, researchers at Oak Ridge National Laboratory and other facilities can purify carbon 12. It's an expensive proposition, but you can now buy isotopes like carbon 12 off the shelf from government labs. To make isotopically pure diamond crystals, scientists usually begin with pure carbon 12, in the form of graphite, and synthesize diamond grit in the usual fashion, with high temperature, high pressure, and a metal solvent. This isotopically pure diamond powder can then be used to grow a large diamond crystal in which every carbon atom is exactly like every other.

Most of the properties of diamond are unaffected by such uniformity. Carbon-12 diamonds produced at GE's Worthington, Ohio, plant are hard, transparent, and beautiful, just like other diamonds. However, one key feature—the diamond's ability to conduct heat—seems to increase enormously in isotopically pure crystals. Heat moves by wiggling atoms. When atoms of different weights, like carbon 12 and carbon 13, occur together, the heat flow is slightly disrupted by the different vibrations of the two isotopes. But when all the atoms are exactly the same, heat is able to travel in steady waves. It turns out that synthetic carbon-12 diamonds, with 99.9 percent or more isotopic purity, are the best heat conductors in the world. These crystals now play a critical role in sensitive electronic gear for high-speed computers and military applications, where cool circuits work better than hot ones.

As the quest to grow large single crystals continued, efforts to develop the exact opposite—extremely fine-grained diamond grit—also gained momentum. Some natural diamonds occur not as isolated crystals but as hard black masses of tiny intergrown crystallites. These forms of diamond, called carbonado and ballas, feature grains that are locked together with diamond-to-diamond bonds, producing a solid that can actually be tougher than single-crystal diamond. The diamond makers realized that while tiny crystals embedded in a saw blade or abrasive wheel work fine for ordinary cutting, grinding, and polishing, solid diamond tools would be much better for more demanding operations. Single-crystal diamonds are too expensive and break too easily along certain crystal planes for use as tools, but large chunks of carbonado are ideal, and many scientists believed they could duplicate nature's carbonado process.

Bob Wentorf and his Schenectady colleague William A. Rocco tackled the problem in 1970, and within a year they had found a solution. Using tried-and-true diamond-making protocol, Wentorf and Rocco subjected a mixture of cobalt metal and extremely fine grained synthetic diamonds to the same temperatures and pressures used in diamond making—roughly 60,000 atmospheres and about 1,400°C. At those conditions, the tiny diamond crystals deform and regrow into a tightly bonded mass that is more than 85 percent diamond, with some interspersed cobalt. The cobalt can then be dissolved away in acid, leaving a hard diamond aggregate that resists fracturing.

Detroit engineers turned Wentorf and Rocco's laboratory procedures into a valuable new product called Compax. Compax tools and wire dies begin as solid black masses. The diamond is then cut and shaped with an electric spark technique that vaporizes the carbon, atom by atom. There are hundreds of uses for these tools, but sintered diamond plays an especially important role in rock drilling, which uses drill bits studded with protruding diamond-cutting teeth. These drill bits have to cut through thousands of feet of solid rock, and every pause to pull up a mile or more of drill rig and replace the drill bit costs thousands of dollars. So long-lived diamond drills save companies (and, one hopes, consumers) a fortune.

With discovery after discovery to its credit, the General Electric high-pressure research laboratory at The Knolls had become famous as "The Diamond Mine." Many prominent high-pressure scientists, as well as astronaut Harrison "Jack" Schmidt, actor Ronald Reagan, and inventor Buckminster Fuller, were among the dignitaries who came to tour the facility.

Throughout the 1960s, General Electric's Detroit diamond-making facility also grew. With a rapidly increasing demand for its Man-Made diamonds, GE quickly added ranks of thousand-ton presses with larger-diameter belts. More personnel were constantly needed to man the new equipment and devise new techniques for machining with diamond and cubic boron nitride. It was obvious that they would soon expand beyond the limits of the Detroit site.

✧　✧　✧

The move to the new facility took place in 1968, when all abrasive production was transferred to Worthington, Ohio. The General Electric pioneers who saw the first glimmer of synthetic diamond in 1954 could scarcely have imagined that modern diamond factory. The sprawling plant, graced by green lawns and a shallow sculpted pool, lies near the northernmost point of the Columbus beltway, just a couple of miles from Francis Bundy's birthplace. The low, flat-roofed tan buildings that house the diamond factory cover acres of central Ohio plains.

For years the purpose of the plant was shrouded in secrecy. Known only as the home of the GE Specialty Materials Department, the facility's actual product was revealed to relatively few people. Even Ohio's governor and legislators were unaware that Columbus had become the diamond capital of the world.

Today, diamond-making is still big business for GE. A few years ago, in a renewed effort to publicize their product and expand markets, the General Electric diamond makers assumed a much higher profile. They changed their name and, for the first time, invited scientists and industrial representatives to tour the factory. Other than the modest GE Superabrasives sign out front, however, there is nothing to suggest the spectacular product created inside.

Behind the security guards and oversized doors lie the heart and soul of GE Superabrasives: the vast rooms where tons of diamonds are grown. Hundreds of workers make their living here, serving row after row of massive presses, each capable of producing pounds of diamonds a day. One room the size of an airplane hangar contains dozens of thousand-ton presses, each standing twice the height of a man, each capable of generating more than 60,000 atmospheres of pressure. An incessant hum of hydraulic devices fills the clean, brightly lit room.

All the presses are equipped with belts remarkably similar to Tracy Hall's original. Perhaps a hundred thousand-ton presses accommodate belts two feet in diameter; four-foot belts fit several much larger presses. The factory also has a few monster presses that are two stories tall and use massive five-foot belts. Open metal stairs lead down to the thick concrete foundations on which the largest presses and hydraulic apparatus rest. Bold warning signs admonish workers to put on ear protection before descending into the deafening pit, where noisy compressors and blowers throb continuously.

The spacious facility is designed for extreme efficiency. The carbide components of the belts are tough, but they do wear out, and once in a while a press will blow out with a percussion that rocks the whole factory. With so many presses in constant use, breakage is a routine occurrence, so the factory walls are lined with sturdy metal shelving, stacked with brand-new anvils and belts just waiting for quick installation, and the factory ceilings are crisscrossed with steel I beams and heavy-duty cranes to aid in repairs.

The thousand-ton presses are astonishingly fast and efficient. In each diamond-making device, as in Tracy Hall's original, two tapered pistons squeeze a carbon-rich sample packed into the hole of the doughnut-shaped belt. It takes a few minutes to load a sample into the hole and a few minutes more to heat and squeeze the sample. The Worthington belts have been equipped with auxiliary sample holding rings to double their productivity. The two rings connect at a pivot point, like the two circles of a figure eight. The belt operator, who wears a blue uniform, protective glasses, and thick gloves, swings the newly loaded belt into position so that the ring of steel and carbide is perfectly aligned, ready to be squeezed between the graceful carbide pistons and heated by a powerful surge of electrical current. As the loaded belt rotates into place and locks into position, the other belt, fresh from the pressure cooker and full of diamonds, swings out over the work area.

Meanwhile, the operator raps the freshly baked sample sharply with his ball-peen hammer, freeing a black cylindrical plug about the size of a wine bottle's cork. He strikes the freed sample again and again, breaking away soft gasketing material and revealing a hard cylindrical mass, three-quarters of an inch thick and studded with tiny diamonds the size of coarse sand—perhaps thirty carats of diamonds in all. Without hesitation the operator pops the diamond-rich slug into a drawer with dozens more just like it. He uses a wire brush to clean off the carbide ring and inserts a new sample assembly into the belt's waiting hole. The entire process, lasting only five or six minutes, is ready to begin again.

Thirty carats per run, ten runs per hour, eight hours per day—a good worker can turn out several pounds of diamond a week. Many dozens of presses operate like that for twenty-four hours a day, three shifts a day, seven days a week. Prodigious amounts of diamond are produced. The annual output of Ohio diamonds—thirty-three tons in 1990 alone—rivals the rest of the world's diamond production, natural and synthetic combined. In a quarter century of operation, General Electric has synthesized hundreds of tons of diamonds, far exceeding the quantity of all diamonds mined since biblical times.

But synthesis is only the first of several processes performed at the Worthington facility. Every day hundreds of diamond-and-metal slugs are processed in huge acid vats. Workers in protective rubber suits monitor the baths and retrieve piles of diamond sand from the caustic brew. Then they wash the diamonds and place them in drying ovens. The concrete floors of the chemical-preparation rooms sparkle from the countless tiny diamond crystals that have worked their way into the hard surface. Worthington employees have learned to change shoes before going home at night; the diamond grit embedded in their soles ruins uncarpeted floors.

After drying, some of the processed diamond is taken to the part of the Superabrasives factory where the fine-grained diamond product Copax is made. There, workers mix diamond powder with metal and subject the carbon atoms to another round of high temperature and pressure. These large presses produce thousands of diamond disks up to two inches in diameter to be used for making tools and dies.

Another area of the facility uses fine-grained diamond as the starting material for producing large, flawless single crystals. Though a relatively minor part of GE's total production, these crystals are in ever-increasing demand for electronics applications. Although they are exorbitantly expensive to make—each one monopolizes a large press for days at a time—the perfection of the synthetic diamond crystals, and their ability to remove heat from sensitive electronic components, is unrivaled.

The final step in preparing GE diamonds for market takes place in a room that is the smallest but most impressive of all. All the synthetic crystals must pass through the sorting room, where they are sized and weighed. It is an immaculately clean place, except for the piles of diamonds everywhere. One container holds 25,000 carats of perfectly sized yellow crystals. Thousands more carats stand in neat conical piles on white paper next to a black binocular microscope. Jars of black-, copper-, and honey-colored abrasives line the shelves. Only two exits lead from the sorting room: one heavily reinforced door to the factory corridors, another to a loading dock designed for armored cars.

In four decades of research, development, and marketing, General Electric's diamond-making venture has gone from a few men struggling with a leaky old press to an international business grossing hundreds of millions of dollars a year. With such extraordinary success, it is no surprise that GE has spawned many rivals in the diamond-making game.

10

The Rivals

Imitation is the sincerest of flattery.   —C. C. Colton

The world's appetite for diamonds is almost insatiable. Diamond mines in Africa produce nearly ten tons annually, roughly matching the output of mines in Australia and Russia, the two other major producing areas. Slightly less than half of this production supplies the annual $4 billion gem market, while the rest provides abrasive material for industry. But this quantity pales beside the world production of synthetic diamond, estimated by GE to exceed one hundred tons each year.

General Electric's success has inspired many rivals to manufacture synthetic diamonds; the business has grown too big and lucrative for just one player, and demand for the abrasive continues to increase each year. Every new automobile consumes about one-quarter carat of diamond abrasive during its production; every truck, plane, or missile uses many times that figure. And diamond-tipped tools have become indispensable for oil drilling, stone polishing, one-hour eyeglass production, and a hundred other operations.

De Beers had long planned to make its own synthetic diamonds in order to protect its diamond monopoly. The company had established the Johannesburg-based Diamond Research Laboratory in 1947, though at the time little thought was given to the synthesis of diamond. The handful of scientists at the lab focused only on investigating the properties of natural stones. Immediately after GE's 1955 announcement, however, priorities at the De Beers facility changed, and the director of research, Dr. J. F. H. Custers, quickly assembled a synthesis research team.

First on board was physicist and crystal expert Henry B. Dyer, a Cambridge-educated South African who worked for De Beers, studying diamond crystals at Reading University in England. Custers also recruited D. B. Senior, a mechanical engineer from Sheffield University; Alan Blainy, who was lured away from the Harwell atomic energy research lab; and a young graduate student from Reading named C. Phaal. The project's new building, the Adamant Research Laboratory, was constructed and equipped in 1957.

None of the team members had any training in high-pressure research, and GE's public announcements gave them few hints about how to proceed. Initially, they tried a piston-and-cylinder device just to get high-pressure experience. After many trials they achieved their first success in October 1958, when a tiny diamond crystal was found in an experiment that used graphite and tungsten carbide as starting materials. Out of dozens of subsequent runs, however, traces of diamond were found only three or four more times.

In late 1958 P. T. Wedepohl, a recent graduate of Witwatersrand University, joined the group and proposed an alternative device with opposed conical anvils, remarkably similar to Tracy Hall's belt. De Beers researchers claim to have developed the idea independently, though Hal Bovenkerk emphasizes that by 1957 belt specifications had been widely copied and circulated inside General Electric in the form of a blue spiral-bound confidential document, and those plans could have leaked out easily. Construction and calibration of the new De Beers device were completed by May 1959, and the first trials were ready to begin in June.

Henry Dyer, who had thought long and hard about the optimal chemical environment for growing diamond, had concluded that nickel or iron would be an ideal solvent for crystal synthesis, and metal thus became a key ingredient in all subsequent experiments. Dyer may have had some help in reaching this conclusion; Hal Bovenkerk is quick to point out that all of GE's commercial product, which had been on the market since 1957, contained telltale traces of these critical metal solvents.

With their new press and revised chemical procedures, the De Beers team created diamonds almost immediately, though not consistently enough to begin marketing them. "Had we patented our apparatus and process then [in the summer of 1959], the legal story would have been considerably different," Dyer laments. "But we were naïve in these matters and merely went ahead with our experiments." They waited until September, when a reliably reproducible procedure was found, to begin the patent process. Without further delay the patent attorneys were brought in, but they were too late. GE had filed its international patents just days before.

It suddenly appeared that all the De Beers research would be for naught. There was little choice for the South African company but to go on the offensive and challenge General Electric's patents in court. No one questioned whether General Electric held valid diamond-making patents in the United States, Canada, and Great Britain; those documents had been filed and then sealed in early 1955. At issue were GE's claims to control diamond synthesis throughout the rest of the world. Could De Beers legally manufacture diamond abrasive in South Africa? If so, then by a quirk of international law they could sell their product freely to American companies, the world's largest consumers.

In the early 1960s De Beers and General Electric commenced a mammoth six-year legal battle. It would ultimately cost millions of dollars; at the time, it was the most expensive court proceedings in South African history. In the most protracted of several separate lawsuits, De Beers challenged the originality of GE's discovery and the accuracy with which they had described it. To make their case, De Beers engaged a number of expert witnesses to discredit General Electric in the South African court. Of these distinguished scientists, none was more colorful or controversial than George Kennedy.

Of the many young physicists and geologists who traveled to Harvard to learn the secrets of high pressure from Percy Bridgman and his colleagues, George Kennedy was certainly the most flamboyant and outspoken. He is remembered as a researcher of great creative power and *joie de vivre*.

Colleagues have described him as outrageous, brilliant, contentious, inspired, aggressive, and just plain rude. Some treated him with awe or fear, others with cautious respect or outright contempt. Only

George Kennedy, circa 1975, in his UCLA laboratory. (Courtesy of Art Montana.)

a few of his colleagues remember him as a friend. Perhaps that isn't surprising, for Kennedy made scores of enemies with his shameless public antics and unrestrained criticism of his peers.

At the end of a particularly aggressive series of long typed letters to Joe Boyd debating aspects of pressure management—letters filled with insults like "stupid," "incompetent," and "dumb"—Kennedy added a conciliatory handwritten note. "Some of my lab help think I was being too heated in my arguments. It's just because I naturally argue eagerly—the real thing is that we both are trying to get at the facts. So *please* ignore any heat in my arguments. It's just my natural way—and I don't want to rewrite the letters."

Such apologies were, by all accounts, rare; even the most senior professors and distinguished scientists were not spared his impolitic scorn. "Dead wood" he'd call them, not caring who overheard. And if he couldn't score a verbal victory, he was willing to settle the debate with his fists. No one enjoyed these confrontations, and a good many of his contemporaries were simply scared of him.

Yet behind his outrageous behavior lay a remarkable flair for intuitive problem-solving and a keen scientific intellect. Raised on a modest Montana cattle ranch, Kennedy was awarded a Harvard scholarship at the age of sixteen and became a Harvard junior fellow in geology soon thereafter. Following B.S., M.A., and Ph.D. degrees and a brief stint teaching at Harvard, he joined the earth science faculty at UCLA in 1953. In decades of top-notch research he gained a paradoxical reputation as a wild man who was nevertheless lionized by the elite of Los Angeles society, a contentious scientific debater unhindered by professional decorum, yet a man dedicated to achieving unassailable accuracy in every measurement he made.

Everyone who knew Kennedy has amazing stories to tell. He was driven by three great passions: conducting high-pressure research, collecting primitive art, and cultivating rare orchids. He once astounded colleagues by presenting three lectures at Oxford in one day —one on the synthesis of high-pressure materials, one on dating pre-Columbian pottery, and one on new species of exotic orchid. Kennedy often boasted of his skill in merging the last two passions. He successfully smuggled ancient South American pottery into the United States by covering them with piles of rare orchids in the back of his car. Customs agents focused on the flamboyant plants, which were legal imports, and missed the priceless art.

George Kennedy was audacious and more than a little unscrupulous. Archaeologists had long been unable to locate the source of a steady stream of valuable burial artifacts being sold by villagers from one little-studied area of Mexico. While most scientists searched for years in an attempt to locate an undisturbed grave, Kennedy used a different approach. He flew by small plane to a local village, rented a Jeep, and stood in the back of the vehicle waving a thousand-dollar bill and shouting in halting Spanish that the bill would go to the first person who took him to an unopened tomb. The very next morning he stood in a pristine chamber lined with precious burial artifacts. Effective as it was, his ingenious solution failed to impress the outraged Mexican authorities. One time, so the story goes, when he was stopped for his illegal exploits by Mexican border police, he dutifully pulled over. Then, as the patrolman approached on foot, Kennedy floored the gas pedal and escaped to the United States.

"How he ever stayed out of jail I don't know," mused Alvin Van Valkenburg, who knew Kennedy as a colleague at Harvard in the early 1950s and as a competing high-pressure researcher in later years.

Kennedy's exploits in search of primitive New Guinea art would seem to rival those of Indiana Jones. On one such trip to the Maprek region he rented a dump truck and headed inland along primitive dirt roads. At each village he stopped and offered cash for ancient wooden carvings. By trip's end a few weeks later, he had amassed two trucks full of art treasures. On another expedition he rented a boat and traveled alone up the Sepic River into the most dangerous part of New Guinea's interior—a region inhabited by headhunters. Official anthropological expeditions to the area required months of planning with government assistance, but Kennedy just took off by the seat of his pants and reappeared a few days later, his boat laden with tons of priceless artifacts. He boasted in a letter to Joe Boyd, "I got most of the loot from two or three crumbling spirit houses . . . and have approximately 40 tons of stuff on its way now. Am setting up my own New Guinea village on our tennis court."

He played the game with abandon. Customs officials in New Guinea had been assured that all the carvings were less than twenty-five years old, and thus not subject to export restrictions. In Los Angeles, equally persuasive evidence was presented that all objects were more than a hundred years old and thus not subject to import duties. Kennedy then avoided paying income taxes by donating the least interesting objects to museums and deducting their value as charitable gifts, while his personal collection of the choicest pieces grew.

Such antics made good stories, but they angered serious archaeologists. When a group of earth scientists nominated Kennedy for membership in the prestigious Cosmos Club, a private society for intellectuals in Washington, D.C., he was soundly vetoed by a lobby of incensed archaeologists.

Kennedy's extravagant lifestyle was enhanced by his marriage to Hollywood heiress Ruth Book. Their relationship got off to a rocky start when he burned her house down while smoking in bed, but to make amends he helped her acquire a magnificent home in West Los Angeles on the crest of the Santa Monica Mountains overlooking UCLA. "It was the least I could do," he explained.

He landscaped the property to include a series of water lily ponds populated by a variety of exotic water birds. As time went by he found that the ponds began to fill up with unwanted algae, and he decided to enlist the services of a small South American fish that he knew thrived on the microscopic plant. Unfortunately, the fish usually died at water temperatures below about fifty degrees, and they couldn't survive winters on the Los Angeles hilltop. The ingenious Kennedy applied to the National Science Foundation for a grant to study and breed the algae-eating fish for resistance to lower temperatures. He used the NSF funds to purchase twenty-five-gallon aquariums with state-of-the-art water temperature controls, stocked with hundreds of fish. Day by day he lowered the water temperature a degree at a time until 90 percent of the fish died. The remaining 10 percent, those most resistant to cold, began the next cycle of breeding. Unfortunately his government-subsidized experiments failed to produce fish that could survive in his private ornamental ponds.

Reflecting back on Kennedy's outrageous exploits, Joe Boyd commented, "After associating with George Kennedy for a while it was clear you could get away with a great deal in life that I hadn't been getting away with."

Kennedy was the perfect gunslinger for De Beers's attack on General Electric. He was a leader in high-pressure research and one of the first to duplicate the diamond synthesis feat following GE's announcement. He brought his flamboyant, aggressive approach into the British-style courtroom as easily as he did to the staid worlds of art, orchids, and scientific debate. Kennedy believed that there were several possible avenues of attack to discredit the GE diamond-making process in court. General Electric had specified a range of pressures and temperatures for diamond synthesis and a variety of starting materials based on carbon plus a metal. If either of these criteria was in error, or if additional sets of viable conditions could be demonstrated, then the GE patent could be circumvented. Kennedy first turned his attention to the question of pressure.

In the early 1950s, when General Electric scientists commenced their studies, everyone used the methods devised by Percy Bridgman to measure pressure. Today we know that Bridgman was wrong. A pressure of 100,000 atmospheres on Bridgman's old scale is, in reality, no more than about 75,000 atmospheres on the corrected scale. For years the GE workers, who used the erroneous Bridgman scale, thought they were achieving pressures well above 50,000 atmospheres, which according to their calculations was more than sufficient to make diamonds. In fact, pressures were closer to 40,000 atmospheres, slightly below the graphite-diamond transition pressure. If the GE team had known about the error, they might have switched to carbide components sooner and thus cracked the synthesis barrier years earlier. Instead, they had focused intensive efforts on trying to make diamond at conditions at which graphite was stable. They had succeeded only when the belt apparatus was fitted with carbide pistons capable of achieving higher pressures, which allowed them to push their work well into the region of diamond stability.

George Kennedy suspected Bridgman's error and he pounced on the chance to discredit General Electric—and Percy Bridgman in the process. In June 1960, Kennedy, along with his graduate-student assistant P. N. La Mori, began to publicize a revised pressure scale. He wrote dozens of letters, proclaiming, "We have very strong suspicion . . . that [Tracy Hall's tetrahedral press] and G.E. apparatus are in gross error at high pressures, probably as much as 30 percent at 100 kb [100,000 atmospheres]. . . . I would not be a bit surprised if G.E.'s 100 kb measurements actually turned out to be 70 or less."

One of the most memorable presentations of these disturbing results occurred at the International High Pressure Conference, held at Lake George's Sagamore Conference Center. It was the first big international meeting on high-pressure science, with delegations present from Russia, Japan, Sweden, and other centers of research. The conference provided the kind of forum at which George Kennedy could be at his most outrageous.

Members of the original GE team remember with chagrin and

wry amusement the contempt that Kennedy showered on them and Bridgman as he pointed out the "stupidity" of their measurements. He repeatedly applied the term "honest kilobars" to his own work, implying something less than honesty in the work of others. These attacks deeply embarrassed General Electric and Bridgman and offended many high-pressure researchers, who saw no need to scorn the earlier work, even if it was in error.

Kennedy repeated his claims in the South African courtroom where De Beers contested GE's diamond-making patents. GE presented strong counterarguments to Kennedy's ruthless attacks. Their patents described diamond synthesis in terms of reproducible experimental procedures, not any absolute pressure scale, for exactly that reason.

Undeterred, Kennedy also challenged GE's description of the chemistry of diamond synthesis. GE scientists claimed that the presence of a metal like iron or nickel was essential both as a way to dissolve the carbon atoms and as a catalyst to stimulate diamond growth. Kennedy argued that iron served only to dissolve the carbon, nothing else. In his capacity as consultant to De Beers, he helped gather more than twenty affidavits from scientists around the world who agreed with his point of view. To counter that challenge, Bob Wentorf performed a series of experiments showing that many molten substances, such as silver chloride and cadmium oxide, dissolve carbon at diamond-making pressures, but they don't make diamonds.

Such subtle scientific arguments made for a complex and protracted legal battle, and George Kennedy was only the most colorful of more than a dozen expert witnesses De Beers put on the stand. The trial dragged on for many weeks until, finally, presiding justice Roberts had heard all arguments. He was expected to deliver his judgment within a few months, but he died suddenly, before his decision was written. After a delay of another year, the entire trial was reheard. The second justice ruled in GE's favor. De Beers immediately appealed, and the case continued.

While De Beers attacked the validity of GE's process patents, a second round of lawsuits and countersuits focused on the belt apparatus. De Beers was so determined to join the synthetic diamond game that it had secretly constructed its own belt-type machines, which some scientists suspected were based on GE patent details. Belt-type devices had been put to work at the well-guarded De Beers plant in Springs, South Africa, just a dozen miles south of the Premier Mine. De Beers successfully operated the plant in secrecy for several years until they foolishly published a photograph of their operation in promotional literature. The photograph showed the distinctive tapered anvils of a belt-type device.

With unequivocal evidence of De Beers's patent infringement, GE sued the South African giant. In a standard legal ploy, De Beers countersued, claiming that GE had themselves revealed details of the belt prior to filing their patent, thus invalidating their claim for protection. The legal battle began again.

In late 1960 the high-pressure experts Tracy Hall, Francis Bundy, Hal Bovenkerk, and Armando Giardini, who had left the army for a professorship at the University of Georgia, were flown to South Africa for the main event. General Electric lawyers had guessed that the De Beers strategy would be based on a key point of patent law: if General Electric had released details of the belt apparatus before the patent date, then their claim was invalid.

Hal Bovenkerk, the first GE witness scheduled to testify, suspected that the De Beers defense would highlight a 1954 GE publicity photograph of the thousand-ton press with a bit of a circular girdle showing. By publishing the photo, De Beers would argue, General Electric had forfeited its rights. What no one outside of the GE team knew was that at the time of the photograph it was Strong's cone apparatus, not the belt, that was mounted in the big press. Bovenkerk played the cat-and-mouse game beautifully, answering four days of intense questions with the traditional "Yes, my lord" and "No, my lord." When the De Beers lawyer at last introduced the key photograph, Bovenkerk was ready.

"Is this a photograph of the General Electric press?" the lawyer asked.

"Yes, my lord." Bovenkerk paused, and then, anticipating the next question, added, "But it's not a belt." The De Beers case was in ruins.

General Electric seized the advantage and pressed De Beers to settle the case. Within a few days of Hal Bovenkerk's testimony, De Beers purchased limited rights to make diamond for a sum that, though not disclosed, was rumored to be about $25 million, many times the total General Electric investment in diamond research. In keeping with industry practice, De Beers also agreed to pay royalties on its diamond production.

Who won the legal battle? General Electric partisans saw the result as a satisfying and long overdue victory for the American corporation. Surprisingly, members of the De Beers group claim that they gained the upper hand and that General Electric's offer of a licensing agreement was merely a ploy to avoid defeat. In one sense it makes little difference, for both companies have since made a fortune selling synthetic diamonds.

Although General Electric and De Beers have remained the major players in the diamond synthesis drama, many others have tried to get into the act. The irrepressible George Kennedy, who approached everything he did with passion, became obsessed with making diamonds in the late 1950s. He was absolutely convinced that the simple piston-in-cylinder arrangement provides the most versatile high-pressure device, and that conviction drove him for almost two decades.

Belt and tetrahedral anvil devices have limited sample volumes; eventually, as pressure is raised, the opposed anvils must come into contact. But a piston-cylinder, Kennedy argued, has the potential for unlimited volume, depending only on the length and diameter of the cylinder. He also believed that the simpler design of a perfect piston in a perfect hole allowed the best control of temperature and pressure, as well as offering the easiest machining and replacement of parts.

George Kennedy was too late to invent diamond making, but he reasoned that if he could make twice as many diamonds with half GE's effort, he would become rich beyond his dreams. For almost twenty years he flitted from corporation to corporation in his quest for diamond. The first abortive attempts were sponsored by Hughes Corporation, the great aircraft builders in Los Angeles. Kennedy oversaw the construction of a press and a piston-cylinder device fashioned from high-grade Maraging steel, with an elegant water-cooling system. The machine could reach diamond-making conditions—just barely—but what Kennedy didn't realize was that Maraging steel corrodes quickly in hot water. Hughes canceled the project when the press exploded, nearly killing two workmen.

Undeterred, Kennedy quickly arranged a project with Teledyne in the mid-1960s and built another piston-cylinder rig, this time with carefully aligned carbide components. Diamonds were readily synthesized, but in the process the strengths and weaknesses of the piston-cylinder apparatus became apparent. On the positive side, Kennedy's Teledyne group was able to obtain large diamond yields with a graphite-and-metal sample four inches long and a half-inch in diameter; each successful run produced more than one hundred carats. But the costly carbide pistons broke constantly, often after only one or two runs, and the group was soon carting away shattered pieces of carbide in wheelbarrows. By the mid-1970s, after almost a decade of expensive research and no clear prospect of a commercially viable process, Teledyne threw in the towel.

Without hesitation Kennedy scouted out his next backer—Kennametal, a company that had extensive experience with carbide products. Ivan Getting, who had worked with Kennedy at UCLA and at Teledyne, was given the design chore: construct a piston-cylinder device with a one-inch-diameter bore and a six-inch-long sample chamber that would fit into the thousand-ton press already at Kennametal's Latrobe, Pennsylvania, plant. Those specifications provided room for a sample five inches long and three-quarters of an inch in diameter—enough graphite to make more than three hundred carats of diamond at a shot.

Though progress was slow, Kennedy maintained management's enthusiasm with his unbridled optimism. He mesmerized Kennametal's executives with promises of piles of diamonds just around the corner. "It's the best idea since the invention of sex!" he would shout. He did have some cause for optimism: Getting's press worked wonderfully well. The principal drawback was the team's lack of expertise in the chemistry of crystal growing. They could make diamond, sure enough, but never with the consistent size and properties essential for commercial use. Perhaps sensing a cooling of corporate enthusiasm, Kennedy jumped ship in 1978, and Kennametal gave up the project within a year of his defection.

For his fourth and final foray into commercial diamond making, Kennedy turned to a local firm, Research and Design Associates (RDA), a Los Angeles think tank, which focused primarily on consulting for the military. Although RDA had no production engineers, no marketing management, and no sales force, Kennedy was a friend of the top RDA management people, and he made them a truly mind-boggling proposal. His grandiose plan was to construct a two-inch-diameter piston-cylinder device in a 3,000-ton press, large enough to churn out more than a thousand carats of diamond—almost a quarter of a pound—at a time. Kennedy's vision was not limited to diamond grit; he envisioned mammoth single crystals, diamond semiconductors, and special diamond components for use in fancy lasers.

But George Kennedy never lived to see the dream fulfilled. At the time of his death in 1980, RDA had authorized only a scaled-back prototype with a half-inch-diameter cylinder—a device that now sits rusting in a Los Angeles warehouse. In almost twenty years of effort, Kennedy produced diamonds in hundreds of experiments but did not see one carat of his synthetic diamond sold commercially.

Several foreign ventures have fared better. Ireland became a major diamond-producing country in 1962, when De Beers shipped twenty-five of its original presses to a new plant, the Ultra High Pressure Units (Ireland) in Shannon, which now synthesizes fifteen tons of abrasives annually. General Electric established a diamond factory in Dublin, Ireland, in the early 1980s. About half the size of the Worthington facility, it too produces about fifteen tons of crystals a year. A brand-new De Beers diamond-making plant on the Isle of Man, rumored to be devoted exclusively to single-crystal synthesis, is said to have created some of the most perfect diamonds ever seen, including a 14.2-carat monster—perhaps the largest diamond ever grown. Diamond production in the rest of Europe, concentrated in France, Germany, and Sweden (an outgrowth of von Platen's original ASEA effort), approaches twenty tons annually.

The former Soviet Union committed vast resources to diamond synthesis, though few details are known regarding their success. Statistics on diamond production were decreed a state secret by the Soviet government in 1956. The former Soviet republics are believed to have operated major diamond production or research facilities at Poltava and Lvov in the Ukraine, Erevan in Armenia, and St. Petersburg in Russia.

Today, several Asian countries are actively developing and operating diamond-making factories. Most Japanese synthetic diamond production is in the form of abrasive crystals, manufactured by Tomei, but remarkable gemstones of more than a dozen carats have been produced by Sumitomo. The Chinese, in contrast, have established a remarkable and unique cottage industry in diamond making. There are reputed to be dozens of individual diamond-making presses scattered around the country. Tracy Hall recalled a 1988 tour of one extraordinary site, a mom-and-pop operation featuring a main building for jade carving and a backyard shed housing a thousand-ton press. The juxtaposition of the ancient carving art with a modern press seemed strange to Hall, but the system has its own logic. Jade carving requires diamond-tipped tools (one word for diamond in Chinese may be translated as "cutting stone"); whenever a new supply of abrasive is required, the carvers can go out back and whip up another batch. Not all Chinese production occurs on such a small scale, however. The Chinese are said to have purchased a single European 5,000-ton press, which they plan to duplicate for a large-scale diamond-making factory.

Of all man's efforts to make diamond, none reveals more about the gem's temptations than the schemes of Chen-Min Sung to establish the industry in South Korea. For the last decade Sung has played a unique and vividly sinister role in the diamond synthesis story. He learned high-pressure technology at MIT in the mid-1970s and eagerly accepted a position as an engineer at GE's Worthington plant in the late 1970s. Sung began as an enthusiastic and ambitious researcher who wanted to improve diamond-making procedures, but, he claims, the management was unresponsive to his ideas. Eventually, disillusioned but rich with GE's secrets, Sung accepted an attractive offer from Norton's vice president in charge of research, Peter Bell. At Norton, Sung was given much more flexibility in research and development and access to their proprietary technology. It now appears that he abused Norton's trust. Adding his knowledge of Norton's proprietary manufacturing and processing methods to his inside information on GE superhard materials, Sung is believed to have secretly sold confidential technology—press designs, synthesis processes, and other confidential data—to a Korean firm.

In 1987, Chen-Min Sung was arrested by the FBI and soon thereafter convicted of transporting stolen property across state lines. His prison sentence now over, Sung and his Korean company face civil lawsuits from General Electric and Norton. Chen-Min Sung's actions shocked and dismayed the high-pressure community, which for the most part adheres to a strict ethical code. But, as Hal Bovenkerk has observed, "Scientists can be crooks as well as anybody else."

"So many people have entered into diamond making only to lose money," Tracy Hall laments. But Hall can tell a very different story. Megadiamond, a company he helped found, survives to this day. Though it claims only a few percent of the market, Megadiamond remains GE's largest domestic rival.

From the moment of Hall's defection in mid-1955, he became a subject of concern to General Electric. No one outside the company knew more secrets or had better cause to share those secrets with others. De Beers, in particular, posed a tremendous threat; with Hall's knowledge they could have easily duplicated all General Electric's apparatus and processes. Yet while Tracy Hall was not about to sell trade secrets, he did have business in his blood. After independently inventing the tetrahedral press, he almost immediately began to build and sell high-pressure devices. In his Provo, Utah, workshop Hall fashioned a dozen big tetrahedral presses of his own design and sold them to government and university labs. But he soon realized that the four-anvil design was not the best for making diamonds. It was possible to get even more diamond-making volume by using six anvils, each pressing on a face of a cubic sample.

Cubic-anvil presses have become the rage in modern high-pressure research. They represent a kind of marriage between von Platen's split sphere, which was awkward to use, and Hall's tetrahedral anvil, which could be tricky to align. The cubic-anvil device features six carbide anvils, arranged in three opposed pairs at right angles to

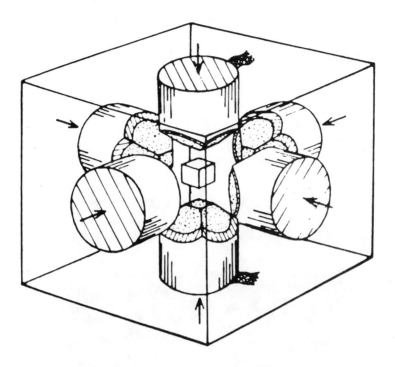

The cubic-anvil press employs six carbide anvils directed at the faces of a cube-shaped sample. This design, which accepts a relatively large sample volume, is preferred by many diamond-making companies and high-pressure researchers. (Courtesy of A. A. Giardini.)

one another. The resulting sample chamber is a cube, just like von Platen's, with each of the six cube faces defined by one of the six anvils. In the early 1960s the cubic-anvil press was an idea waiting to happen, and several groups hit upon the design at more or less the same time. Tracy Hall's innovation was a complex arrangement of guide pins that kept all six anvils aligned precisely while pressure was raised or lowered.

While General Electric continues to use the belt to make diamond, several small American operations rely on cubic-anvil presses of Tracy Hall's design. U.S. Synthetic Corporation (USS) in Provo's East Park industrial center is a prime example of a small-scale producer. Its facility could hardly be more different from General Electric's vast Worthington plant. At USS a dozen workers occupy one section of a module in an unimposing village of one-story corrugated metal buildings. On the outside, the simple shelters are nondescript

The cubic-anvil Ultrapress, designed by Tracy Hall, features six pistons that compress a cube-shaped sample. U.S. Synthetic Corporation in Provo, Utah, markets the eight-foot-tall press and manufactures diamond inserts for rock-drilling bits. (Courtesy of U.S. Synthetic Corporation.)

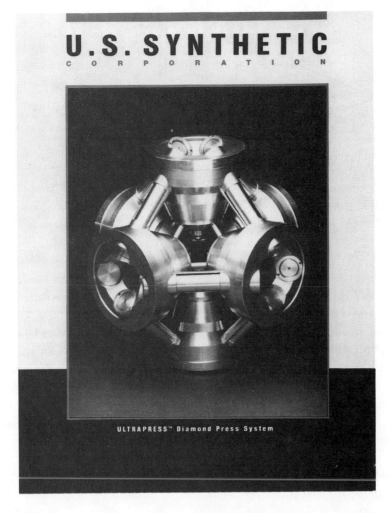

except for occasional company logos on the doors—a modest USS in an oval frame next to a plain door is all that marks the corporation's main entrance. The door opens onto a small reception area with a thin industrial carpet and spartan furnishings. A narrow corridor leads past cubicle offices to the production area.

This is no-frills diamond making. Clean concrete floors, unadorned metal walls, and minimal fluorescent lighting create a simple environment well suited to the work. A dozen employees feed and maintain two cubic-anvil presses, designed and built to Tracy Hall's specifications. The USS presses, crafted from gleaming stainless steel, stand eight feet tall, alien in their massive symmetry. They operate twenty-four hours a day, six days a week, and churn out 180 runs each on a good day.

On a nearby set of metal shelves, one-inch cubes of rusty red wonderstone are stacked like a pile of children's blocks. The press operator selects a cube, which has been drilled through the center and packed with a sample of diamond powder. He places the assembly at the center of the press's six massive carbide anvils, each aimed at one of the sample's six flat sides. With inexorable force, the cube is crushed in the cubic vise, and then heat is applied. The operator retreats behind a protective shield to begin the pressurization; once every few hundred runs—perhaps once or twice a week—an anvil will break. At such times it's best to be behind something solid.

It takes only a few minutes for temperature and pressure to do their work. The wonderstone cube has become noticeably smaller and has turned gray from the heat. The press operator attacks the assembly with a hammer, easily shattering the gray shell and revealing a dense diamond core—a bullet-shaped drill piece, ready to attach to a drill bit that will slice through thousands of feet of solid rock.

From the modest beginnings in 1955, when the world's supply of synthetic diamond could have been dispersed by a sneeze, to today's thriving industry, the diamond makers have made dramatic strides. Almost one hundred tons of diamonds are synthesized every year, providing nine out of ten carats used in the world today. In just three decades synthetic diamond production has exceeded the historical output of all the world's mines several times over.

Yet even that extraordinary output may pale beside the astonishing advances of the next generation of diamond makers.

11

✧

The New-Age
Diamond Makers

As the last remaining dinosaurs neared their end, a dusting of microscopic diamonds apparently fell from the sky, according to a scenario
proposed by two Canadian researchers who found extremely tiny diamonds in 65-million-year-old rocks from Alberta. . . . The researchers
suggest the diamond dust was either brought to Earth by an impacting
meteorite or created during the high-pressure collision.

—Science News, September 5, 1991

In the roughly rounded mountains
of Pennsylvania's Appalachian Mountains there are mines of one of
the most sought-after of all geological treasures. Deep into the earth
men have carved their caverns—drilling, blasting, and moving countless tons of rock. These prospectors seek neither precious metals nor
gemstones; they labor for gravel. Gold and silver may be good for
making trinkets, but you can build a nation with crushed stone.

The Madison Formation of western Maryland and central Pennsylvania makes great gravel. Its massive blue-gray limestone beds,
remnants of an ancient coral reef, blast free into neat layers a foot or
two thick, a perfect size for transport to the steel-jawed rock crusher.
Sieve-like sorters guide the shattered rock to conveyor belts, each
ending in a great conical gravel pile: fist-sized for drainage, walnut-
sized for septic systems, pea-sized for driveways and walkways.

The mining strategy is simple, but the results are epic. First,
geologists find a mountain with limestone layers near its base. A great

pit is cut into the mountain's flank, exposing a sheer wall of limestone. Crushing and sorting equipment is then installed close to the pit for easy access to the rock. Miners tunnel deep into the mountain, removing every bit of limestone except for a few widely spaced rock pillars, four feet on a side and several stories tall, that support the vast underground chambers. The imposing cavern's fifty-foot ceilings and pavement-smooth rock floors define the top and bottom of what was once a solid limestone layer. Mammoth trucks with wheels taller than a man ferry freshly broken rock to the outside world. Deeper and deeper the operation extends, sometimes the better part of a mile laterally beneath the wooded slopes.

Eventually a limestone mine must give out; a mountain can only be undercut so far before the risk of collapse becomes too great. The deeper the excavation, the more costly the operation. But abandoned limestone mines are not without their uses. The open pits are meccas for an army of amateur fossil hunters, who comb the weathered rock rubble for beautifully preserved shells of strange, extinct sea animals. The ancient reef rock breaks with a pungent sulfur smell, letting fossil hounds breathe in the atoms of life that were entombed a third of a billion years ago.

One spent Madison quarry, about fifty miles southeast of Pittsburgh, serves a very different purpose. This mine, with its carefully guarded gates and prominent NO TRESPASSING signs, serves as a chamber for making diamonds. In this underground limestone mine Pennsylvania workers pack pipes full of graphite and metal powders and then surround the pipes with tons of explosives. When detonated, each massive explosion creates the tremendous temperatures and pressures needed to convert the graphite to a solid mass of submicroscopic diamond crystals.

This violent process mimics nature's most catastrophic events. Almost all the world's natural diamonds grow deep beneath us in the hot, dense rocks of the earth's mantle. There, carbon atoms coalesce over aeons to form magnificent gems. But nature has found another way to play the diamond game. Every so often—perhaps once every few thousand years—the earth's gravitational field captures a massive chunk of rock from outer space. The extraterrestrial boulder picks up speed as it approaches the earth. Plummeting through the atmosphere at several miles per second, the rock glows white hot and then begins to vaporize in a spectacular trail of fire. While a smaller rock would burn up in the atmosphere, this massive rock survives the fire to smash into the planet's surface in a terrible explosion, more powerful than a fleet of nuclear missiles.

Most large meteorites hit deep water, since oceans cover more than two-thirds of the earth's surface. Perhaps one in three meteorites strikes land or shallow water, where the projectile blasts and craters rock and soil in an instant of unimaginable pressure and temperature. In such a catastrophe rocks are transformed into an exotic dust of high-pressure minerals. Common quartz changes into coesite or even denser forms; under just the right circumstances, everyday carbon compounds become diamond. Everywhere there is life there is carbon, ready to be transformed instantaneously by such an impact into microscopic diamond crystals.

Layers of natural diamond dust offer clues to the scope of epic catastrophes in the earth's past. Recently, Canadian geologists David B. Carlisle and Dennis R. Braman extracted microscopic grains of diamond from a layer of sediments 65 million years old—rocks deposited at the very end of the age of dinosaurs. The diamond dust is so fine that many scientists suspect it was caused by meteorite impact. Did those diamonds form in the same collision that caused the extinction of dinosaurs and countless other life forms? While the verdict is still out, a majority of scientists believe that such an impact propelled huge quantities of fine dust into the atmosphere, blackening the skies for months and profoundly disturbing the growing cycles of plants, and thus the lives of the animals that depended on them for food. As the diamond-bearing dust settled, it left a layer of fine sediment in 65-million-year-old rocks around the world.

Scientists discovered meteoritic diamonds more than a quarter century ago at the famous Canyon Diablo site at Meteor Crater, Arizona—the same place that first yielded coesite, the high-pressure form of quartz. Unlike South African or Brazilian stones, meteoritic diamond crystals are small, usually the size of fine sand grains, or about a hundredth of an inch across. While most Canyon Diablo particles display all the characteristics of ordinary fine-grained diamond, some of the grains do not. Meticulous analysis of the material in late 1966 revealed an extraordinary find: hexagonal diamond, a new crystal form of carbon different from both graphite and diamond.

Apparently, almost 30 percent of the meteorite diamond, including crystals up to a few hundredths of an inch across, occurred in this intriguing form.

The find was newsworthy but not entirely unexpected. As early as 1962 scientists had predicted the existence of hexagonal diamond, and in the mid-1960s General Electric scientists had detected traces of the new material (they called it delta-carbon) in the product of some synthetic runs at pressures above 130,000 atmospheres. In fact, Francis Bundy and coworkers were able to make nearly pure hexagonal material by subjecting carefully oriented graphite crystals to extremely high pressures.

Upon careful examination, the GE team realized that the natural meteoritic material, their synthetic delta-carbon, and the predicted hexagonal diamond were the same beast. Mineralogists, always searching for new species, pounced on the find and gave it the name lonsdaleite, in honor of British mineralogist Dame Kathleen Lonsdale, who had contributed much to the study of natural diamond crystals.

In many respects, lonsdaleite and diamond are remarkably similar. They have virtually the same density and almost the same hardness. But the x-ray patterns they produce, while similar in some ways, are nevertheless quite distinct, indicating significant differences in their atomic arrangement.

The relationship between the structures of normal cubic diamond and the new hexagonal crystal—both of which are built from pyramids of four carbon atoms—is hard to describe but easy to demonstrate. There are two simple, systematic ways to stack layers of same-sized spheres. The first layer is easy—just pack the balls close together so that each one touches six others. This close-packing arrangement is used for efficient shipping of all kinds of round objects, from soup cans to sewer pipe.

The second layer is also straightforward; you build it by placing one ball in a depression formed by any three adjacent balls in the first layer. You'll notice that there are lots of spots to choose from, and that it doesn't matter at all which one you select initially. From then on the second layer is formed just like the first, with close packing of balls.

Next comes the tricky part. Where do you start the third layer?

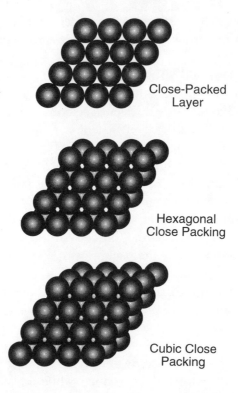

Close-Packed
Layer

Hexagonal
Close Packing

Cubic Close
Packing

In a close-packed layer, each ball touches six others. A second layer fits only one way on the first, but there are two different ways to place the third layer: either directly over balls in the first layer (hexagonal close packing) or over the spaces between balls (cubic close packing).

You must begin this layer by selecting a depression formed by three balls in the second layer, but now there are two different kinds of spots to choose from. Look carefully and you'll see that half the depressions are directly above the center of a ball in the first level, while half are centered over the space between two balls in that layer. If you choose to place a ball directly above one in the first layer, you end up with an alternating arrangement, often described as ABABAB in the literature of crystals—the result is hexagonal close packing. A quite different pattern arises if you make the other choice—it creates an ABCABC sequence of layers known as cubic close packing. Diamond and lonsdaleite differ simply in the way the layers of carbon atoms are stacked. Diamond adopts ABCABC cubic close packing, while lonsdaleite displays ABABAB hexagonal close packing. Under most natural circumstances the cubic arrangement prevails, but under special conditions, such as the almost instantaneous shock of a meteorite impact, lonsdaleite can also form.

While most researchers agree that the Canyon Diablo diamonds formed from carbon atoms contained in the meteorite itself, two rival theories compete to explain their origins. One group contends that Canyon Diablo diamond represents transformed meteoritic graphite: they say that black graphite grains originally embedded in the iron-rich body were converted to diamond by the pressure and temperature of impact. Others disagree, theorizing that most meteoritic diamond was formed in the vacuum of space, where they believe carbon atoms condensed directly into diamond. The debate continues, but scientists have found that both methods—explosive shock and vapor deposition—can be used to make diamond.

Humans are quite adept at making explosions. The highest pressures available on earth come courtesy of the military, whose high-velocity projectiles and nuclear weapons explode to create many millions of atmospheres of pressure, even if only for a fraction of a second. In mid-1959, Paul S. De Carli, scientist at the Stanford Research Institute in Menlo Park, California, and his visiting colleague John C. Jamieson, geology professor from the University of Chicago, attempted to duplicate nature's feat and create diamond by violent impact. They packed explosives behind a solid plate of aluminum metal and detonated the device with an electrical pulse. With a deafening boom, the explosively propelled metal plate plowed into a sample of graphite at supersonic speed, generating transient pressures greater than 300,000 atmospheres. In experiment after experiment, the resulting shock wave transformed graphite into diamond.

De Carli and Jamieson's success suggested an alternative route to commercial diamond synthesis. Du Pont, a leader in explosives technology, decided to try. For almost two decades they have produced millions of carats of diamonds annually in a process reminiscent of the early efforts of Hannay and Noble.

Although it might seem that any big explosion can produce diamonds, the process is in fact subtle and complex. As a shock wave passes through graphite, the intense heat and pressure can indeed create diamond, but since the pressure drops rapidly after the shock wave passes, the crystals can just as easily convert back into graphite while they are still hot. The key is to dissipate the heat as quickly as possible so that the high-pressure material doesn't have a chance to change. Du Pont originally employed a special starting mix of iron carbide and graphite, using the iron carbide to draw heat away from the carbon. Eventually, they switched to a graphite-copper mixture. Originally, the Du Pont process produced hexagonal diamond along with cubic diamond, but recently modified synthetic runs only produce the preferable cubic diamond.

The most striking feature of Du Pont's synthetic diamond, trade-named Mypolex, is its extremely fine grain size—typically less than a millionth of an inch—which makes it ideal for polishing gemstones. Du Pont synthesizes only about two million carats (less than half a ton) of Mypolex each year, and the product costs significantly more per carat than other synthetic diamond abrasives. Nevertheless, Mypolex enjoys a steady market because it is uniquely suited for high-precision polishing.

Today, high pressure is the key to all commercial diamond synthesis, but that situation may soon change. Scientists have learned that under the right conditions flawless diamonds will form in a vacuum, where the pressure approaches zero. At the earth's surface, carbon atoms invariably arrange themselves in a particular pattern with three nearest neighbors producing the structure of graphite. In the near vacuum of deep space, however, hot carbon atoms often wind up bonding to four carbon neighbors, thus forming interstellar diamond dust. What has happened in space for billions of years can now be duplicated in the laboratory.

The secret to the new diamond-making technology, known as chemical vapor deposition, or CVD, lies in forming a gas of single, isolated carbon atoms usually by heating carbon to very high temperatures, and then fooling those atoms into adopting the "wrong" structure as they cool. In successful CVD, the carbon vapor condenses so that each atom has four nearest neighbors—the distinctive structure of diamond—rather than the usual three of graphite. This strategy is an old one, familiar to chemists, who often play such tricks on atoms. Even before World War I some scientists had suggested that diamond could be grown at the low pressures at which graphite would normally form.

Though it seemed less promising than the high-pressure route, low-pressure synthesis would be much less expensive and thus well worth the effort to develop. The first concentrated efforts to make diamond at low pressure took place shortly after World War II, when research programs were established at Union Carbide's Linde Air Products Division and at General Electric. The two groups adopted similar approaches, trying to grow diamonds by vaporizing hydrocarbons in a vacuum. The General Electric effort, conducted primarily by researchers David Turnbull and Richard Oriani, began in 1950, almost simultaneously with Project Superpressure. The vacuum research continued with strong corporate backing but no appreciable success until 1957, when the breakthrough of high-pressure synthesis obviated the vacuum process.

Union Carbide scientist W. G. Eversole also spent the better part of the 1950s trying to grow diamond; he eventually learned to deposit layers of carbon atoms on hot diamond surfaces late in the decade. He placed diamond particles in a vacuum and exposed them to hot, carbon-rich gas. His procedure, which under the best circumstances increased the weight of his starting material by only about 2 percent every hour, received the first patent for a low-pressure method of diamond synthesis in 1961. Eversole's discovery, anticipated by decades of theory and experiment, marked a major advance in diamond making, but it came at a time when brute-force high-pressure methods seemed to be the best path to synthesis, and the vacuum process generated relatively little excitement.

Eversole's approach was resurrected six years later by John C. Angus and his students at Case Western Reserve University in Cleveland, Ohio. Angus and coworkers meticulously cleaned natural diamond powder in acid and sealed it in a vacuum. New diamond was grown when carbon-rich natural gas at a pressure of less than a thousandth of an atmosphere was heated to 1,050°C and passed over the diamond powder.

The Case Western Reserve research was widely heralded as a milestone—in the authors' words, the first "evidence conclusively demonstrating that diamond crystals can be grown at subatmospheric pressure." Their report was submitted to the *Journal of Applied Physics* in November 1967 and appeared in print half a year later with the title "Growth of diamond seed crystals by vapor deposition." The three authors, Angus and his colleagues Herbert A. Will and Wayne S. Stanko, gave ample credit to Eversole's earlier research, which they had successfully duplicated. They commented, "It is surprising that this remarkable work has received so little attention."

In spite of this pioneering research, there was little follow-up in North America. Instead, Russian and Japanese scientists took the lead in exploring the potential of CVD diamond in the 1970s and early 1980s. B. V. Derjaguin and his colleagues in Kiev learned to grow faceted diamond crystals in a vacuum, while S. Matsumoto and S. Sekata at Japan's NIRIM laboratories produced transparent diamond disks. These programs enhanced the earlier research by establishing the key idea that the presence of hydrogen atoms in the low-pressure environment greatly enhances the quality and growth rate of CVD diamond.

Penn State's Rustum Roy, who visited Japan in 1985 and returned to establish a research consortium of universities and industry, rekindled American interest in CVD diamond. Roy and others realized that the vapor deposition techniques widely used to manufacture silicon-based semiconductors, in which computer chips are built up atom by atom, are also ideally suited to making CVD diamonds. Inspired by these ideas, hundreds of scientists have tackled the CVD diamond challenge, and dozens of technical papers every year announce a steady stream of laboratory advances. Researchers have learned to deposit clear, hard diamond coatings on a wide range of materials, including metals, semiconductors, and glass. The procedures were at first confined to temperatures so high that they could damage plastics, but effective lower-temperature techniques are now being devised.

The most exciting potential use of CVD diamonds is still just a glimmer in researchers' eyes. Some day diamond films, which are tough, durable, and resistant to heat damage, may become the ultimate semiconductor—the new critical material of the electronic age.

One major roadblock remains, however—a barrier that is consuming vast amounts of research time and energy in today's high-tech labs.

Every electrical device, whether run by flashlight batteries, a gasoline generator, or electric power from the wall, functions by the artful control of electrons. To use electricity we must first learn to control the movement of these electrons. We need conducting materials like copper wire in which electrons flow easily, so power can move from the electric plant to homes without dissipating. At the opposite extreme of the resistance scale we need insulators like plastic and glass to stop the flow of electrons and protect us from dangerous electric currents.

But if conductors and insulators were all we had to work with, the electronics field would be rather dull. Fortunately, there is another class of materials—semiconductors—that conduct electrons, but not very well. The behavior of electrons in a semiconductor is somewhat analogous to that of cars in a crowded parking lot where every driver is looking for a better space. Each car idles as its driver waits for a spot to open. When every space is filled, nobody moves. Pure silicon, with just enough electrons to fill all the electronic parking places, keeps electrons from moving, making it a poor electrical conductor.

Add just a few extra cars to the lot and the situation looks very different. Those cars without a parking spot rush around, looking for a place to stop. In a silicon crystal scientists achieve the same effect by removing a few silicon atoms (just one in ten million will do) and replacing them with phosphorus atoms, which have an extra electron. Suddenly there are a few mobile electrons that can't be held and, bingo, you have an *n*-type semiconductor (because those extra electrons carry a negative charge).

A similar phenomenon occurs in the parking lot when there are a few empty parking spaces. For every hole, some eager driver dashes out of his space to grab what he thinks might be a better one. The vacated space is quickly filled by another car, and so on. In a silicon crystal you can mimic that situation by substituting aluminum atoms for one out of every few million silicons. Aluminum has one too few electrons and so contributes the "holes" that inspire electrons to move around. The result is called a *p*-type semiconductor (because the holes are positively charged).

Taken by themselves, *n*- and *p*-type semiconductors are just poor conductors, but when pieces of the two types are combined something remarkable happens. Electrons travel easily from *n* to *p*, because negatively charged electrons seek the positive holes, but if you try to push current the other way, nothing happens, since negatively charged electrons resist flowing to a negatively charged site. The composite semiconductor behaves very differently from simple insulators and conductors. The junction of an *n* and *p* semiconductor—technicians call it a diode—acts like a one-way street for electrons. Certain combinations of three semiconductors—*npn* or *pnp*—are called transistors, and they can be used to amplify, detect, or switch electric signals. In modern microelectronics, large numbers of *n* and *p* semiconducting regions form the complex integrated circuits that lie at the heart of all electronic gear.

Diamond has the potential to become our most reliable, efficient, long-lasting, and durable semiconductor. Of course, pure diamond won't do; like pure silicon it is a poor conductor. But add just a bit of boron to the carbon lattice and you get a superb *p*-type semiconductor. The only missing link is the lack of an easy-to-make *n*-type diamond semiconductor. Until one is found, there can be no diamond integrated circuits, but keep watching the news. Hundreds of researchers are working on the problem, and the age of revolutionary diamond semiconductors manufactured by CVD technology could be close at hand.

Some materials scientists question whether CVD diamond will ever become commercially important. They argue that vapor-deposited diamond is expensive to produce and that its properties, while unique, do not yet satisfy any obvious critical need. But other, more optimistic researchers envision wonderful uses for CVD diamonds. Easily cooled diamond-coated integrated circuits may be only a few years away. Saws and knives that almost never need resharpening, lifetime razor blades, scratch-proof lenses, unbreakable watch crystals, and crash-proof computer disks could become everyday objects of the twenty-first century.

Most CVD technology is now limited to depositing a thin diamond layer on an existing substrate, but what is difficult now may become routine in the decades to come. As our ability to deposit diamond increases, we may eventually learn to grow large, perfect diamond crystals of any size and shape. Imagine an era of diamond manufacturing when we could build any object, atom by atom, in solid diamond. Diamond semiconductors, a durable alternative to silicon, would be foremost in many scientists' minds, but solid-diamond technology could lead to the ultimate ball bearings, light-weight permanent artificial joints, and even solid diamond household tools. Sculptors would possess a new medium of unrivaled brilliance, while artisans could shape solid diamond jewelry of breathtaking beauty.

Thanks to CVD techniques, the day may come when diamond, the most prized of all gems, becomes as familiar in everyday life as plastic or glass.

PART II

⋯⋯⋯⋯⋯⋯⋯⋯⋯⋯⋯⋯⋯⋯⋯⋯⋯⋯
✧

The Diamond Breakers

12

The Magical
Diamond Cell

You can observe a lot by watching.   —Yogi Berra

For the better part of a century sci-
entists relied on the earth to learn how diamonds were made. Today,
they rely on diamonds to learn how the earth was made.

Diamond's utility in modern research stems in large measure
from its strength and hardness, but the mineral possesses another
extraordinary property. Diamond is unique in its transparency to all
kinds of light.

All of us, every moment of our lives, are surrounded by a surging
sea of electromagnetic radiation. Light—energy in the form of waves
that travel at 186,000 miles per second (in a vacuum, remember)—
pervades every nook and cranny of the universe. Our eyes sense
only a tiny fraction of this energy; there is more—much more—out
there.

More than a century ago, James Clerk Maxwell predicted the
existence of invisible kinds of light. He realized that waves of light
could be any length at all, from the diameter of an atom's nucleus to
the size of stars, the same way ocean waves can range from microscopic ripples to globe-spanning swells. Like sailors clinging to a bob-
bing boat, who can only sense a small range of the ocean's waves, our
eyes see only a small portion of the electromagnetic spectrum—the
part where the waves are about a ten-thousandth of an inch long.

Red, orange, yellow, green, blue, violet—the colors of the spectrum are nothing more than thin slices of the vast radiation continuum.

The discovery of the other kinds of electromagnetic radiation—radio waves, microwaves, infrared radiation, ultraviolet light, x-rays, and gamma rays—propelled science and technology into the twentieth century. Scientists and engineers quickly learned that each kind of light energy can be absorbed, scattered, or transmitted to advantage.

In order to manipulate light you first have to know how it interacts with matter. With so many materials and such a wide range of light, it's a huge job that continues to consume the research lives of tens of thousands of scientists, who call themselves by lots of fancy names like spectroscopists, crystallographers, and radio-astronomers.

Research on matter and light has revealed an extraordinary fact about diamond. Of all known solids, nothing is more transparent to a wider range of light. Not only can you look right through a diamond with visible light, but the gemstone is also largely transparent to radio waves, microwaves, x-rays, gamma rays, and most kinds of ultraviolet and infrared light. Diamond is the ultimate window. High-pressure scientists, armed with knowledge of diamond's unique transparency, didn't take long to devise a completely new use for diamonds. For them, the gemstone provided an unparalleled way to measure volume.

Scientists have observed many unexpected phenomena at high pressure, but one fact is always true—squeeze on anything and it will get smaller. Whenever you apply force to a pencil, push a button, or blot a paper, the atoms under stress will, for a time, move a little closer together. Scientists quantify this effect with graphs of pressure versus volume—the meat and potatoes of high-pressure research—which identify the abrupt atomic rearrangements called phase transitions, such as the transformation of graphite to diamond, or water to ice. High-pressure workers are always looking for new phase transitions, and they know that pressure-volume data are often the best tools for spotting them. They also ask lots of questions about their compressed samples: "Which atoms get closer together?" "How much closer do they get?" "Do some kinds of atoms compress more than others?" Such questions about atoms and how they are arranged are usually the intellectual territory of the scientists known as crystallographers.

Crystallographers focus x-ray beams at tiny crystals and study how the energy scatters. Each type of crystal yields a distinctive pattern of scattered x-rays. The crystallographer's job is to work backward—measure the x-ray pattern and deduce the atomic structure. By the close of World War II x-ray crystallography was routine, and most common atomic structures had been thoroughly described. Enterprising researchers, always seeking fresh turf, looked to the intriguing problem of atomic structures at high pressure. What they needed was a material strong enough to hold a pressurized sample and transparent enough to allow scientists to zap the sample with x-rays. The answer was diamond.

In 1946, many of the tens of thousands of physicists, chemists, engineers, and technicians who helped make the atomic bomb during the epic Manhattan Project were looking for new opportunities. Scientists at the innocuous-sounding Institute of Metals at the University of Chicago were among those who spent the war working on the bomb, but the end of hostilities didn't end their involvement in weapons research. In 1947 they received a modest grant from the Office of Naval Research to study the behavior of metals and other materials at high pressure. Their work was hardly arcane—you can't build submarines or calculate the destructive effects of explosives without knowing how metals behave under pressure.

Physicist Andrew W. Lawson, like so many of his colleagues, spent much of the war years on atomic bomb research at Chicago. He proved an able leader and, in spite of his youth, was named head of the Chicago high-pressure project in the spring of 1947. Within a few weeks Lawson took the logical first step—a pilgrimage to Harvard to confer with Percy Bridgman. In typically generous fashion Bridgman gave Lawson the blueprints for his press and pump and provided all sorts of advice on laboratory procedures. Inevitably, their pressure conversation turned to the question of volume.

The classic problem for high-pressure researchers is how to measure the volume of a sample crushed inside a massive metal device. Bridgman and others did it by the simple method of piston displacement: they measured the amount the piston moved in response to changes in the sample's volume. The technique worked reasonably well, but told scientists nothing about what individual atoms were up to. Lawson and Bridgman knew that x-rays, which can probe a sample's atomic structure, could give them the answer. Now all they needed was a material that could sustain high pressure while transmitting x-rays.

X-rays are not absorbed by atoms themselves, but by the clouds of electrons that surround each atom's nucleus. One key to finding a material transparent to x-rays is to find atoms with only a few electrons. Nature hasn't given us many workable choices. The lightest atoms, hydrogen and helium, with one and two electrons per atom, respectively, are both gases, so they don't make very good pressure cells. The third element, lithium, is an extremely soft and chemically reactive metal, so it won't work either. Which takes us to the fourth element, the metal beryllium, with four electrons per atom.

Beryllium is a shiny, silvery metal with a slight bluish sheen; it looks a lot like stainless steel at first glance. It's easy to machine, though potentially quite toxic to the machinist if precautions against beryllium dust aren't taken. The University of Chicago group built a pressure cell entirely out of the expensive metal and obtained reasonably good x-ray patterns at 15,000 atmospheres. After a few trials, however, it was clear that the metal cell would always be limited by the thick beryllium walls; there were simply too many atoms in the way. The cell absorbed most of the x-rays and scattered much of the rest to fog their x-ray film. Lawson and his crystallographic colleague Ting-Yuan Tang thus turned to diamond, formed from the six-electron element, carbon. They reasoned that the great strength of diamond would permit a much smaller pressure device with lower x-ray absorption.

These two scientists pioneered the use of diamonds in high-pressure x-ray research. Their rudimentary device, first assembled in 1949, consisted of a small diamond cut in half and then clamped together in a steel vise. A hole no larger than the diameter of a pin was laboriously drilled through the diamond halves, along their surface of contact, to form a cylindrical sample chamber. Two short lengths of steel piano wire or tungsten carbide, inserted at opposite ends of the hole, compressed powdered samples to more than 20,000 atmospheres. Following the century-old tradition of high-pressure researchers familiar with explosions, Lawson and Tang dubbed their invention the split-diamond bomb.

In trial x-ray experiments on calcite (the common white mineral that composes most limestone and marble), they demonstrated the feasibility of taking x-ray pictures through diamond. Lawson and Tang inserted a powdered sample into the cylindrical hole and compressed it. They focused an x-ray beam through the diamond onto the pressurized sample and recorded the resulting diffraction on special x-ray film. The split-diamond bomb proved that diamonds were an ideal window for high-pressure x-ray work, but the device failed to take full advantage of the crystal's strength. By splitting the diamond in two, the Chicago researchers weakened the cell and limited the maximum attainable pressure. As so often happens in science, an eager graduate student took the next step.

John C. Jamieson, who would later work with Paul De Carli to create diamond by violent impact, was a jovial, genial man who approached each new experimental challenge with cheerful optimism.

The split-diamond bomb of Andrew Lawson and Ting-Yuan Tang consisted of a cleaved diamond held together by a screw-tightened metal clamp. A hole drilled through the diamond served as a sample chamber, while a stiff wire piston compressed the powdered sample from either side of the hole. (Courtesy of the American Institute of Physics.)

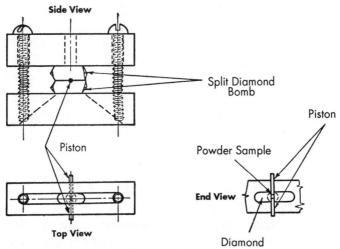

Upon joining the University of Chicago high-pressure team in 1951 as a doctoral candidate he immediately set to work on the high-pressure calcite problem. Jamieson reasoned that a hole drilled through a single crystal of diamond would be stronger, and therefore confine higher pressures, than a halved diamond. He selected a three-carat gem, worth more than $50,000 in today's dollars, and took it to a Chicago company that specialized in drilling holes in diamond for extruding wire of uniform diameter. Shortly before his death in 1983, Jamieson recalled his uncharacteristic impatience at having to wait eight months for the process to be completed. With a twinkle in his eye, he told of making phone calls every few weeks to track the progress of the quarter-inch-long hole. Eventually, bit by bit, as diamond drill abraded diamond crystal, the hole was completed.

The new cell worked beautifully, achieving 30,000 atmospheres and allowing Jamieson to discover a previously unknown phase transition in calcite. He also heated samples in the diamond bomb and thus was able to mimic the behavior of minerals in the hot, compressed interior of the earth. Jamieson's single-crystal cell could do things no other device could, and other labs rushed to make diamond cells of their own. Yet, as clever as the miniature piston-cylinder was, it just missed the full potential of diamond for achieving high pressures. The real diamond cell breakthrough took a brilliantly different approach.

Few scientists have had to resist greater temptations than Alvin Van Valkenburg and Charles Weir, who formed the high-pressure research team at the National Bureau of Standards (NBS) in Washington, D.C. It was there that Van Valkenburg and Weir were given unlimited access to fistfuls of gem diamonds.

Van Valkenburg came to NBS just after World War II, having studied geology, mineralogy, and x-ray crystallography. There he joined forces with Charles E. Weir, probably the only African-American to play a major part in postwar high-pressure research.

Van Valkenburg's career had progressed easily, but Weir had struggled all his life against racial prejudice. His scientific credentials were impeccable: an undergraduate physics degree from Chicago and graduate work at Howard University and Caltech. The NBS newsletter referred to him euphemistically as "one of those rare native Washingtonians," but even in the community of supposedly objective physicists racism was pervasive. The restaurant at the National Bureau of Standards made it clear that Weir was not welcome, so Van Valkenburg and Weir usually ate sandwich lunches together in their office. Discrimination was even more blatant at many professional meetings, where Weir was forced to eat and sleep away from the conference center. In New York City he always ate at the coin-operated cafeterias, where everyone was treated the same.

Van Valkenburg and Weir formed a lasting friendship at the NBS, where they had one unusual advantage over other high-pressure workers. As government researchers, they enjoyed a steady supply of fine diamonds confiscated from would-be smugglers. There have always been gem smugglers, but the greatest diamond hoard came to America following Britain's decision to pull out of Palestine in 1948. Before escaping the danger zone, many people had converted their wealth into diamonds, and many of those stones were illegally carried into the United States. Customs agents in New York and Florida confiscated millions of dollars' worth of smuggled stones, which the government refused to release onto the carefully regulated commercial market. Boxes full of these precious stones were instead offered to the scientists at the National Bureau of Standards.

"When you do science you have to give credit to all who helped," Van Valkenburg reminisced. "The smugglers made my career." He never learned their names, though he was told that more than one had been sent to jail. Thanks to them, the two NBS researchers had thousands of diamonds at their disposal—valuable gems just sitting there for the taking. Most of the diamonds were small, weighing only a fraction of a carat, but there were scores of larger stones as well. The standout was a magnificent 7.5-carat cut gem of a particularly rare type that displayed unusual transparency to infrared radiation.

Van Valkenburg and Weir handled their treasure casually. Scientists often keep messy offices, but Van Valkenburg and Weir were worse than most. The desks in their small shared office were always piled high with unread papers and unanswered mail. To make matters worse, Charlie Weir smoked incessantly and scattered ashes everywhere. Amid this chaos, diamonds were just lying around, waiting to be studied.

Van Valkenburg recalled one diamond delivery—perhaps a million dollars' worth—that arrived by courier late one afternoon. It was too late to arrange for proper security, and the night watchman refused to take responsibility for the gems, so Van Valkenburg just stuck them in the back of his desk drawer, where they lay forgotten for several days. Given all the government lab regulations of the 1990s, it's difficult to imagine such lax supervision, but there were few controls on NBS scientists in the 1950s.

One time Van Valkenburg accidentally dropped a small diamond —no more than a third of a carat but still worth a week's pay—on the dusty floor. In spite of a careful search, the gem seemed to have vanished; it turned up a week later in the far corner of the lab and was plopped back into its box. This cavalier attitude was prevalent throughout the NBS; one by-product was the bureau's almost total lack of environmental concern. Smokestacks at the NBS glass group's suburban lab site spewed all sorts of toxic fumes—beryllium, arsenic, lead—right in the middle of a quiet residential Washington, D.C., neighborhood. No one said anything about it.

With so few regulations and so many diamonds, Van Valkenburg and Weir first thought about how to study the mineral itself. They knew that not all diamonds are alike. While the great majority absorb a broad range of invisible infrared radiation, perhaps one of every hundred natural gems is transparent to infrared wavelengths. Scientists could easily shine an infrared beam onto stones to sort diamonds into type I (opaque to infrared) and type II (transparent), but they didn't have a clue about what caused the difference. Some said it was a subtle structural difference, while others argued for the presence of an unknown impurity.

Van Valkenburg favored the impurity hypothesis, and he burned dozens of diamonds, analyzing the resulting gas and hoping to identify the contaminating substance. The mystery element wasn't boron, oxygen, aluminum, phosphorous, or sulfur. After incinerating dozens of gems, he gave up in frustration. (Nitrogen, an element Van Valkenburg couldn't detect with his apparatus, would eventually be shown to be the culprit.)

As Alvin Van Valkenburg was busy cremating precious stones at the National Bureau of Standards, another government agency was vying for the diamond hoard. George Switzer, gem curator at the Smithsonian's National Museum of Natural History, was desperately trying to work a deal to acquire the Hope diamond, the most notorious of all blue diamonds. Switzer thought a trade including the multimillion-dollar stockpile of smuggled diamonds might convince its owner, Harry Winston, to part with the fabulous jewel. Thus, for a time in the mid-1950s, there was considerable pressure on Van Valkenburg and Weir to produce something more useful from the stones than carbon dioxide. Although the Hope diamond trade never came to pass (in 1958 Winston finally decided to donate the famous stone to the Smithsonian), the episode did cause the NBS scientists to look for better uses for their horde of cut diamonds.

Having burned numerous diamonds to no avail, Van Valkenburg and Weir discovered other ways to destroy the gems. They selected the magnificent 7.5-carat, emerald-cut type-II gem—worth perhaps a

Alvin Van Valkenburg, NBS research technician Elmer Bunting, and Charles Weir (from left to right) pose with their drilled-diamond cell. The device (inset, lower right) was made from a 7.5-carat gemstone that finally shattered at high pressure. (Courtesy of Eric Van Valkenburg.)

quarter of a million dollars in today's retail market—for their copy of Jamieson's drilled-diamond cell. If Jamieson got 30,000 atmospheres with a 3-carat stone, they reasoned, NBS should be able to go even higher with a 7.5-carat jewel. It took four solid months of drilling and 16 carats of diamond dust to craft the tiny hole—one-quarter of an inch long and one sixty-fourth of an inch wide—but for a short while the NBS team had the world's most glamorous pressure cell. Soon, however, they faced the friendly rivalry of other high-pressure groups. General Electric pressure experts, not wanting to be left out, constructed their own drilled cell, but with slightly tapered holes for an even tighter fit and even higher pressures. In the mid-1950s, drilled-diamond cells at Chicago, NBS, and GE set records for the best x-ray and infrared spectra results at the highest pressures. Until 1957, that is, when the NBS team made their big mistake.

Pressure workers are greedy; they always want to reach higher pressures. The NBS team, hoping to establish a new record, literally pushed their cell to the breaking point. With a sickening crack, the 7.5-carat gemstone shattered into four pieces. Too late they had learned a critical lesson: a diamond is incomparably strong when under compression, but place it under tension—push from the inside out—and it shatters.

Van Valkenburg and Weir were dismayed at their costly failure. What could they do? Drill another diamond, with the constant worry that it, too, might shatter? Abandon high-pressure research altogether? They debated their options for a few depressing days and made their decision: it was time to try something new.

The diamond-anvil cell, affectionately nicknamed the DAC in many high-pressure labs, was an idea waiting to happen. The diamond cell is so simple in design and construction that it could have been built centuries ago. Isaac Newton could have watched matter transform at thousands of atmospheres of pressure. Thomas Edison could have discovered new materials with extraordinary properties. But it was not until 1959 that two research teams, independently and virtually simultaneously, hit upon the idea that transformed high-pressure research.

Perhaps the easiest way to enclose a sample and subject it to pressure is by using a piston-and-cylinder apparatus. Bridgman and others adopted this approach in their large presses, where sturdy metals formed the cylindrical walls of the chamber and carefully machined steel or carbide pistons drove into the confined sample. The split- and drilled-diamond cells of the Chicago high-pressure lab incorporated the same strategy, with diamond acting as a strong and transparent cylindrical chamber and stiff wire acting as miniature pistons. It wasn't the best use of diamonds, but it was the logical first step to try.

Bridgman had used another strategy—opposed anvils—to obtain the highest pressures of his career. That geometry was also adopted in one form or another by most of the early diamond makers—Tracy Hall's belt, Herb Strong's cone, even von Platen's split sphere incorporated pairs of anvils. With that history in mind, workers at both NBS and Chicago, stimulated by two very different experimental objectives but both committed to using transparent diamond windows, converged on a single, elegant solution. They devised a diamond-anvil cell based on Percy Bridgman's opposed-anvil design.

John Jamieson created the new apparatus in the hope of achieving higher pressures for his x-ray studies. His drilled-diamond cell, with a maximum pressure of only about 30,000 atmospheres, could duplicate conditions of only the first fifty or sixty miles of the earth's outer layers—representing only a pitiful 4 percent of the solid earth's total volume. He became increasingly frustrated by the significant partial absorption of x-rays by his large drilled diamond, as well as the diamond-induced scattering of x-rays, which darkened his film before sufficient data could be obtained. He reasoned that in the drilled-diamond cell the diamond served only as a passive chamber, not the active element in applying pressure. Much better, he thought, to apply pressure using the diamonds as anvils, with the sample squeezed between.

Thus the Chicago diamond-anvil cell was born. Jamieson took a bit of sample, put it on a diamond surface, placed a second diamond on top, stuck the whole works in a screw vise, and squeezed like crazy. X-rays reached the sample by passing through the sides of the relatively thin diamond anvils, parallel to the anvil faces, thus minimizing x-ray absorption. Jamieson and Lawson completed a prototype cell in late 1958, optimistic that 100,000 atmospheres would soon be within their reach.

The University of Chicago scientists used their diamond cell to produce excellent x-ray patterns of a new form of bismuth found at 35,000 atmospheres, a record for x-ray work, and they were only a little discouraged when one diamond cracked as they reached for higher pressures. The small anvils, only a fraction of a carat each, were easily replaced. The Chicago pressure cell represented a significant advance, and it received prominent exposure in the November 1959 issue of *The Review of Scientific Instruments*. But Jamieson and

John Jamieson and coworkers at the University of Chicago pressurized their samples by squeezing them between the faces of two diamond anvils, using two large screws to change the pressure. The entire assembly could be mounted onto an x-ray machine, which irradiated the sample from the side of the opposed anvils. (Courtesy of the American Institute of Physics.)

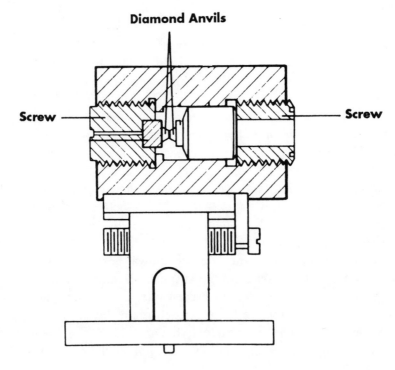

Diamond Anvils

Screw   **Screw**

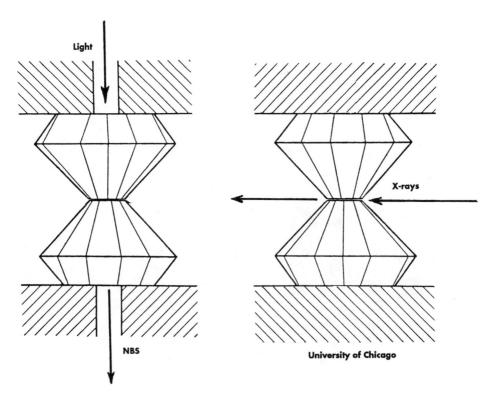

Research groups at the University of Chicago and the National Bureau of Standards adopted different strategies in their diamond-anvil research. NBS scientists directed their infrared beams through the two diamonds perpendicular to the flat faces, while Chicago workers passed an x-ray beam parallel to the diamond-anvil surfaces.

Lawson just missed the full potential of the opposed-diamond arrangement. The NBS team would have to show the world what diamonds could do.

The University of Chicago scientists had designed their diamond cell for x-ray studies, but Van Valkenburg and Weir at NBS attacked the high-pressure problem from the perspective of the infrared spectroscopist. The Chicago team had passed an x-ray beam through the side of their diamond anvils, in an arrangement analogous to the earlier drilled-diamond setup, but to do spectroscopy you have to see the sample, and to see a high-pressure sample you have to be able to

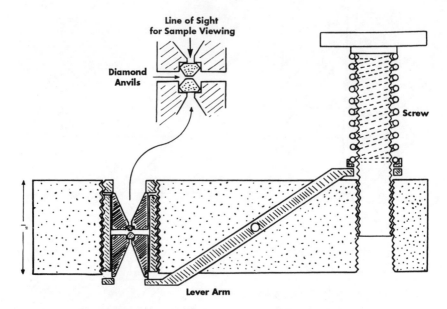

The National Bureau of Standards's lever-arm diamond-anvil cell employed a pair of opposed diamond anvils mounted in steel pistons. The screw acted on the lever arm to change pressure. This device, designed for spectroscopic work, allowed scientists to look directly at their pressurized sample. (Courtesy of the National Institutes for Standards and Technology.)

look *through* the sample chamber. In late 1958 Van Valkenburg hit upon the simple idea of cutting off the tips of brilliant-cut gem diamonds and using them as tiny transparent anvils. By leaving a hole in the steel anvil supports, he could look right through the anvils at the compressed sample with no distortion or interference.

Charlie Weir, who counted machining skills among his credentials, built the first NBS opposed-diamond-anvil device in 1958. He attached type-II diamond anvils to two steel pistons, which fit into a precisely machined cylinder. The pistons were clamped together by a slick lever-arm arrangement that Van Valkenburg described as "little more than an elaborate nutcracker." The NBS group believed that exceedingly high pressures might be achieved in their machine with the simple turn of a screw.

The new diamond-anvil cell with its type-II diamonds seemed

ideal for infrared studies. The device fit snugly into their infrared machine, and Van Valkenburg and Weir were confident that obtaining infrared data would be a straightforward task. Poised to do great things, the two scientists decided to seek the help of a widely respected authority on infrared spectroscopy. They approached Ellis R. Lippincott of the University of Maryland's chemistry department, a gentleman scientist who spent a long and productive career teaching chemistry and contributed a great deal to our understanding of how matter absorbs and scatters light. Lippincott was immediately drawn to the NBS proposal. He knew that pressure forces subtle shifts in atomic positions and alters the way light rays of different colors travel through a solid. Apply pressure and a material's spectrum will change ever so slightly. Study high-pressure spectra, Lippincott thought, and you'll discover a lot about matter.

Lippincott, Van Valkenburg, and Weir performed their first infrared experiments on a pinhead-sized mound of potassium chloride. The NBS researchers, nervous and excited, piled their sample on one diamond face, crushed the white powder between the machine's vise-like anvils, and placed the cell in their spectrometer. No spectrum appeared. They shifted the pressure cell this way and that, refocused the beam, and adjusted its intensity, but to no avail. Van Valkenburg remembers wasting more than an hour in fruitless fiddling. In frustration, he removed the cell from the spectrometer and placed it under a microscope to see what had gone wrong.

At that moment, he became the first human to watch matter transform at thousands of atmospheres of pressure. The potassium chloride around the edges of the diamond remained colorless, but at the center of the flattened disk-shaped sample was a circle of darker material—clearly a new form of the chemical. One by one the NBS team looked in amazement at the microscopic phenomenon. "It seems odd," Van Valkenburg recalled, "but when we designed that diamond cell we never actually thought about *looking* at the sample." But look at samples they did. The Lippincott, Van Valkenburg, Weir patent for a high-pressure optical cell ushered in a new era of high-pressure research. For the very first time researchers could not only measure spectra at a wide range of wavelengths—they could also actually watch an amazing variety of high-pressure phenomena at pressures greater than 100,000 atmospheres. Early photographs taken by the NBS group through their cell show striking phase transitions in materials at pressures corresponding to depths of more than two hundred miles beneath the surface of the earth.

As powerful as their first diamond-anvil cell was, the NBS team had just gotten started. "We tried everything," Van Valkenburg remembers, "and we broke diamonds left and right." But they eventually achieved pressures of more than 300,000 atmospheres.

Van Valkenburg realized that the diamond-anvil cell was greatly limited because it crushed the samples completely. Single crystals, with their special directional properties, thus could not be studied. The system also could not confine and probe liquids or gases. Van Valkenburg devised an elegant solution—one he views in retrospect as almost trivial, though it radically changed high-pressure science.

Van Valkenburg observed that two flat diamond anvils aren't enough to confine a sample—they only form a contact surface. So he

Alvin Van Valkenburg enhanced the flexibility of the diamond-anvil cell by incorporating a metal gasket between the two diamonds. This gasketed cell enabled him to study fluids and uncrushed single crystals at ultrahigh pressures.

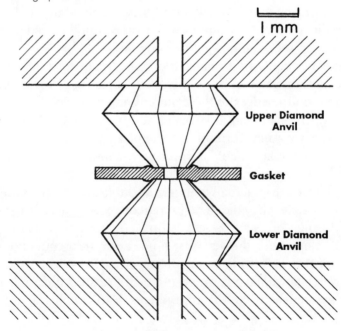

204

took a thin metal sheet of nickel alloy, drilled a hole in it, and used it as a gasket. By placing the metal gasket between the two anvils, he formed a tiny cylindrical sample chamber about the size of a sand grain. Van Valkenburg simply filled the chamber with a pressure-transmitting fluid like water or oil and squeezed. As the metal gasket deformed, the pressure increased.

Alvin Van Valkenburg saw wonderful things in his gasketed diamond cell. Simple water, squeezed to 10,000 atmospheres at room temperature, formed rectangular crystals of a new kind of ice that no one had ever seen before. Then, at 25,000 atmospheres, another new form with cube faces appeared in the cell. He saw everyday liquid chemicals like benzene and toluene form crystals; he dubbed the blade-like crystals of pressurized alcohol "gin-sickles."

Metal gaskets also allowed the NBS researchers to study tiny single crystals without the grains being crushed between the diamonds. NBS researchers placed crystals of calcite and other minerals in the gasket chamber, surrounded them with liquid, and closed the cell up. Squeezing the diamonds didn't smash the crystals; it just compressed the liquid, which in turn compressed the crystal equally on all sides like a deep-sea diver. A ton of rocks will crush the life out of you, but a ton of water pressure distributed over your entire body causes little discomfort.

Nitric acid formed beautiful crystals in the cell, while benzene, a liquid at room pressure, revealed at least four different high-pressure crystal forms. By heating the diamond cell while he changed pressure, Van Valkenburg learned to change crystals from one form to another so he could map out the pressures and temperatures at which they are stable.

The success of the diamond-anvil cell forced a new breed of high-pressure workers square up against a long-standing problem—the same problem that Percy Bridgman had faced a half century before. How could they measure a pressure that had never been measured before? Up to a few thousand atmospheres the task is fairly straightforward, because gas compression behaves like the mechanical compression of a spring: if you double the pressure, you halve the volume. But that rule breaks down as gas molecules are jammed close together and atoms begin to repel each other. Solids are no better, because the way they compress at low pressure is not always the way they compress at high pressure.

Alvin Van Valkenburg examines a pressurized crystal in his diamond-anvil cell, circa 1964. (Courtesy of Eric Van Valkenburg.)

Once again, the National Bureau of Standards came to the rescue. Lippincott's spectroscopic studies had shown that certain spectral features shift regularly with pressure. One such effect occurs in the bright red fluorescence of ruby crystals: when bathed in blue, violet, or ultraviolet light, ruby crystals give off a brilliant red fluorescence. The exact shade of red, which can be measured with an ordinary spectrometer, shifts steadily with pressure. In early 1972 members of an expanded NBS high-pressure team introduced their ruby fluorescence method of pressure calibration, the method still used almost universally today.

In spite of its power and simplicity, the diamond-anvil cell was slow to catch on. Most researchers who had spent their lives using impressive large-volume presses just couldn't get very excited about working on tiny volumes under a microscope. Charlie Weir made a special trip to New Hampshire, partly to show off the new device to the vacationing Percy Bridgman. Bridgman was politely interested but hardly enthusiastic, and the visit was brief. Alvin Van Valkenburg received similarly unenthusiastic responses when he presented a series of lectures on the diamond-anvil cell. His low-key style and the prevalence of big presses conspired against its immediate acceptance.

Of the three diamond-cell inventors, Ellis Lippincott had the widest reputation. If the novel device was to gain new adherents, he was the one to promote it. But just as the diamond cell was coming into its own, Lippincott's reputation was destroyed by the polywater fiasco.

The scientific community was astounded in the late 1960s when Russian chemists N. N. Fedyakin and B. V. Derjaguin announced the discovery of a completely new kind of water that seemed to form easily in narrow capillary tubes. The new water froze at $-50°C$, boiled at $300°C$, and appeared to be considerably more dense than ordinary water. The Russian researchers theorized that the new form of H_2O possessed a distinctive new atomic structure.

Ellis Lippincott and his coworker, Robert R. Stromberg of the National Bureau of Standards, were skeptical but sufficiently intrigued by the unlikely Soviet reports to examine the new water themselves. They followed the Russian recipe and examined the minute sample with infrared spectroscopy—a sensitive probe of molecular structure—fully expecting to see the familiar spectrum of water. Instead, they stared in amazement at a totally new spectrum, unlike anything they'd seen before. This new form of water had all the traits of a polymer, a chain-like collection of atoms. Lippincott and his coworkers rushed their manuscript, "Polywater," into print with a feature article in the June 27, 1969, issue of *Science.*

For a brief time polywater was the rage, the subject of intense study and wild speculation. Scientists at the University of Southern California hinted at polywater's potential biological effects on skin pores, calling it a possible "fountain of youth." Frank Donahoe, a researcher at Wilkes College in Pennsylvania, gave readers of *Nature* a sober warning: a tiny amount of polywater released into the oceans, Donahoe argued, might cause all the water to transform. "I regard the polymer as the most dangerous material on earth. . . . Treat it as the most deadly virus until its safety is established." The *National Enquirer* picked up on the hype with the headline "Scientists have discovered a new type of water that could poison the world!"

The conclusion to the sorry affair came at the hands of Dennis L. Rousseau of Bell Telephone Laboratories, who noted the similarity of the polywater spectrum to that of sodium lactate, a common ingredient in human perspiration. Rousseau wrote, "Determined to understand polywater's infrared spectrum, I turned to my athletic passion, handball. After a lively game, I returned to the laboratory with my sweaty T-shirt and wrung the perspiration into a flask. When I placed the sweat in an infrared spectrometer, the spectrum looked strikingly similar to that of polywater." A year and a half after the appearance of Lippincott's first article on polywater, *Science* published Rousseau's crushing rebuttal, "Polywater and sweat: Similarities between the infrared spectra."

Polywater was Ellis Lippincott's last hurrah; a short time later he became ill with Hodgkin's disease. In spite of the ridicule prompted by his intensely embarrassing error, Lippincott remained a gentleman. He could have exploited his initial findings to create personal publicity, but he avoided the circus-like atmosphere that has characterized the recent cold fusion fiasco. He could have retaliated against his critics, but he refrained from antagonism or personal attacks. He just quietly slipped away in 1974, a sad and broken man.

✧ ✧ ✧

Although scientists showed little interest in the Van Valkenburg, Weir, and Lippincott diamond cell at first, the inventors knew they had a good idea. In 1960, the three scientists filed for a patent and formed a company to build and market the cells. High Pressure Diamond Optics was founded in 1961 with an initial investment of $125 from each of the three coinventors.

Sales were slow in those first years, and one by one the partners dropped out. Charlie Weir retired in the late 1960s to engage in his favorite hobby, joining the color-blind world of amateur radio operations. Ellis Lippincott died in 1974. Only Alvin Van Valkenburg stayed with the business long enough to see its success.

The diamond-cell business took off in the mid-1970s for a reason few could have foreseen. Diamond cells can generate very high pressures, but that is not their only use. The opposed-anvil arrangement is also ideal for crushing soft samples into a uniform thickness ideal for spectroscopic identification. If you want to determine the origin of a chip of paint, a piece of mud, or perhaps a trace of white powder, the diamond cell is perfect for preparing the sample. The first major buyer of diamond cells from High Pressure Diamond Optics was the Royal Canadian Mounted Police. Today, forensics experts around the world use the device routinely in their investigations.

The company founded by Van Valkenburg, Weir, and Lippincott is now a thriving concern that has sold more than a thousand diamond cells. Their main business remains producing forensic devices for laboratories around the world. But High Pressure Diamond Optics also offers state-of-the-art lever arm cells, modified versions of the original NBS pressure cell that achieve the highest sustained pressures of which man is capable.

In his final years, Alvin Van Valkenburg passed the daily business responsibilities to his son Eric, but he never lost his unbridled enthusiasm for the diamond-anvil cell. He loved to travel to conferences and conventions, where he'd set up a diamond-cell display to show high-pressure phenomena to anyone who wanted to peer down his microscope. He would enthusiastically relate the story of his first glimpse of the high-pressure world and the sweep of his many subsequent discoveries.

And he would say, over and over again, "We had such a wonderful time!"

13

$\diamond$

Transformations

Unwary readers should take warning that ordinary language undergoes modification to a high-pressure form when applied to the interior of the Earth; a few examples of equivalents follow:

High-Pressure Form	Ordinary Meaning
certain	dubious
undoubtedly	perhaps
positive proof	vague suggestion
unanswerable argument	trivial objection
pure iron	uncertain mixture of all the elements

—Francis Birch, "Elasticity and Composition of the Earth's Mantle,"
1952

Most scientists think of high pressure as a fascinating curiosity, but to geophysicists, who devote their lives to probing the earth's deep interior, pressure is the name of the game. Pressure triggers violent earthquakes as the earth's brittle outer layers warp and crack; it creates volcanoes as underground reservoirs of molten rock squeeze to the surface; and it produces diamonds and scores of other exotic minerals—materials that make the inner earth very different from the world we know.

Our planet's dynamic interior is forever in motion. Its white-hot metallic core is overlaid by almost 1,800 miles of soft incandescent rock, slowly flowing like hot taffy in great subterranean currents. On this vast restless ocean floats a thin, brittle crust, relentlessly propelled across the planet's face like scum on the surface of a boiling pot of soup. Thousand-mile slabs of crust collide, break apart, or scrape by one another at the whim of the turbulent rock underneath.

The women and men who study the earth's interior know that there is little hope that anyone will ever actually travel hundreds of miles straight down, where a thousand degrees of temperature and hundreds of tons per square inch of pressure transform ordinary rocks to high-density forms. The deepest mine penetrates less than three miles beneath the earth's surface, and the deepest drill hole reaches less than ten miles down. The technical problems of probing much deeper are insurmountable, at least with present technology. Geophysicists must rely on indirect methods to study their planet.

Most of what we know about the earth's deep interior comes from seismologists, who use the energy of sound to probe the earth. Seismic waves—waves of sound triggered by earthquakes or explosions or even the passing of a heavy vehicle—travel through rock at a little more than five miles per second. The exact speed depends on the density and kind of rock encountered on the journey, so each time geophysicists measure a wave's travel time they learn something about the rocks through which it passed. Through millions of measurements at thousands of listening stations, scientists have gradually built up a sonogram of the earth's inner structure.

Seismologists tell us that the earth is layered like an onion. The deeper you go, the denser the rock. The thin outer crust, our home, is the hard, brittle residue just a few miles thick that overlies the hot, plastic interior. Next is the rocky mantle, composed primarily of minerals composed of the elements silicon, magnesium, and oxygen. At the center of the earth is the core, a ball of white-hot iron (plus unknown amounts of other elements) about 4,000 miles in diameter.

Seismologists are very good at calculating the thickness and properties of these layers. They know, for example, that the mantle is made up of three major layers: an upper mantle with relatively low seismic velocities (about five miles per second), a transition zone in which velocities increase rapidly with depth, and a lower mantle with uniformly high velocities of more than seven miles per second. What scientists don't know is the nature of the stuff that makes up each of the layers. Were the upper mantle, the transition zone, and the lower

mantle formed from the same elements? Do pressure and temperature cause minerals to transform to new denser types in different
layers? If so, what are the properties of those new minerals? Without
experiments on minerals at deep earth conditions, there's no way to
know for sure. That's where mineral physics comes in.

Mineral physicists spend most of their research lives in the laboratory, studying the properties of materials at high temperature and
pressure. They ask what happens when you squeeze on a mineral, or
heat it, or add a little bit of iron. Does the volume change? Do sound
waves travel through it faster? Does heat pass through it easily? Armed
with that knowledge, and the insights of seismology, mineral physicists try to understand the earth's many layers.

Seismology has been around, in one form or another, for as long
as people have worried about earthquakes, but mineral physics is a
post–World War II science; until the 1950s no one could duplicate
the environment of the earth's mantle. The geologists' efforts were
thus inextricably linked with those of the diamond makers, for both
groups were striving to reproduce conditions deep within the earth.
Loring Coes's synthesis of coesite and other high-pressure minerals
pointed the way for many geologists, and General Electric's successful diamond synthesis proved that mantle conditions could be reproduced in the laboratory. But Percy Bridgman's protégé, Francis
Birch, first saw the true implications of high pressure for understanding the earth's deep interior.

Birch fertilized the field of mineral physics with scores of intriguing ideas about the behavior of rocks at high pressure. Perhaps better
than anyone else of his generation, he understood that the dense
minerals within the earth must adopt structures different from those
of their near-surface counterparts. Though he didn't publish much,
his work transformed the way people thought about the earth's interior.

Francis Birch knew that the observed increase of seismic wave
velocities from the crust to the lower mantle pointed to profound
differences between the minerals at the surface and those deep within
the earth. His "Elasticity and composition of the earth's mantle," a
revolutionary sixty-page article published in the June 1952 issue of the
Journal of Geophysical Research, included the bold suggestion that
the speed of sound waves within the earth is closely related to density.

If you know wave speed at a particular depth, he argued, you can estimate the local rock density. Using this theory, Birch predicted the existence of seven distinct rock layers in the earth. He calculated that about a third of the planet's mass is concentrated in the dense metallic core, while almost all of the remaining two-thirds is found in the multilayered mantle.

Forty years ago Francis Birch provided geophysicists with persuasive evidence to support the conventional wisdom that the earth consists of several concentric layers of increasing density, but he did not stop there. He transformed the study of our planet's deep interior by focusing on the nature of deep-earth materials at the atomic level. The dramatic density changes implied that common minerals in the crust are replaced by new forms—dense minerals never before seen. Extrapolating in part from the well-known fact that carbon transforms from graphite to the much denser diamond at high pressure, Birch theorized that rocks would also adopt new, denser forms deep within the mantle. Long before anyone could prove or disprove his conjectures with experiments, Francis Birch suggested that deep mantle rocks are made of dense oxides—primarily forms with magnesium and silicon—in which oxygen atoms adopt an efficient, close-packed arrangement.

Francis Birch established a bridge between seismology and mineralogy, and he showed geophysicists what they must do to understand the earth's inaccessible interior. Discover what minerals form at high pressure, he said, and you will know the earth. It was a message that mineralogists around the world took to heart.

In 1960 Russian mineralogist Sergei Stishov made a most extraordinary discovery. Following Francis Birch's lead, he synthesized a new, dense form of silicon dioxide, the commonest of all oxides. The announcement brought Stishov instant fame and recognition in the high-pressure community, but he paid a harsh price for his glory. Soon after publication of the details of his discovery, his name all but disappeared from Russian scientific periodicals. No one in the West knew what had happened to Sergei Stishov, and for more than twenty years his story remained unknown.

Only in the recent era of *glasnost* was the Soviet scientist able to visit the West and talk freely of his ostracism.

In 1960 Sergei Stishov, then a graduate student in Moscow State University's Department of Geochemistry, engaged in thesis research at the nearby Institute of High-Pressure Physics. With his training in the earth sciences and mineralogy, Stishov was especially interested in learning what happens to common minerals at deep-earth conditions. While most researchers at the institute squeezed metals, carbon, and other elements, Stishov was intrigued by Birch's predictions and elected to look at quartz, a form of silicon dioxide and one of earth's commonest minerals. Quartz is everywhere. It constitutes the sand at the beach, the pebbles in almost every stream, and a considerable fraction of most rocks you're likely to step on.

Loring Coes had already shown that at pressures near 40,000 atmospheres quartz becomes a denser form of silicon dioxide, the mineral others had quickly named coesite. If Birch's conjecture was correct, then coesite should become an even denser form of silicon dioxide at much higher pressure. Stishov planned to squeeze silicon dioxide to more than 100,000 atmospheres to find out. Stishov's mundane experiment did not capture the imagination of high-pressure physicists, and they pretty much left the young student alone.

The routine experiment yielded remarkable results. Stishov used a copy of Tracy Hall's tetrahedral press to subject quartz to 130,000 atmospheres and 1,500°C. At such extreme conditions quartz became a colorless, hard mineral more than 60 percent denser than the sand he had started with. The silicon and oxygen atoms had rearranged themselves into a new atomic structure similar to that of titanium dioxide.

In every silicate mineral in almost every rock on the face of the earth, each silicon atom is surrounded by four oxygens in a regular pattern called a tetrahedron. Stishov's new phase was completely different. Six oxygens surrounded every silicon. This new arrangement allowed for much denser packing of atoms. Birch's radical prediction had been proven correct—high-pressure silicates could indeed adopt dense structures with more efficient oxygen packing.

Shortly after the key experiments had been completed, Sergei Stishov was transferred to a group in the institute headed by Vasiliy Andreevich Galaktionov, a distinguished physicist and winner of the Lenin prize. In an effort to impress his new boss, Stishov told him all about the exciting discovery and its profound geophysical implications. At the time, Stishov remembers, Galaktionov said little. Two weeks later, however, Stishov was informed that his "discovery" had already been made long before by Galaktionov's high-pressure group.

Stishov was in a state of shock. Why hadn't they published their results? he asked. "Because the work was classified," he was told. The next day, institute officials first delayed the start of Stishov's heavily attended seminar on the new material, then unceremoniously canceled the event and sent the audience away. In spite of the project's classified status, Stishov was asked to write up his results for publication and was told that he *might* be included as a coauthor as a "courtesy," even though he had done nothing original.

Stishov could have played along with the lie, doing his part for the Soviet scientific collective, but he chose instead to challenge Galaktionov's claim to priority. He demanded an internal hearing to compare his data with Galaktionov's "secret" results. As the confrontation with the venerable Galaktionov approached, young Stishov felt increasingly isolated. "I went around like a leper. People in the corridor scattered like cockroaches when I appeared."

The hearing was officially witnessed by several institute officers. The format was simple; each scientist could ask questions of the other.

Stishov first: "Vasiliy Andreevich, what is the density of the material you synthesized?"

"The same as yours," Galaktionov replied.

"Yours is four point three five, too?" Stishov asked with undisguised skepticism.

Galaktionov simply repeated the correct value Stishov had just given. It was time to adopt a different tactic.

"Vasiliy Andreevich, what is your refractive index?" Stishov knew that this optical property, one of the first things scientists checked in a new material, differed significantly in the two forms of silicon dioxide.

"The same as yours," Galaktionov responded.

"What exactly?"

Stishov recalls that Galaktionov replied with confidence, trying to bluff his way out of the lie: "Something like one point four or five," he said.

The lie had been uncovered. Stishov's phase had two distinct refractive indexes, both much higher—close to 1.8. Enraged, Stishov accused Galaktionov of lying. "You have done nothing; this is all a trick," he declared. The brief meeting was over; Sergei Stishov was vindicated.

Stishov went to the institute's director, Leonid Vereshchagin, to ask for permission to publish news of the discovery and to request formally that the director accept coauthorship.

Vereshchagin seemed cordial and attentive to Stishov during their June 1961 meeting. He instructed the young scientist to forget the unpleasantness with Galaktionov and publish his data quickly, but what impressed Stishov most was Vereshchagin's odd response to the question of authorship. Even three decades later Stishov vividly recalls the incident. "He began to explain to me how he would eclipse me if he were coauthor, and how noble it was from his point of view to refuse to be listed as a coauthor." In retrospect, Stishov suspects that Vereshchagin was accustomed to making such a speech and then having his name included anyway out of respect. Ambitious and naïve, the unfortunate graduate student took Vereshchagin's words at face value.

Sergei Stishov wrote up his results and, with his adviser and coworker Svetlana Popova as the sole coauthor, submitted his historic paper, "A New Dense Modification of Silica," to *Geochemistry* in July 1961. Reprints of the paper posted at the Institute of High-Pressure Physics evoked little comment, but other copies were rushed to Joe Boyd, Bob Wentorf, and George Kennedy. Word of the discovery spread quickly throughout the American geological and high-pressure communities.

Armed with knowledge of the new phase's properties, Edward Chao and his U.S. Geological Survey collaborators went back to the dense Meteor Crater residues in which they had discovered coesite several years before. It was a simple matter to extract crystals with density of 4.35 and refractive index of 1.8. On December 14, 1961, less than two weeks after Stishov mailed his article to the United States, details of Chao's meteor discoveries were whisked to the *Journal of Geophysical Research*, where they were published a month later. In record time the remarkable new mineral had been found in nature.

Stishov, unaware of Chao's efforts, proposed to name the new compound birchite in honor of Francis Birch. That idea was quickly squelched by Russian officials, who had been stung by the anti-Soviet rhetoric of the John Birch Society. Meanwhile, Ed Chao exercised the prerogative of the natural mineral's discoverer and selected the name stishovite.

By naming a major new mineral after him, the geological community had bestowed an extraordinary honor on Stishov. But his impolitic triumph over Galaktionov and his rapid recognition by the West did not sit well with the rigid Soviet scientific bureaucrats. Russian science was organized around all-powerful institutes, with their all-powerful institute directors. Graduate students were expected to remain subservient and humble; Stishov had overstepped the accepted bounds of professional behavior.

In late 1961 Stishov's work finally received Director Vereshchagin's full attention. Who was this upstart graduate student to challenge a Lenin prize winner? he asked. Who was he to publish under the institute's jurisdiction but not include the director as coauthor? Why wasn't the new mineral named vereshchaginite? And if not that, then why not popovaite, after the more senior author?

An example had to be set, and Sergei Stishov paid the price for his fame. Upon learning that the new mineral was to be called stishovite, an incensed Vereshchagin terminated Stishov's position at the Institute for High-Pressure Physics. His work was cut short, his desk cleaned out, and access to the facilities denied. For many years, the West had no contact with the scientist who had proved that Francis Birch was right.

Squeezing oxides of silicon represented only the first small step toward understanding the minerals that form the earth's mantle. Many other elements—iron, magnesium, calcium, aluminum, and a dozen more—occur in abundance in the earth. Thanks to Stishov, scientists had good reason to believe that these elements formed dozens of novel high-pressure minerals deep within the earth.

The diamond-anvil cell provided geologists with an ideal window for studying the interior of the earth. For the first time, they could observe the effects of the earth's immense pressures and watch minerals transform before their eyes. William A. Bassett, a geophysicist at Cornell University, became one of the first earth scientists to succumb to the allure.

As a young researcher at the University of Rochester, Bassett had begun a high-pressure research program with his fellow junior faculty member Taro Takahashi. Takahashi had equipped his lab with one of Tracy Hall's tetrahedral-anvil presses, but Bassett wanted to do high-pressure x-ray work as well. After hearing Alvin Van Valkenburg give a talk about the diamond-anvil cell at a New York scientific meeting, Bassett knew he had to see for himself. Late that year he and Takahashi drove down to Washington, D.C., for a visit to the National Bureau of Standards, where they saw the new cell at first hand. Charlie Weir and Alvin Van Valkenburg demonstrated the cell, showed them the infrared setup, and gave them plans to construct one of their own.

A few months later, Bassett and Takahashi became the first geologists to build their own version of the NBS cell, one specially designed for x-ray work. Their diamond-cell research focused on the structures of simple materials—silver iodide, which transforms at moderate pressure; and iron metal, the dominant metal of the earth's core. They also discovered how to use a laser to heat their pressurized samples to thousands of degrees, devised new ways to measure spectra through the cell, and pioneered the use of the cell in a variety of x-ray techniques.

By the early 1970s the dynamic Rochester high-pressure laboratory had attracted several bright young graduate students, including Lin-gun ("John") Liu, one of the few scientists since Percy Bridgman to engage in high-pressure research without frequent collaborators. Liu learned the diamond-cell trade at Rochester and then took off for the Australian National University under the sponsorship of A. E. ("Ted") Ringwood.

In the early 1960s, following Francis Birch's lead, Ringwood predicted an earth full of totally new minerals. He described the earth's interior as a place very different from the crust—a place in which every atom competes for a tiny volume. His marvelously speculative paper, "Mineralogical Constitution of the Deep Mantle," appeared in the *Journal of Geophysical Research* in 1962, exactly a decade after Birch's seminal contribution.

The earth's mantle, which accounts for perhaps 80 percent of the planet's volume, is composed mainly of silicon, magnesium, and oxygen, in a ratio of one to one to three. Ringwood guessed that at very high pressure the preferred atomic structure for this combination of elements would be identical to that of the dense synthetic compound strontium lead oxide. This idea intrigued John Liu, who arrived in Australia ready to put Ringwood's ideas to the test. Day after day, in a frenzy of experiments, he loaded a small sample of earth material, squeezed and heated it in his diamond cell, and then x-rayed the powdered products to identify any new high-pressure minerals that formed. Almost every sample produced something new, because almost every mineral transforms at high pressure. John Liu feasted on high-pressure discoveries; for a time in the mid-1970s, he was the only researcher pursuing this work. Each new experiment produced a research paper, typically a two- or three-pager in the journal *Earth and Planetary Science Letters* or, if the news was really big, in *Nature*.

But of all John Liu's findings, the discovery of silicate perovskite is the one that will ensure his fame. In the summer of 1974 he demonstrated that a sample of silicon, magnesium, and oxygen atoms in a ratio of one to one to three adopts a new structure above about 250,000 atmospheres and 1,000°C. Liu identified the unknown substance as possessing the perovskite atomic structure, in which each magnesium is surrounded by nine oxygens, while each silicon is surrounded by six oxygens, just like in stishovite. Liu startled the geophysical world with a concise paper in the October 1974 issue of *Geophysical Research Letters* in which he proposed: "Since the density of perovskite is greater than that of any other phase postulated . . . it is probable that this structure predominates in the lower mantle."

Then, in the only paper he coauthored with Ted Ringwood, Liu reported in 1975 that a mixture of calcium, silicon, and oxygen in an atom ratio of one to one to three also adopts the perovskite form. Subsequent studies on silicates with magnesium and iron—minerals that compose more than 90 percent of the earth's mantle—revealed that they, too, transformed to a silicate perovskite structure at pressures near the 300,000-atmosphere limit of his diamond cell. The December 11, 1975, issue of *Nature* contained Liu's conclusion: "The lower mantle is composed mainly of the perovskite phase, which may represent the last stage of the mineralogical evolution in the Earth's mantle."

His discovery was so simple. John Liu had done little more than crush and heat microscopic specks of silicates in his diamond cell, but from those experiments he made a sweeping, historic conclusion. More than half of the earth's vast bulk consists of silicate perovskite, a dense high-pressure mineral that we will never see at the earth's surface—a mineral whose natural crystals will never grace a collector's cabinet.

By the mid-1970s, thanks in large measure to the research of Bassett and Takahashi and their gifted students, the diamond-anvil cell stood poised to dominate high-pressure research in the geosciences. But many earth scientists had devoted their lives to big-press work, and not everyone was pleased at the diamond cell's ascendancy.

The conflict between diamond-cell and big-press research had come to a head in the mid-1960s, when the issue of a national high-pressure lab arose. George Kennedy, the leading opponent of the diamond cell, had formulated his own master plan for American high-pressure research. Naturally, he was to be the inspiration, founder, and director of his proposed National High-Pressure Laboratory, to be funded by the National Science Foundation. His glorious vision—a single laboratory filled with the best large-press apparatus, available to anyone with a good idea—ultimately failed, a casualty of Kennedy's sledgehammer approach to science.

The grandiose idea failed in part because the diamond-cell people were left out. George Kennedy didn't like the diamond-anvil cell; he thought big, which the diamond cell wasn't. "It isn't going to amount to anything," he would say, simply dismissing a growing community of diamond-cell users. He'd argue strenuously with Alvin Van Valkenburg and Bill Bassett, never really conceding a point in their favor, so there was little enthusiasm in return for Kennedy's idea. In fact, his aggressiveness seemed to polarize the situation: "Why do you need large volumes anyway?" Van Valkenburg responded to Kennedy's scheme.

Kennedy also offended the sizable community of scientists who studied high-pressure phenomena with explosive shock waves. In spite of the extremely high pressures and temperatures generated by shock-wave experimenters, Kennedy scorned their methods and mistrusted their results. As a result, shock-wave scientists from across the country rallied against his proposal as well.

Even some American experts in the large-volume technology that Kennedy promoted so fervently were skeptical of the idea. Harry G. Drickamer, a professor at the University of Illinois and one of the leading chemists doing large-volume high-pressure work, questioned Kennedy's leadership. The scientists' mutual dislike, which had developed while the two were graduate students at Harvard, continued throughout their rival careers. Drickamer, vastly the more conservative of the two, had spent a lifetime using high pressure to perform painstaking studies of chemical reactions. In the process, he had become one of the leading spokesmen for the high-pressure establishment. Drickamer had little patience with Kennedy's controversial style; Kennedy in turn resented the fact that Drickamer, who was often asked to summarize high-pressure advances at meetings and in review articles, virtually ignored developments in earth science research. Whatever the underlying reasons, Drickamer argued that a "national" laboratory under the control of one biased and contentious director was not the best way to spend limited National Science Foundation research dollars.

Kennedy also had to contend with a rival proposal for another national high-pressure facility. Lawrence Livermore Laboratory, a secretive government facility that devotes much of its energy to military research, eagerly sought to secure its own high-pressure center. As the government reviewed the two proposals, each group explained why the other shouldn't get the center—a process that seems to have helped to discredit both.

Kennedy sealed the fate of his center when he pushed for joint development of the center's state-of-the-art apparatus with Soviet scientists. The well-funded Institute for High-Pressure Physics in Moscow had initiated several important studies, and Kennedy saw many advantages in collaboration. At a time of cold war tensions and national rivalries, however, such an idea proved unlikely to win political support.

The final blow to George Kennedy's plans came at the hands of Alvin Van Valkenburg, who joined the National Science Foundation as a program director in 1964. Program directors spend most of their time trying to figure out how to give too few research grant dollars to too many qualified researchers. For every grantee, Van Valkenburg found, there were several "disgruntees" who had to be mollified, cajoled, encouraged, and dismissed with efficiency. Van Valkenburg saw Kennedy's project as a potential disaster that might set back American high-pressure research. He pointed out to Kennedy's vocal supporters at the NSF that most members of the high-pressure community didn't want the center, that the giant Russian-style presses, which were to be the centerpieces of the lab, didn't work very well, and that few people in the high-pressure community got along with George.

By the end of 1965 the National High-Pressure Laboratory was dead. George Kennedy, never one to turn the other cheek, learned of Van Valkenburg's opposition through his Washington contacts, and he remained hostile to Van Valkenburg for the rest of his life.

The year 1965 marked a turning point in American high-pressure research. The diamond-anvil cell—easy to use, cheap to deploy, and capable of the highest sustained pressures—was inexorably replacing large-volume presses. By 1970, with the extraordinary excitement generated by the Apollo lunar samples, many geologists abandoned the costly large-volume high-pressure work altogether. Diamond-cell advocates lobbied for diamond-cell funding, inevitably at the expense of the big presses, and they made a persuasive point to funding agencies. After all, when scientists could achieve hundreds of thousands of atmospheres for $5,000, who would spend twenty times that amount for a quarter the pressure? Richard Kerr, news writer for *Science*, underscored the point in a prominent August 1978 article, in which he wrote that "massive machines [for high-pressure research] have fallen out of favor . . . as the diamond cell has demonstrated its superiority."

"The diamond cell ruined it for us," argues Stony Brook geologist Tibor Gasparik, a champion of large-volume work. "I was a dinosaur. I couldn't get a grant because the diamond cell took all the money." The large-press legacy of Percy Bridgman and Tracy Hall was left to the Japanese, who embraced the tradition and for two decades have led the world in large-press design and use.

....

George Kennedy never lived to see research with large-volume apparatus regain its once-proud status in North America. In mid-1979 he was diagnosed as having mesothelioma, at the time an invariably fatal form of cancer. Outspoken and optimistic to the end, Kennedy treated his disease as just another bold confrontation. In 1979 Joe Boyd received a typical Kennedy letter, rich with enthusiastic details of lab work, orchid growing, and yet another collecting expedition to South America for primitive art. "Let me give you a quick run down on my medical problem," he wrote. "I have a strange cancer known only among asbestos workers which involves about ½″ of cancerous cells on the outside of my left lung and between the lung and the pleural cavity. I am on a heavy dose of chemotherapy. There is a good chance it will contain or stop it from further growth. . . . It sure can kill you fast if you let it get out of control." Kennedy's lifelong pack-a-day cigarette habit had caught up to him. Inexplicably, he had ignored the warning signs of the cancer for a full year.

On September 19 and 20, 1979, Kennedy's UCLA colleagues quickly organized a conference of high-pressure researchers, ostensibly to celebrate the scientist's sixtieth birthday. Everyone there knew the meeting's real purpose was to provide a last chance to say goodbye to a remarkable man. Though he was in poor health, he remained a feisty combatant in the discussions. At the banquet in his honor he displayed his characteristic disregard for convention by unbuttoning his shirt to show fellow scientists the painted marks on his body that guided his radiation therapy.

George Kennedy died on March 18, 1980. It was the end of an era in high-pressure research.

14

❖

Megabar

Pressures [approaching a megabar] have not been reached. In fact . . .
claims of pressures as high as [half a megabar] should leave doubt.
—A. L. Ruoff, "Linear Pressure Scale and One Megabar," 1979

A million—a thousand thousands —is almost inconceivable. You will blink a million times next month; a million grains of fine beach sand easily fit in a glass; a tennis pro could play a million points in a long career; and, if you're very lucky, you might live close to a million hours. You wouldn't want to count a million of anything, but you could if you had to.

To most people, a million is a glamorous figure. You might guess that scientists are more sober-minded, that to them one number is as good as the next. But scientists are human, too, and when a million of anything seems an impossible barrier, there's a scientist who's going to try to break it.

One million times atmospheric pressure—a megabar to high-pressure researchers—was just such a barrier. A megabar does amazing things to everyday matter. At one million atmospheres all the air in a typical living room will squeeze down to a solid chunk the size of a loaf of bread. At a megabar a gallon of water becomes a dense quart of ice. Subject an ordinary rock to that crushing pressure—14 million pounds per square inch—and it will compress to half its normal size. A megabar is the pressure you'd feel underneath a stone monument roughly 2,000 miles tall; it is a pressure beyond imagining.

Reaching and sustaining a megabar, like synthesizing diamond, was a feat more easily claimed than accomplished. More than one scientist announced success before the barrier was unequivocally broken. All of the researchers who aspired to break high-pressure records faced one daunting problem—a problem even more imposing than achieving a million atmospheres. They first had to discover a convincing, reproducible method for measuring that pressure. But how do you measure a sample encased in layer upon layer of steel and carbide?

In 1970 Naoto Kawai, an energetic and ambitious physicist at Japan's Osaka University, became the first researcher to announce achieving a sustained pressure of a megabar. Kawai brought an intense, intuitive approach to his science, solving problems and reaching conclusions without the mathematical rigor employed by many of his colleagues in the Department of Materials Physics. The passion with which he tackled his work reminded some of George Kennedy. Kawai would show off his high-pressure laboratory with great animation and then display the same enthusiasm as he gave visitors a tour of his nearby dog-breeding facility.

Kawai and his laboratory staff used a modification of Baltzar von Platen's split-sphere device that focused pressure from six massive steel anvils onto a second set of eight carbide anvils, which in turn crushed a tiny sample to extreme pressures. Kawai's team placed their split-sphere assembly in a giant press, two stories high. Half the device was sunk below the lab floor; the other half soared up to the lab's high ceiling. The researchers claimed to have gradually increased the pressure this assembly could achieve from 800,000 atmospheres in 1968 to more than a megabar in 1970.

Kawai's multianvil press was a creative effort, but there was no way to see the samples it compressed and absolutely no way to confirm the reported megabar pressure. Still, using the equation that pressure is force divided by area, the Japanese team could make a rough calculation of the maximum pressure possible by dividing the total force they applied to the large external sphere by the surface area of the tiny interior sample. This simple theory breaks down at extreme pressures, however, when metal and carbide components bend, flow, and fracture, absorbing and redistributing force. There was no way for Kawai and his coworkers to be sure of the pressure they achieved, and their reports of a megabar, while impossible to disprove, were disputed. The high-pressure community proved completely unreceptive to the megabar claims, and Kawai's team eventually described their high-pressure experiments without reporting pressures at all.

Kawai's experience underscored the difficulty of the endeavor, but there were any number of practical reasons for a country to support research to break the megabar barrier. Without a doubt, any successful superpressure project would produce new materials. Powerful solid rocket fuels, ultrahard abrasives, blast-resistant metal alloys, and high-temperature superconductors might all be produced by squeezing matter. All high-pressure research scientists knew of these possibilities and they used these speculations without hesitation to tweak more money out of government research coffers. Leonid F. Vereshchagin, director of the Moscow Institute of High-Pressure Physics, was no exception. He used the strategy to build a high-pressure facility like no other in the world. For Vereshchagin, becoming the first to reach a megabar was, quite simply, a matter of pride.

Achieving a megabar became one of Vereshchagin's driving passions, and he used the vast resources of his institute to tackle the problem from two radically different directions. On the one hand he thought large—larger than any high-pressure researcher had ever thought before. Others had constructed five-thousand- and ten-thousand-ton presses two stories tall, but Vereshchagin oversaw construction of a fifty-thousand-ton press requiring a hundred-foot-tall steel frame and its own special five-story building. Kawai and von Platen had designed complex two-stage pressure chambers in which multiple anvils compressed sample assemblies with large volumes; Vereshchagin's team built a vastly more complex five-stage monster with even larger sample volumes—reportedly as much as a full liter.

The Soviet superpress required a small army to operate and maintain it, and each experiment cost a fortune to assemble and run, but the Soviets were confident they could perform experiments no other lab could do. But by all accounts, the monster press was a dismal failure. The multistage device was fiendishly difficult to assemble and align, subject to frequent and expensive breakage, and dangerous to boot. Furthermore, with their sample encased in so many layers of metal and carbide, the scientists were unable to measure the properties of their pressurized samples. Today, the mighty machine has been relegated to measuring the crushing strength of huge concrete blocks.

But the Soviet researchers were by no means defeated. They also thought small in their quest for a megabar—smaller than anyone had thought before. This second megabar project was organized by Evgenii N. Yakovlev, who reasoned that if very high pressures can be obtained from two opposed flat anvils, in the manner of Bridgman and Van Valkenburg, then even higher pressures could be sustained if one of the anvils was slightly conical, thus forming a much smaller area of contact. The result of this logic was the diamond indentor, a miniature device of the utmost simplicity. Yakovlev and his colleagues pushed a sharp diamond point like a phonograph needle onto a flat polycrystalline diamond surface. A minuscule sample, caught at the point of contact, could be squeezed to unprecedented pressures.

In 1972 Vereshchagin, Yakovlev, and their associates claimed to have achieved contact pressures close to five megabars, based on assumptions about their large applied force acting on a tiny assumed area. In the next several years they published numerous reports of experiments in the megabar range, but the world's high-pressure community was not convinced. There was no known way to calibrate pressures at the tip of a pin, much less produce meaningful measurements of material properties at the contact point. The Soviets continued to use the diamond indentor, but within a few years they too stopped trying to guess their pressures.

It is possible that the megabar barrier had indeed been broken by the mid-1970s. Both Kawai's split-sphere device and Vereshchagin's diamond indentor were capable, at least in theory, of such extreme pressures. But without the ability to make internal measurements, their claims could never be confirmed and their experiments would remain historical curiosities. The world would have to wait a little longer for the breakthrough.

✧ ✧ ✧

Of all the scientists who studied matter at high pressure, no group had better reason to seek a megabar than the geophysicists. Most of the earth's inaccessible interior experiences immense pressures of up to 3.5 megabars, and full understanding of the earth's core and lowest mantle regions requires an intimate knowledge of pressures of a million atmospheres and more. Yet in the early 1970s most earth scientists remained content to focus on much lower pressures, corresponding only to the outer few hundred miles of the planet. There was so much to learn about rocks at 300,000 atmospheres, there seemed little urgency to reach for a million.

All that changed in 1968 when Ho-Kwang ("Dave") Mao came to the Geophysical Laboratory to work with Peter M. Bell. It would be hard to imagine two more different scientists. Mao, the son of a Nationalist Chinese general, was born in Shanghai in 1941 but grew up in Taiwan after his family fled the mainland with the defeated Nationalists. His remarkable career in high-pressure research came about by pure chance. All students enrolling in Taiwan's university system listed their choices for school and subject major and then took a difficult six-part entrance examination. The highest scorers received their first selections. Mao placed in the top 5 percent, but by the time his score came up, his top choice—the physics department at Taiwanese National University—was filled. In fact, he had to settle for the university's geology department, his eighth pick. One point higher on the six-hundred-point exam and Mao would have studied food production as an agricultural chemist; one point lower and he would now be a vet.

After graduation in 1963 and a year as a second lieutenant in the Taiwanese air force, Mao came to the United States for graduate studies. He enrolled at the University of Rochester because it had no application fee, and by chance he ended up working with Bill Bassett and Taro Takahashi just as they were establishing their high-pressure diamond-cell program. Upon graduation he was offered a postdoctoral fellowship at the Carnegie Institution of Washington's Geophysical Laboratory.

There may be many high-pressure workers who envy Dave Mao his skill and success, but he has few enemies. He never speaks unkindly of other scientists—even those who have labored to discredit his work. Such a gifted scientist required only one thing to succeed—insulation from everyday pressures of students, grant preparation, committees, and departmental politics—insulation that was provided by the research environment of the Geophysical Laboratory and by his longtime colleague, Peter Bell.

Bell's outgoing, dynamic style contrasted dramatically with Mao's quiet introspection. Bell was born in 1934 in New York City but grew up in exotic ports in Trinidad, the Bahamas, and Venezuela, where his father served as an executive in a shipping company. His education included exclusive New England prep schools and culminated with a doctorate in geophysics from Harvard. Together, Mao and Bell forged one of the most productive high-pressure research teams in history.

It's not always easy to analyze what makes a successful collaboration, but Mao and Bell's contributions resulted, at least in part, from their remarkably complementary scientific backgrounds. Mao, having worked at Rochester, knew the diamond cell as well as anyone and had applied it to fundamental problems in the earth sciences. Bell, who had studied under Francis Birch (and under the influence of Percy Bridgman) at Harvard, was an expert in big presses—the opposed-anvil squeezer and a variety of piston-cylinder designs—and had a broad background in earth and planetary physics. Mao wanted nothing more than a quiet laboratory and the time to perform experiments. Bell reveled in giving talks, securing grants, and welcoming visitors to the lab. Both men were exceptionally bright and creative thinkers; together they worked high-pressure magic.

If Mao and Bell had the desire and ability, the Carnegie Institution of Washington gave them the opportunity. After decades of accumulating steel-company profits, Andrew Carnegie spent the last years of his life giving away his fortune. At the beginning of this century he built hundreds of libraries, endowed museums, established foundations, and funded dozens of philanthropies. Carnegie knew that his millions had been earned in large part by taking advantage of a scientific discovery—the process that turns ordinary iron into steel. Some of his vast wealth, he reasoned, should be put back into scientific research. So on January 28, 1902, the Carnegie Institution of Washington was established "to encourage, in the broadest and most liberal manner, investigation, research, and discovery, and the application of knowledge to the improvement of mankind." To accomplish this objective, Carnegie poured $22 million into the institution for the creation of several laboratories and observatories.

Carnegie's endowment supported earth science research almost from the first day. The Geophysical Laboratory, situated on a hilltop in northwest Washington, D.C., opened for business in 1907, one of the first research centers to be organized by the institution. Almost from the start, pressure research had been a priority; Dave Mao and Peter Bell were merely continuing a tradition of three scientific generations when they began their twenty-year high-pressure collaboration.

At the time Mao joined the institution in the late 1960s, the diamond-anvil cell created by Van Valkenburg and his colleagues at the National Bureau of Standards had remained almost unchanged for more than a decade. There were so many fascinating experiments to be tried in its routine 300,000-atmosphere operating range that a thousand scientists could have spent their entire lives without running out of work. But there was an even more basic reason for sticking to the original design: at such high pressures, the samples were already almost too small to measure. Higher pressures would mean even smaller samples, beyond the capabilities of then current instruments.

But experimental possibilities and priorities inevitably change over time. The early 1970s saw the widespread introduction of powerful new light sources. Portable, affordable lasers and high-intensity x-ray sources provided scientists with new tools to probe microscopic samples. In 1974, with several years of experience under their belts, Mao and Bell decided to extend the diamond cell's pressure range.

Mao was sure he could obtain higher pressures with larger samples. In the NBS design, pressure was limited by the relatively soft steel backing the diamonds. Above a few hundred thousand atmospheres the diamonds sank into the deformed steel support, and no further pressure increase was possible. Mao reasoned that a harder backing material such as tungsten carbide would greatly increase the pressure range, but he also knew that direct diamond-to-diamond contact at those pressures would almost certainly cause diamond breakage. Van Valkenburg's metal gasketing technique provided an elegant solution to the dilemma. As diamond anvils deform a gasket, the metal automatically behaves like a binding ring, providing additional support to the stressed diamond tip. It is no coincidence that the gasketed diamond-anvil cell looks a lot like a miniature version of Tracy Hall's belt apparatus.

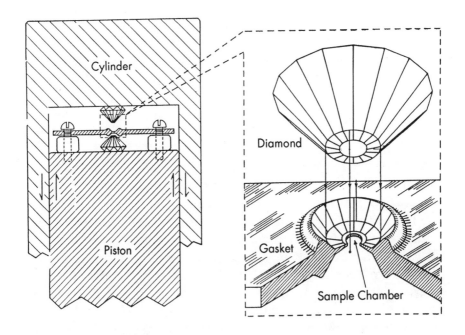

Pressures exceeding a megabar were achieved by Dave Mao and Peter Bell, who used a diamond-anvil cell with a precisely aligned metal gasket and beveled diamond anvils. (Courtesy of H.-K. Mao.)

Perfect alignment of the diamonds was another critical factor in reaching a pressure record. The two diamond-anvil faces had to be exactly parallel or the gasket would deform unevenly and catastrophically, squirting the sample out sideways. The two anvils also had to approach each other along the exact same central axis to maintain stability as pressure increased. To accomplish that difficult mechanical feat, Mao and Bell devised a piston-cylinder device to hold the diamonds—a clever configuration that ensured proper diamond support and alignment.

To perfect their diamond cell Mao and Bell engaged in a long process of trial and error, breaking diamond after diamond. Dave Mao remembers the all-too-familiar sickening snap, the muted but distinct sound of yet another diamond destroyed by pressure. Eventually they hit upon a felicitous combination of components that permitted much larger samples and much higher pressures. With this improved design, the megabar goal seemed within their reach. Their new device would not only sustain a million atmospheres of pressure; it would also let them look at the pressurized sample and measure its properties with laser light or x-rays.

For their first experiments they decided to crush ruby, whose characteristic brilliant red fluorescence (when excited by a blue laser beam) would serve as their megabar marker. Mao and Bell knew that based on the calibration work done at the National Bureau of Standards to about 300,000 atmospheres, a wavelength shift of 37 units in ruby fluorescence corresponded to an increase of 100,000 atmospheres in pressure. Therefore, they needed to observe a total ruby shift of about 370 units to stake the megabar claim.

The critical experiment took place just before Christmas 1975, during the Geophysical Laboratory's annual holiday vacation. The lab was quiet. The newly modified diamond cell held its compressed cargo of crushed ruby, ready to fluoresce and reveal the changing pressure. The first turns of the screw were routine: a 30-unit shift meant 83,000 atmospheres; then 45 more units to 206,000 atmospheres. It took only about twenty minutes to make and measure each pressure step. Two more increments and the cell soared to almost half a megabar. Bell and Mao knew the diamonds could break at any time, but they were determined to push the cell to its limits.

The next turn took them to 619,000 atmospheres. Now each increment brought the nervous scientists a new world's record pressure, though there was no way of predicting how much the pressure might rise. With another twist the pressure shot up to nearly 800,000 atmospheres, with a 290-unit shift in the ruby fluorescence line, but the next turn brought only a slight rise, to 820,000 atmospheres. Mao feared that diamond failure was near, that the cell could take no more and had begun to bend. It was literally a megabar or bust, and with another two twists they did it. The ruby line had shifted a record 370 units. They'd achieved—and documented—a pressure of 1,018,000 atmospheres.

On December 29, 1975, the two elated researchers submitted a terse eight-hundred-word report to *Science*. Short and to the point, the paper staked its claim to the one-megabar mark. They described "the highest pressure ever reported for a static experiment in which an internal standard was employed." Their historic article appeared just two months later, in the February 27, 1976, issue.

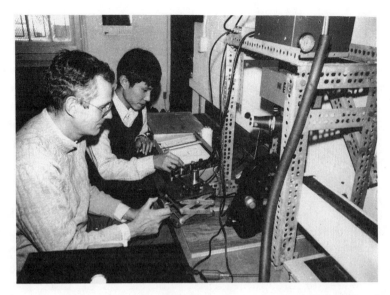

Peter Bell (left) and Dave Mao adjust a diamond-anvil cell capable of more than 1 million atmospheres pressure. (Courtesy of the Geophysical Laboratory.)

The story might have ended there, with Mao and Bell's triumph, but almost as soon as it was staked, the megabar claim was challenged.

Arthur L. Ruoff directs the productive high-pressure research program at Cornell's Department of Materials Science and Engineering. He is a burly man with a big laugh and a big temper. By all accounts he loves his science, but he is also a pragmatic man fascinated by the stock market. His Cornell office is filled with an odd mixture of research monographs and books on investing.

In the mid-1970s his principal objective was clear: he wanted more than anything else to be the first person to reach a megabar. He even went so far as to affix a bold gold-on-black sign, THINK MEGA-BARS, on the wall of his Cornell high-pressure laboratory. At a time when pressures of 300,000 atmospheres were becoming routine, the Cornell team made a major commitment to surpass the 1-million-atmosphere mark.

The skillful and creative Cornell researchers pursued two radically different approaches to the megabar problem. They first thought very small, using a modified version of the Vereshchagin diamond indentor. Ruoff knew that he could generate large pressures by pushing very hard on a pinlike point, so his group built a diamond-tipped anvil and jammed it against a flat diamond surface.

The diamond indentor was appealing for its simplicity and low cost. The large, flat diamond surface, though pitted by each experiment, could be used over and over again by moving the sample to undamaged areas, while the tiny diamond tip, only one five-hundredth to one one-thousandth of a carat, was cheap and easy to replace if it failed. With such a tiny tip, the Cornell scientists needed only a moderate force, up to a few hundred pounds, instead of the thousands of tons required in large-press research.

But trade-offs are a constant frustration in high-pressure work. Ruoff's team ran into the same problem that stymied the Soviet workers: the advantages gained by the diamond indentor's small scale were in many ways offset by its minute sample volume. The tiny amount of crushed sample was much too small to x-ray, it could not be viewed microscopically, and there was no way to measure the sample pressure directly. The Cornell researchers were able to make some measurements of electrical properties, and they guessed at pressures based on assumptions about the size of the diamond tip and the applied force, but many felt that the experiments lacked the rigor of internally calibrated diamond-cell studies.

The second Cornell megabar strategy fared no better. Ruoff's plan was to build a very large split-sphere device similar to those designed by von Platen and Kawai. His calculations indicated that with appropriate scaling of components a maximum pressure of 8 million atmospheres—eight megabars—might be generated in a split-sphere press. But rather than adopt the complicated two-stage arrangement used by Kawai, the Cornell team relied on a single stage with six sharply tapered anvils that defined a cube-shaped sample chamber just one-sixteenth of an inch on a side. Preliminary runs in 1974 and 1975 failed to produce the hoped-for record, due to defor-

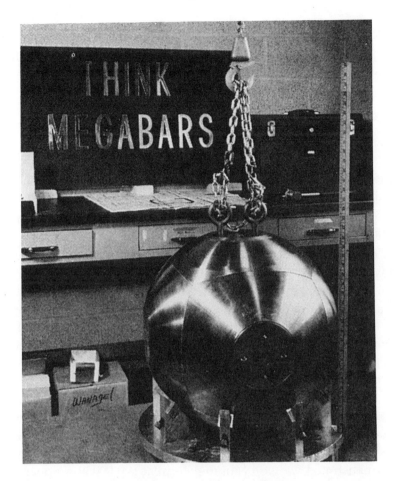

The Cornell University split-sphere device was designed by Arthur Ruoff and his colleagues and used in their attempts to break the megabar barrier. The metal sphere is approximately two feet in diameter. (Courtesy of Arthur Ruoff.)

mation and failure of the tungsten carbide anvils. But improvements were proposed to alleviate this problem, and the researchers were optimistic that a megabar was within reach.

In late 1975, when the Geophysical Laboratory broke the megabar barrier, both Cornell devices were still being tested, and both seemed poised to push past the megabar mark. If the Cornell University team was to take the megabar honors, only one path remained.

First, discredit Mao and Bell's announcement by casting doubt on the Geophysical Laboratory methods; then announce Cornell's own success. It was a desperate but common strategy in the research game, and Ruoff was a master player.

The perfect forum for Ruoff's assault took place in the summer of 1977, when scientists from around the world traveled to Boulder, Colorado, for the sixth biannual meeting of the International Association for Research and Advancement of High Pressure and Technology—at the time, the largest high-pressure conference ever organized. As the scientists sat atop a brown sandstone promontory overlooking Boulder, eating a barbecue feast of chicken and ribs, they first heard the startling news: Mao and Bell had grievously erred. The crushing announcement came complete with equations and graphs and talk of diamond strengths and defects. According to Ruoff, no diamond-anvil cell could ever even approach a megabar.

Ruoff boldly attacked Mao and Bell's claim, arguing that the ruby pressure scale on which the megabar calibration was based was fatally flawed. To prove his point, the scientist cited well-known values of diamond's hardness and elastic behavior along with theoretical equations relating to material strength and failure. Any natural diamond, he demonstrated, would begin to deform at 500,000 atmospheres because of the gem's inevitable crystal defects. At a pressure of 700,000 atmospheres megabars or so, he continued, all natural diamonds would fracture or distort, thereby becoming useless as high-pressure anvils.

These calculations seemed to prove beyond a doubt that the Geophysical Laboratory scientists could not possibly have exceeded 500,000 atmospheres. According to Ruoff, even the most perfectly designed diamond-anvil cell would shatter at well below the 1-million-atmosphere mark. The very fact that the Mao and Bell diamonds *didn't* fail provided ample proof that the ruby calibration grossly overestimated pressure.

The logic behind his double-edged reasoning could not be lightly dismissed. No one had ever measured fluorescence of ruby (much less any other property of any material) at a megabar, so there was no certain way to verify Mao and Bell's results. One could only describe the low-pressure behavior of the ruby fluorescence shift as precisely as possible and then extrapolate it to high pressures. Like the tower built by an acrobat who balances and then climbs chair after chair, the whole structure becomes more precarious the higher you go. The ruby-pressure scale appeared ready to tumble down around Mao and Bell.

Ruoff's presentation was phrased with the formalisms of science, but his unspoken meaning seemed clear to the earth scientists. Theoretical physics is a lot more convincing than the experiments of a couple of geologists, he seemed to imply. Deep down, many must have felt that he was right; the sturdy empiricism of earth scientists is no match for the sophisticated computations of theorists. For my own part, as a recently added member of Mao and Bell's research team, it was my first bitter taste of physicist envy.

In the coming months and years a number of advocates of the diamond cell suffered Ruoff's calculated scorn. Alvin Van Valkenburg was invited to Cornell to give a lecture about the diamond cell and its extraordinary pressure range, and he was treated to a humiliating public harangue—a scientific mugging that Van Valkenburg remembered with uncharacteristic bitterness to the end of his life. "I couldn't argue with Ruoff because he could snow me with equations," he recalled.

For a time the bold attack proved a good strategy for the Cornell researchers: when exposed to such a clearly delineated conflict, most spectator scientists will not immediately take sides. Better to let everyone have his say and wait for the dust to settle, then see where things stand. For more than a year Ruoff lectured at conferences and departmental seminars around the world, patiently explaining flaws in the ruby calibration system and showing why the diamond-anvil cell couldn't have done the megabar trick. Ruoff also published pointed rebuttals of Mao and Bell's claim in a series of articles whose objective seemed to be the step-by-step destruction of both the ruby pressure scale and Mao and Bell's megabar claim.

All the while, Ruoff was pushing his own lab team to the limit, until finally, in the fall of 1977, they succeeded. A short article published in the December 9, 1977, issue of *Science*, "High Pressures on

Small Areas," described a series of diamond-indentor experiments that appeared to soar above the megabar mark. However, there was no pressure standard, which made it impossible to determine experimental pressure with any precision. Pressures were crudely calculated by assuming a figure for the area of contact between diamond tip and diamond flat. Using this method, five experiments appeared to have approached or exceeded 1 million atmospheres.

It seemed ironic to some that Ruoff, who had gone to such lengths to discredit the use of diamond anvils in megabar research, should so soon thereafter claim a megabar from his own diamond device. But Ruoff pointed out that diamond anvils fail because of defects that are inevitable in any *large* diamond crystal. With a small enough diamond tip, he reasoned, weakening defects may be avoided and much higher pressures attained. Not the slightest mention of Mao and Bell's megabar paper of twenty-two months earlier was made.

For a few years Arthur Ruoff succeeded in muddying the waters of megabar research. He had effectively cast doubt on the 1976 Carnegie announcement and within two years had made his own megabar claim in a prestigious scientific journal. If asked in early 1978 who was ahead in the megabar race, most high-pressure researchers would have probably called it a toss-up between Cornell and the Geophysical Laboratory.

Undeterred, Mao and Bell continued their intense research at a megabar and beyond. Driven by the need to answer Ruoff's objections, they tested and retested the ruby scale. Although no one had ever measured material properties at a *sustained* pressure of a megabar, scientists had made many measurements in that range with explosive shock waves, which create large pressures for a millionth of a second. Physicists John Shaner and Daniel Steinberg of the Lawrence Livermore Laboratory's Shock Wave Physics Group, for example, had used shock waves to measure the compressed volumes of metals like copper and silver at pressures up to a megabar. In fact, in the late 1970s, measuring metal volumes at pressure appeared to be the only way to confirm megabar claims.

Mao and Bell took advantage of those shock-wave measurements by mixing copper, silver, and other metals with ruby powder. At high pressure they x-rayed the metals to determine their atomic spacings.

From that figure they could calculate metal volumes and thus estimate pressure. Then they measured the wavelength shift of the ruby line to calibrate the fluorescence method. This essential process proved tedious and exacting, but it seemed to show beyond any reasonable doubt that with only minor correction the ruby scale could be extrapolated to a megabar. Mao and Bell carefully wrote up their results, added Shaner and Steinberg's discussions to beef up the section on shock-wave theory, and sent off a manuscript to the prestigious *Journal of Applied Physics*.

Still, the battle wasn't over. Following standard policy, the journal's editor, Lester Guttman, selected two anonymous reviewers for the twenty-five-page manuscript. The first reviewer supported it enthusiastically. But the second reviewer, obviously George Kennedy by his characteristic handwritten marginal scrawl and well-known prejudices, had wholeheartedly joined the Ruoff camp. An unabashed large-press supporter, he had never forgotten the role that diamond cells and shock-wave researchers had played in derailing his National High-Pressure Laboratory. He made point after point against publication, noting discrepancies between "reliable" large-press studies and the diamond-cell results. He criticized assumptions underlying shock-wave measurements of metals and reiterated Ruoff's arguments that natural diamonds would inevitably fail well below a megabar. "I am as of now, and have continued to be, exceedingly skeptical of pressures of one megabar," he wrote.

Kennedy's objections succeeded in delaying publication of the extended ruby scale for months, but a revised version finally appeared in the June 1978 issue of the *Journal of Applied Physics*. Then, following this breakthrough, Mao and Bell continued to shatter their own records. They reached 1.2 megabars early in 1976, then 1.5 megabars. Arthur Ruoff had claimed a possible high pressure of 1.6 megabars for his indentor, but Mao and Bell topped even that with the publication of "High-pressure physics: sustained static generation of 1.36 to 1.72 megabars" in the June 9, 1978, issue of *Science*. At that higher pressure, Mao and Bell observed the plastic deformation of diamond —a dimpling of the diamond anvil face that Ruoff had predicted at much lower pressures. "Diamonds Flow Like Butter" a *New York Times* article proclaimed, in an exaggeration of the subtle high-pressure effect. This time there was no rebuttal from Cornell.

The conflict had been resolved. Within a matter of months most high-pressure workers were convinced of the validity of the Geophysical Laboratory's original megabar claim. Dave Mao attended a high-pressure conference that summer. "Pete and I were all prepared for lots of arguments, but when we talked about a megabar everybody just sat there. Nobody made an objection at all." The consensus was that the values Art Ruoff had used for diamond strength, or perhaps the way he applied his equations to large diamond crystals, were invalid.

Few other groups ever adopted the Cornell diamond indentor, and Ruoff's early claims of large pressures have never been verified. The Cornell scientists, who worked so hard to discredit Mao and Bell's diamond-anvil cell and the validity of the ruby-pressure scale, eventually purchased their own lever-arm diamond cell from Alvin Van Valkenburg and built their own ruby calibration system.

Science, like any other human endeavor, does not always advance smoothly from discovery to discovery. Conflicts and rivalries inevitably arise, and false paths deflect researchers from their goals. But science is underpinned by the truth, which eventually will out.

15

....

✧

Journey to the
Center of the Earth

The achievement of sustained pressures of about 1.5 million atmospheres . . . has shown that the study of rocks under conditions prevailing at the boundary between the earth's mantle and core is practical.
                                    —Richard A. Kerr, *Science*, August 4, 1978

In this age of technological miracles it might seem that nothing is beyond our grasp, no feat beyond our ambition. But scientists believe that there are limits to what we can achieve. Unless our understanding of the physical universe is very wrong indeed, there are some feats we can never perform, some places we can never go.

Science fiction notwithstanding, there is no known way to travel faster than the speed of light or backward in time. No known physical laws permit teleportation of matter, nor do we know of any way to neutralize the force of gravity. Based on our understanding of matter and energy, we can imagine no way that a spaceship could survive a visit to the nuclear fires of the sun's surface. And, to the scientists who study our planet, it is absolutely inconceivable that anyone will ever travel to the center of the earth.

Geophysics can be a strange and frustrating endeavor. Most scientific research deals with matter we can see and experiments we can perform. We can measure the boiling temperature of water, the speed of light, or the distance to the nearest star. But we will never be able to determine the precise temperature at the earth's core or the exact ratio of the elements that exist there. Instead of conducting an impossible search for the correct answers to such questions, geophysicists spend most of their lives eliminating incorrect answers, thus narrowing the range of possible truth.

Any information we gather about the earth's inaccessible interior must come from indirect observations. Therefore, describing the earth's deep interior is a game with only a few rules; you can propose almost any model for the earth that you want as long as you play by them. First of all, your model has to account for the present state of the earth, including its total mass, rotational characteristics, gravitational and magnetic features at the surface, and the inner layering as deduced by seismology. Your model has to conform more or less to standard ideas about the chemical composition of the earth, based on studies of meteorites, the moon, and other planets; it can't contain lots of some unknown element X; and it should include rocks and minerals that we know, or at least suspect, might occur at high pressure and temperature.

To play the game well, you also have to explain the extraordinary dynamics of our planet, in which soft, hot mantle rocks slowly convect and, in the process, shuttle thin plates of brittle rock across the surface. You need to explain why volcanoes and earthquakes occur with regularity in some places and not at all in others, and you should be able to explain the chemistry of volcanic rocks, the formation of the moon, and other distinctive traits. Bonus points are awarded for originality.

The most widely accepted models of the earth assume a 2,000-mile-diameter solid inner core, composed mostly of iron and nickel, surrounded by a 1,100-mile-thick outer core of iron-rich liquid metal. Geophysicists calculate that the core accounts for slightly less than a third of the earth's mass. The majority of the planet's mass and volume remains locked in the mantle's three major zones—the olivine-rich upper mantle, the spinel-rich transition zone, and the dense lower mantle. Mantle rocks, consisting primarily of the elements silicon, magnesium, and oxygen, plus some iron and calcium, provide a dramatic contrast to the core's metallic composition. Like a pot of water rolling and boiling in slow motion, the convection of the mantle rocks drives the process we call plate tectonics, by which the thin, brittle plates of rock that form the earth's outer solid layer are shunted about by the mantle's stately cycles. The earth's great oceans and mountain ranges, along with its most destructive earthquakes and volcanoes, are merely side effects of this activity.

Geophysicists have known about the multilayered structure of the earth for most of this century, but they still fiercely debate the nature of the boundaries between the great layers. Standard textbook illustrations of the planet's cross section show sharp, concentric zones like an idealized onion, but these stylized drawings are not the whole truth. Are the boundaries smooth and plain-like or rough and mountainous? Do the layers sharply separate different kinds of materials like the interface between ocean and atmosphere, or is there a fuzzy zone of mixing like the water-saturated sediment at the bottom of a lake? Does matter pass freely back and forth across the different boundaries? Have the thicknesses of some layers changed over time, and are they still changing?

Although we may never know exactly what lies inside the earth,

The layered earth. (Courtesy of *The Washington Post*.)

Journey to the Middle of the Earth

Below the cold, thin crust that encloses the earth lie layers of geologic mystery. As geologists envision it, a cross section of earth would look something like the diagram.

1 **Crust**—Consists of hardened, lightweight rock. Thickness varies from 6 miles to 30 miles.
2 **Lithosphere**—Solid (but ductile or deformable) rock in which crust is embedded. Thickness varies from almost none (where asthenosphere pushes through) to about 45 miles.
3 **Asthenosphere**—A mixture of solid and molten rock that pushes through the lithosphere to spew molten rock along mid-ocean ridges (causes sea-floor spreading). Extends down about 125 miles.
4 **Upper Mantle**—Consists mostly of a solid mineral called olivine. Lies between 125 miles and 250 miles.
Boundary Layer—A solid layer where greater pressure causes olivine crystals to be squeezed into a more compact crystal called spinel. 250 to 280 miles.
5 **Transition Zone**—Solid layer dominated by spinel crystal form. 280 miles to 420 miles.
Boundary Layer—Still greater pressure becomes enough at this depth to wrench spinel crystals into perovskite. 420 miles to 435 miles.

6 **Lower Mantle**—Consists mainly of solid perovskite mineral. 435 miles to 1,800 miles.
7 **Outer Core**—Liquid iron and nickel. 1,800 miles to 2,930 miles.
8 **Inner Core**—Solid iron and nickel. 2,930 miles to 3,925 miles, the center of the earth.

BY JOHNSTONE QUINAN—THE WASHINGTON POST

we can narrow the range of possibilities by doing experiments and collecting data. Geophysicists, constantly seeking new ways to probe the earth and to mimic its high temperatures and pressures in the laboratory, jumped at the chance to use the diamond-anvil cell. Finally, they had an instrument that allowed them to study suspected mantle minerals at unprecedented pressures and extraordinary temperatures. For the first time scientists could reproduce most of the earth's deep environment in their laboratories.

Bill Bassett and Taro Takahashi at the University of Rochester got the diamond-anvil movement rolling, while their students, John Liu in Australia and Dave Mao at the Geophysical Laboratory, helped spread the gospel. Soon workers in France and Japan followed suit, making important discoveries about the nature of the inner earth. But of all the geophysicists who adopted the diamond-anvil cell, no one has tackled the problem of the deep earth and its makeup with more brilliant gamesmanship than Raymond Jeanloz.

Jeanloz is often described as "creative" and "controversial," but those adjectives are too bland and simple. Of the many different ways to excel at experimental research, the most tried and true is to develop a new experimental method when you are young and then spend most of your career applying it to lots of obvious problems. Scientists like Percy Bridgman, Loring Coes, and Alvin Van Valkenburg, who were among the best at exploiting their own technical innovations, are justly revered in the scientific community. But Raymond Jeanloz doesn't play the game that way. Rather than rely on a single technique, he seizes whatever experimental or theoretical approach might help him answer key scientific questions. He doesn't hesitate to ask epic questions that few have dared ask before. Then, sometimes on the basis of a single tenuous experiment, he offers his best guess at the right answer.

If everyone did science the way Jeanloz does it, the result would be chaos. There would be so many new theories flying around that we'd never sort them all out. But if nobody did science like Jeanloz, it would be a deadly dull world indeed.

Raymond Jeanloz's individualistic approach to science is in some ways a reflection of his life. He speaks of his work with casual assurance. "We've been accused of speculating too much," he once told *Science* reporter Richard Kerr. "It's a matter of style. Some groups will put out the numbers and that's it. We try to wave our hands a bit about how they apply to the Earth." At a recent scientific session of the American Geophysical Union, Jeanloz sat in the third row, even though he was chairing the series of lectures. When asked why he was positioned away from the traditional spot up front, he smiled and replied enigmatically: "Harassing people. That's what I'm paid for."

He dresses comfortably in jeans and an open-neck shirt. His gold wire-rimmed glasses, full beard, and ponytail bespeak a man who came of age in the early 1970s. He is good-natured, easygoing, and quick to smile or nod his head in agreement. But his eyes reveal the intensity of purpose that drives him to spend seven days a week in a laboratory seeking the hidden workings of our planet.

Jeanloz began his undergraduate education at Deep Springs College, a unique educational institution in central California where two dozen students spend two or three years in monastic seclusion. An accomplished violinist, he thought of a career in music, but he also excelled in literature, mathematics, and science. A half year of hitch-hiking around the country provided time to sort things out, and he realized that science was his calling.

In 1975 Jeanloz enrolled as a Ph.D. candidate at the California Institute of Technology, where he became a student of Thomas Ahrens, a leading geophysicist in shock-wave research. Ahrens built giant gas-powered shock-wave guns in the basement of his laboratory building and used them to subject rock and mineral samples to multi-megabar pressures for brief instants.

Jeanloz used the shock-wave technique to discover a phase transition in simple calcium oxide, which normally has the same atomic structure as table salt. In normal calcium oxide, every calcium and oxygen atom is surrounded by six neighbors of the other element, but shock-wave data suggested that at high pressure calcium oxide adopts a much denser structure. Jeanloz decided he needed a different experimental apparatus—the diamond-anvil cell—to study the new phase. Though he had never used one before, he felt committed to solving the problem and would do whatever it took to get the answer. He wrote to Peter Bell at the Geophysical Laboratory and proposed a two-week diamond-cell study of calcium oxide at megabar pressures.

It was an audacious request. At the time, Mao and Bell had obtained megabar pressures in only a few runs, and each run had cost months of time, not to mention several broken diamonds. Even with everything working well, it could take as long as two weeks just to produce a single high-pressure x-ray pattern. Nevertheless, Jeanloz came to the Geophysical Lab in 1978 for a brief preliminary attempt. Under Dave Mao's expert supervision, he loaded the calcium oxide into the diamond cell, and together they raised the pressure. At about 0.6 megabars Mao noticed a subtle change in the appearance of the sample—a possible sign of transition—and he suggested that they x-ray the powdered sample at that point. After a week's exposure the freshly developed x-ray film confirmed Mao's suspicion. The pattern showed one set of lines characteristic of calcium oxide's room-pressure salt structure, but there were several new lines that suggested a different form. The calcium oxide had partially transformed into a dense structure in which each atom had eight atomic neighbors instead of the usual six. From that point on, Jeanloz was sold on the diamond-anvil cell.

Ph.D. in hand, Jeanloz accepted a junior faculty appointment at Harvard University in the summer of 1979. He put considerable effort into establishing a diamond-cell program and then developing reliable techniques for measuring pressure and temperature in his laser-heated device. Two and a half years later, in January 1982, he was lured back to California to a tenured professorship at Berkeley. For a decade Jeanloz and a succession of outstanding students have tackled big questions about the earth—research that has earned Jeanloz several prestigious honors, including a MacArthur Foundation award. Jeanloz quickly credits his students for any success, and his students invariably return the compliment.

Jeanloz's research addresses the biggest questions in geophysics. In a recent highly publicized diamond-cell experiment, Jeanloz collaborated with his Ph.D. student Elise Knittle on her thesis project to study the nature of the earth's core-mantle boundary, a zone about two thousand miles down where iron-rich liquid is believed to contact silica-rich rock at more than

3,000°C and pressures greater than a megabar. To duplicate that region, Knittle and Jeanloz simply loaded their diamond cell with a tiny piece of iron foil surrounded by powdered magnesium silicate perovskite, a mineral suspected by most earth scientists to be the dominant lower mantle phase. They raised the pressure to almost a megabar and zapped the mixed sample with a laser beam powerful enough to melt the iron. The result was a distinct reaction zone between the perovskite and liquid metal—a zone that contained iron oxide and an unusual iron-silicon compound.

Some scientists would have written up these data with a conservative title like "Possible reactions of (Mg, Fe) SiO_3 perovskite and liquid-Fe at high pressure and temperature" and sent it off to a specialty journal. But in the hands of Jeanloz and Knittle the results were transformed into a lead article with the sweeping title "Earth's core-mantle boundary" in the March 22, 1991, issue of *Science*. On the basis of a single simple series of experiments, they predicted a core-mantle boundary with astonishing topography—mountains of iron-rich minerals perhaps a hundred miles tall floating on the liquid core. They noted that such irregularities could explain several of the earth's most curious features: the location of hot plumes of rock like the one beneath the Hawaiian islands, a number of seismic anomalies that suggest a blurred core-mantle boundary in some places but a sharp one in others, and the puzzling surface variations in the earth's magnetic field.

The flamboyant *Science* article attracted the attention of the national press as well as earth scientists around the world. *The New York Times* featured the work in a front-page story illustrated with a startling cross section of the earth showing exaggerated core-mantle mountains and twisted magnetic field lines. It was fascinating stuff, but many geophysicists questioned the experiments and their interpretation. The pressure was too low, the temperature too uneven, the time too short to draw such grandiose conclusions, they argued. Jeanloz and Knittle had measured a pressurized sample no larger than a flyspeck and yet had boldly extrapolated the results to answer problems on a global scale. But whatever scientists thought about the experimental details, the research had a profound influence on the conventional view of the earth and forever altered the way many scientists pictured our planet.

In 1989 Jeanloz and his graduate student Charles Meade devised another simple diamond-cell experiment to duplicate deep-focus earthquakes, among the most destructive and least understood natural phenomena. Rocks behave a lot like taffy: at cool temperatures both are brittle—bend a piece of cold rock or taffy too much and it will break with a snap. But heat them up and they will soften and bend. It's this latter phenomenon that allows mantle rock to flow and convect. Earthquakes result when stressed rock snaps, so they should logically occur in cooler brittle rocks within a few miles of the surface. But scientists, who can pinpoint the exact depth and location of any earth tremor, find that some regions experience strong earthquakes located as much as four hundred miles below the earth's surface, well below the region that would support any conventional mechanism for rock breaking. For years scientists have wondered how these violent, often destructive deep earthquakes could occur.

In 1989 Raymond Jeanloz and Charles Meade set out to mimic deep earthquakes by subjecting various minerals to mantle pressures and temperatures. They attached a sensitive microphone to their diamond-anvil cell to listen for telltale sounds, and they squeezed their tiny samples. Nothing unusual happened when they compressed dry minerals; they did not hear the pop associated with a sudden energy release like that of an earthquake.

But Jeanloz and Meade weren't through. They next tried squeezing and heating serpentine, a mineral that has molecules of water locked into its crystal structure. As they pressurized their sample to 250,000 atmospheres, they were gratified to hear a series of audible pops—miniature earthquakes in their diamond-anvil cell. Again and again they observed the effect, and they soon realized that the sound occurred as water was expelled from the serpentine sample, thus demonstrating that serpentine could be the culprit in deep-focus earthquakes.

Jeanloz and Meade's report on deep-focus earthquakes rated a prominent position in the April 5, 1991, issue of *Science*. The two geophysicists proposed to startled colleagues that the ocean might continuously feed water into the mantle.

It was an extraordinary idea. At first glance the earth's oceans seem forever isolated from the earth's deep interior, but ocean water does react with rocks, and some of those rocks are carried down into the mantle by the dynamic processes of plate tectonics. By the same token, volcanoes spew forth vast quantities of water vapor and other gases, thus replenishing the surface supply. In the 4.5-billion-year history of the earth, all the water in all the earth's oceans could have recycled four times over, and several oceans of water could be locked in the present mantle.

The waters of the earth's oceans may actually be part of an immense, dynamic system that extends deep into the mantle. It is an astonishing proposition, made all the more remarkable by the tiny shred of evidence on which it's based—the behavior of a tiny sample squeezed between two gem diamonds.

16

···

✧

Squeezing Hydrogen

There have been many claims in the past of the successful metallization of hydrogen, one of the key problems in physics, but none so far pass the absolute requirement of . . . reproducibility.

—Neil W. Ascroft, *Science*, August 3, 1989

Before there was a sun to fire the heavens, before there was a planet to transform its radiance into life, even before the first galaxy danced through the heavens, there was hydrogen. The simplest of all atoms, hydrogen carries but one proton and one electron, yet from this simplicity arose all the complexity of creation—stars, continents, black holes, and life. If you were asked to design a universe, and you had but one element with which to begin your cosmos, you should, without hesitation, select hydrogen.

To physicists, no element is more glamorous. Created in the aftermath of the big bang, hydrogen coalesced to fire the first star; God said, Let there be hydrogen, and there was light. Hydrogen burned in nuclear fires to forge the elements of life: carbon, nitrogen, and oxygen. More than 500 million tons of hydrogen burn in our sun every second, giving heat and light to our planet.

Physicists know that understanding hydrogen is a key step to understanding more complex matter. They devise elaborate formulas to predict the behavior of protons and electrons and program their supercomputers to calculate models of reality. The physicists' equations tell us something extraordinary: if you squeeze hydrogen gas hard enough, it will become a solid metal.

There is a theory, buttressed by impressive mathematical models and decades of research, that all kinds of matter will turn into metal if subjected to enough pressure. British scientist J. D. Bernal first proposed the idea in 1928, and more than thirty years ago chemist Harry Drickamer and his students at the University of Illinois became the first to demonstrate that pressure can transform simple compounds like table salt to metal. Now scientists believe that everything —beach sand, a plastic spoon, a mug of beer, even the air you breathe —would become a shiny metallic solid like aluminum or copper at very high pressure.

This theory arises from our understanding of atoms and the way they bond together. At the center of every atom lies a small, heavy nucleus made of protons and neutrons. The atomic nucleus is surrounded by one or more whizzing electrons, which may be thought of as orbiting around the nucleus at a great distance. If the nucleus could be enlarged to the size of a pea and placed in the center of a football stadium, electrons would be like gnats flying around the cheap seats. When you pick up an object, the nuclei of its atoms provide almost all of the weight (about 99.95 percent), and the electrons in their orbits account for almost all of the volume.

Electrons provide the glue that holds atoms together in solids, liquids, and gases. In most everyday materials, each electron remains close to one atom or molecule, seldom moving far away. Metals are different. In every metal some electrons are free to wander throughout the solid. These nomadic particles tend to reflect light, giving metals their distinctive luster, and they move easily in an electric field, which is what makes metals good electrical conductors. The electricity you use in your home is nothing more than electrons moving back and forth through metal wires.

Physicists, using the elegant wave equation of Erwin Schrödinger, have learned to describe the behavior of electrons and thus predict the properties of any collection of atoms. But so far the equation cannot be solved exactly except when applied to a single, isolated hydrogen atom. Countless scientists have spent decades thinking up clever ways to find approximate solutions to Schrödinger's equation for more complicated systems, but no one has exact answers. As a result, if ten theoretical physicists try to calculate the property of a material—the density of table salt or the boiling point of water, for example—chances are they will give you ten different answers, depending on how they set up their equations. This situation has, for many years, been a great solace to those of us who do experiments on the real stuff.

For these theoretical methods to have any validity, they have to be able to predict the behavior of the simplest electron system—two hydrogen atoms joined to form the hydrogen molecule. Theory predicts that at extreme pressures, when atoms and their electrons are confined into smaller and smaller volumes, electrons have less and less room in which to move. At the pressure of metallization, some electrons would be forced from their atomic homes and left to wander forever—or until the pressure is lowered.

Is theory good enough to predict what happens to the simplest element of all? What is hydrogen's pressure of metallization? What will scientists see when they get there? These are among the most compelling questions in physics.

More than half a century ago, Princeton University scientists Eugene Wigner and Hillard B. Huntington predicted the existence of metallic hydrogen. Their admittedly crude calculations yielded a lower limit of 250,000 atmospheres as the transition pressure, but since then many other groups have published their own calculations. By the early 1970s dozens, if not hundreds, of theoretical physicists had thought about the metallic hydrogen problem. Naturally enough, they came up with dozens of different predictions of the transition pressure, ranging from less than one megabar to more than ten megabars. Most theorists favored a value somewhere between one and a half and three megabars, a pressure almost within reach of the diamond-anvil cells of the late 1970s.

Metallic hydrogen has become the holy grail of high-pressure research. Of all the substances imagined by scientists, none should be stranger or more wonderful than metallic hydrogen. For one thing, it could be a superconductor—a material that transmits electricity with absolutely no loss of electrical energy—at room temperature. In an energy-hungry world, where every power cable and wire eats a bit of any passing current, superconductors could save us billions of dollars and usher in fabulous new technologies. Lots of materials are superconductors near absolute zero (about −273°C), a temperature so impractically cold that large, expensive refrigerators would have to surround every superconducting component. Recent discoveries of "high-temperature" superconductors, which work at about 180°C below zero, have improved matters considerably, but a room-temperature superconductor would be the ultimate electronic material.

That's not all metallic hydrogen is predicted to do. Theorists calculate that it could be the most concentrated form of chemical energy imaginable. As a rocket fuel it could store hundreds of times more thrust per pound than any other material; as an explosive it would be thirty-five times more destructive than TNT; and, the military was quick to realize, there could be no better way to pack hydrogen atoms into a hydrogen bomb than in its dense metal form. Keenly aware of such vast potential for destruction, some scientists raced to produce metallic hydrogen with a new dark urgency. They were driven not so much by curiosity of the unknown as by fear that others might exploit the substance first.

Theorists cannot even guess at some key questions about the metal hydrogen. Once made, will the metal persist after pressure is released? Could you hold a chunk of metallic hydrogen in your hand, or would it be unstable and revert immediately to the gas form? Only the scientists in high-pressure laboratories can provide the answer.

In spite of the potential applications, most physicists view high-pressure hydrogen research primarily as a crucial test of theory. Every new measurement on hydrogen constrains the modelers and guides their efforts. But scientists who probe the planets see another payoff. The giant planets of our solar system—Jupiter, Saturn, Uranus, and Neptune—are made almost entirely of hydrogen. Just like stars, they are immense, pressurized balls of condensed hydrogen, with minor amounts of helium and a few other light elements, surrounding a relatively small rocky core. The only difference between giant planets and small stars is that pressures and temperatures in the planets aren't quite great enough to trigger the nuclear fusion reactions that convert hydrogen to helium plus energy. If Jupiter had been just a few times larger, our solar system would have had two stars.

If hydrogen does become a metal at a few megabars—just a small fraction of these planets' interior pressures—then metallic hydrogen is surely the most abundant mineral in the universe.

The quest for metallic hydrogen has occupied a small army of researchers for the past twenty years. For half a century the metallic hydrogen goal has been clearly in view —we know it's there, but we just can't quite reach it.

The early unconfirmed claims of a megabar—by Kawai in Japan and Vereshchagin in the Soviet Union—were accompanied shortly thereafter by the researchers' equally spurious announcements of metallic hydrogen. Both groups based their findings on detecting a sharp increase in hydrogen's electrical conductivity when their samples were compressed. The teams published their claims almost simultaneously in 1975.

In both cases, it is now suspected that the drop in resistance ascribed to metallization was simply a short in an electric circuit that had been crushed and drastically deformed by pressure. George Kennedy spoke with scorn of what he saw during his visit to the Japanese lab. "I couldn't believe it. You could see when the wires shorted out," he said.

The Russians fared no better in the eyes of fellow scientists. Vereshchagin died in 1976, shortly after the questionable hydrogen experiments, but his successor as director of the Institute of High-Pressure Physics, Evgenii N. Yakovlev, pursued the false result with a vengeance. During his ten years as director, from 1976 to 1986, he pushed his scientists to use the diamond indentor instead of the diamond-anvil cell, and he reported metallization of just about everything—ruby, table salt, water, even diamond—at close to a megabar. All the measurements were suspect. The diamond tip and flat that the Russians used were bonded to a piece of metal. If they pushed hard enough, the diamond tip contacted the diamond flat and the current flowed through the metal. Long after many Soviet scientists, including the ostracized Sergei Stishov, scoffed at the director's sloppy work, Yakovlev continued to promote his ideas from his privileged position. One embarrassing Soviet news exposé even called him the man who "was able to make metal even out of absolute vacuum." Yakovlev became the symbol of ineptitude in the Soviet science establishment.

But even if Kawai or Yakovlev had been successful in making hydrogen metal, there was still no real hope of measuring its physical properties with any precision in their devices. In 1978 a group of workers from Lawrence Livermore Laboratory reported results from their studies of hydrogen that had been explosively compressed and just as rapidly decompressed. Their experiments provided intriguing evidence that electrical conductivity increases dramatically above about two megabars, but their experiment recorded changes only during the fraction of a second when the sample was at an unknown high temperature and pressure. Most researchers agreed that significant progress on the hydrogen metal question would depend on reaching and sustaining higher pressures. The diamond-anvil cell was the obvious choice for the job.

In 1979 Dave Mao and Peter Bell's diamond cell held the world's static high pressure record of 1.7 megabars, and they seemed to have the best chance to document the nature of hydrogen at a megabar and above. Unfortunately, the hydrogen experiment is vastly more complicated than merely squeezing rocks. With rocks, Mao and Bell could simply pulverize their sample to a fine powder and place it in the gasket hole; with a gas like hydrogen, the sample cannot be loaded so easily. Mao and Bell had to condense the hydrogen—to load enough hydrogen atoms into the gasket hole—*before* closing the diamond cell.

Their first approach was to cool the hydrogen to −253°C, creating a liquid a thousand times denser than normal gas. Adapting well-established methods for handling liquefied gases, Mao and Bell loaded their diamond cell into a six-foot-tall insulated glass container, just like a giant thermos bottle. They poured ultracold liquid hydrogen into a gasketed diamond cell, which was then tightly sealed. A sprinkling of fluorescent ruby powder in the chamber provided built-in pressure calibration. A simple turn of the diamond cell's screw raised the pressure to 50,000 atmospheres, more than twice the previous pressure at which accurate measurements had been made on hydrogen. Mao and Bell discovered that increased pressure causes hydrogen to solidify. They watched the element change from a colorless liquid to a colorless solid, and they became the first humans to look at solid pressurized hydrogen at room temperature.

Hydrogen at a megabar seemed to be just a turn of the screw away. Unfortunately, it wasn't that easy. Pressurized hydrogen relentlessly exploits every opportunity to escape the confines of a gasket chamber. It penetrates and cracks ordinary metal gaskets, which leak or split after a few hours; Mao finally had to build gaskets of special stainless steel. Even diamond anvils fell prey to hydrogen's destructive effects: anvils with the tiniest invisible surface flaws shattered at pressures as low as 50,000 atmospheres.

Despite these difficulties, Mao and Bell were able to make slow and methodical progress. High-pressure hydrogen remains colorless, so normal light spectra don't reveal much. Furthermore, because x-rays only scatter off electrons and hydrogen has only one electron per atom, it is almost impossible to x-ray the substance. But there were other options. Indian physicist Shiv K. Sharma, an expert in optical measurements who joined the high-pressure team for a two-year postdoctoral fellowship in 1977, provided a new kind of probe—Raman spectroscopy, the ideal tool for studying pressurized hydrogen.

A beam of light—from a laser, for example—can either pass right through a sample or be partially or completely absorbed by it. The infrared spectroscopy used by Van Valkenburg, Weir, and Lippincott at the National Bureau of Standards measures that absorption. But laser light can also scatter sideways off a sample, thereby indicating the way the atoms or molecules are vibrating. These vibrations slightly change the energy of the scattered light—changes that can be measured by a spectrometer. In the hands of Shiv Sharma, Raman spectroscopy gave scientists their first glimpse of how hydrogen molecules behave at high pressure.

The scientists at the Geophysical Lab knew that solid hydrogen forms from molecules shaped like tiny dumbbells, with a hydrogen atom at each end. Sharma learned that at high pressures, these dumbbells rotate freely in the crystals, as expected. But the researchers were astonished to find that the bond holding the two hydrogen atoms together seemed to become weaker at higher pressure. This discovery suggested to Sharma and his coworkers that the hydrogen molecules could perhaps be on their way to becoming a metal.

Throughout Sharma's spectroscopic studies the liquefied-gas-loading system worked reasonably well, allowing measurements to be made up to 600,000 atmospheres. But it was never easy. Sometimes the gasket wouldn't fill completely, or the liquid would escape as soon as the cell warmed up to room temperature. In 1980 Dave Mao visited Los Alamos National Laboratory to learn how scientists there had been loading diamond cells with hydrogen and other gases with a much simpler high-pressure system. The Los Alamos researchers inserted their cell into a thick-walled steel vessel—a foot-long cylinder of metal, five inches in diameter, with a two-inch bore, open at one end. They sealed the chamber with a massive metal screw cap and pumped up the gas pressure to 2,000 atmospheres. It would be a simple matter to seal the cell while it was pressurized and then remove it for study—or at least that's what Mao and Bell thought.

The Geophysical Lab's high-pressure team built their own copy of the Los Alamos gas-loading system in 1981 and had used it for more than a year when Dave Mao and his research associate, Ji-an Xu, first tried to load hydrogen. Lab scientists had loaded more than a hundred cells with other gases like argon and neon and methane without a hitch. The operations had become so routine that many of the usual high-pressure safety precautions—remote operation of pressure valves, wall braces for pressurized tanks, and protective armor barriers for workers—were observed only halfheartedly. Mao and Xu's preparations were straightforward: align the cell, mount the gasket, add a bit of ruby powder for pressure calibration, position the diamond cell in the big cylinder, and seal it up. They started to pump hydrogen gas into the container and waited behind a curved metal barrier of protective armor.

Suddenly the entire building shuddered as the thick steel cylinder exploded, propelling a fist-sized metal chunk across the room and sending out a ricocheting shower of smaller shrapnel. The noise deafened Mao and Xu, who had been casually standing in the projectiles' paths just moments before. It took the stunned scientists days to recover from their narrow escape, for they had been literally inches away from horrible injury or death. "I was so shaken that I almost had a car accident going home," Mao remembers.

The explosion reminded the scientists of a sobering fact: hydrogen isn't an ordinary gas. Its molecules had exploited tiny defects in the steel cylinder. Mao and Bell almost learned too late that only specially fabricated steel should be used for high-pressure hydrogen work.

The explosion was only a temporary setback. Dave Mao designed an improved version of the cylinder with remote loading features, and the lab's machine shop went to work building the prototype with hydrogen-safe steel. In six months they were ready to try again.

The hydrogen project took on a new dimension in 1984 with the arrival of postdoc Russell Hemley, who had just received his Ph.D. in chemistry from Harvard. Hemley is a quiet, serious scientist with a business-like façade, which nevertheless fails to hide his gracious and generous nature. Hemley brought a dual expertise in Raman spectroscopy and theoretical chemistry to the Geophysical Laboratory—skills that paid tremendous dividends for Mao and Bell's research. Hemley, in turn, welcomed the chance to work on high-pressure hydrogen—easily one of the most exciting experimental subjects in materials science. Together, the scientists went to work pushing hydrogen to higher and higher pressures.

The first step was to set up a new spectroscopy lab specifically geared to measuring still-smaller samples in the diamond cell at even higher pressures than before. With funds from the National Science Foundation and the Carnegie Institution, Hemley obtained a new argon laser and a state-of-the-art spectrometer and detector, which he equipped with specially designed microscopes for studying samples in diamond cells. Within a year the men were ready to take hydrogen to a megabar—the region where most physicists predicted metallization would occur.

Mao, Bell, and Hemley pushed their system to the limit, knowing full well that the experiment would end in a shattered diamond anvil. They breezed past a megabar and the hydrogen spectra continued to reveal the surprising trend found by Shiv Sharma: the bond between hydrogen atoms continued to weaken. The experiment went higher and higher—1.2, 1.3, 1.4 megabars and still no dramatic spectral changes. The all-too-familiar *pop* of breaking diamond finally occurred as they attempted to push the cell above 1.5 megabars.

Even though the hydrogen sample remained a clear, colorless solid and no metallization seemed to have occurred, the experiment was nevertheless a resounding success. The Carnegie scientists had more than doubled the previous pressure record for solid hydrogen, and they had pushed to within sniffing distance of the predicted metallic form. They submitted a short paper to the influential *Physical Review Letters* describing their findings.

That 1985 publication of their paper marked a high point in hydrogen research, but the small Geophysical Laboratory team felt uncertain about the future of their hydrogen research. Without a major new commitment of time and money there was little hope of pushing the pressure much higher. Rus Hemley was still a postdoctoral fellow, and soon it would be time for him to find a permanent job; his departure would further reduce chances for the lab's success. Furthermore, Mao and Bell sensed an undercurrent of resentment from more tradition-minded Carnegie geologists, who saw any excursions into physics research as a violation of the Geophysical Laboratory's mandate. In late 1986, Peter Bell decided to leave the Geophysical Laboratory for a well-paid position as the Norton Company's vice president of research. Dave Mao was sorely tempted to abandon the Carnegie Institution for a post at the Lawrence Livermore Laboratory, where a major government-sponsored effort to make metallic hydrogen was about to begin.

However, the high-pressure team was saved by a strong commitment of support from the Geophysical Laboratory's director, Charles T. Prewitt. Rus Hemley was given a staff position in the summer of 1987, and Dave Mao was given free rein to pursue the hydrogen problem—or any other high-pressure research of his choosing. Together, the new team of Mao and Hemley set off to make high-pressure history.

✧　✧　✧

Beginning in the spring of 1988, the two scientists tackled the hydrogen problem with renewed effort. Diamond failure remained the key problem. They had pushed their diamond cells close to 3 megabars with three mineral samples, but every time they tried hydrogen the diamonds broke at about 1.5 megabars.

There had to be a way to prevent such failures. They decided to try cold.

Mao and Hemley reasoned that extreme cold would reduce the penetrating power of hydrogen. They could simply dunk the entire diamond cell in a bath of liquid nitrogen, a readily available colorless liquid that boils at a temperature almost two hundred degrees below zero. Commercially available containers for liquid nitrogen were the wrong size and shape, so Mao fabricated a crude holder of white polystyrene from an old packing crate. The scientists then loaded the diamond cell, immersed it, and repeated the familiar ritual of measuring pressure and turning the screw. The process worked: with liquid nitrogen they were able to push hydrogen above 1.5 megabars for the first time.

On April 14, 1988, Mao and Hemley broke the record. A hydrogen sample had been loaded the previous day, and by 6:00 P.M. on the fourteenth the sample was confined at a record 1.8 megabars. Mao and Hemley were exhausted; they had been at it for more than twenty-four hours straight, raising and measuring pressure over and over again. They planned to continue until the diamonds broke and the apparatus destroyed itself. An oversized yellow envelope marked "Comptroller of the Treasury, Income Tax Division, Annapolis, Maryland 21411-0001" lay empty and ignored next to the assorted blank federal and state forms that were strewn about on a lab bench. They were too close to stop, even though the income-tax deadline was only a day away.

The liquid nitrogen coolant created an unforeseen problem. The slightest leak in the nitrogen cooling jacket would allow the cell's temperature to rise, causing ice to condense on the diamonds, perhaps even cracking them and destroying the experiment. Because they needed to monitor the cooling system so closely, Mao and Hemley couldn't leave the lab for more than an hour or so at a time. Fortunately, the nitrogen-cooled cell seemed to be working beautifully.

Rus Hemley's Raman spectroscopic lab was located behind the main lab building in an antiquated structure about the size of a one-story cottage. Though sometimes grandiloquently referred to as "the Experiment Building" in grant applications, the cheaply made cinderblock and wood-frame structure had actually been designed as a bunker for testing machine-gun barrels during World War II. So many discarded gun barrels are buried beneath the site that sensitive magnetic experiments have to be conducted elsewhere.

Mao and Hemley had filled the old bunker with sophisticated experimental hardware and computer terminals. A ten-foot-long lab bench with four massive legs dominated the room. On the near side, computer terminals monitored experiments and stood ready to store and analyze data. Behind the terminals was an array of lasers that directed their brilliant beams through a maze of mirrors and lenses to focus on the tiny pressurized sample. Two large spectrometers, black metal boxes about the size of a footlocker, measured the interaction of the laser light with the hydrogen sample, revealing the behavior of the sample's atoms under pressure.

The lab had grown chilly from a combination of boiling liquid nitrogen and cool evening air, and both scientists dressed for warmth and comfort. No one at the Geophysical Lab—or in practically any other physical science lab, for that matter—wears a white lab coat anyway.

In spite of the excitement at setting new hydrogen pressure records with every turn of the cell's screw, the results seemed rather dull. There had been no obvious change in the transparency of the hydrogen—it certainly didn't look metallic. The hydrogen spectrum, which appeared on the computer screen as a single well-defined peak on a gently sloping background, changed smoothly and continuously with pressure, confirming the trends of earlier studies. For the past two dozen hours the new data had been, in one sense, a negative result—for more than a day nothing unusual had happened. But when Mao turned the screw and pushed the pressure above 1.8 megabars, they caught their first glimpse of a dramatic change.

Two peaks suddenly appeared on the Raman spectrum where before there had been only one. At first Hemley suspected experimental error; perhaps one part of the sample was at 1.8 megabars but another part was somehow at a much lower pressure, giving two distinct positions for the one strong hydrogen peak. Hemley attacked the computer terminal controlling data collection, urging the spectrometer to define the positions of the two peaks more precisely. As the machine's gears whirred he wrote furiously in his notebook. Mao stood by the diamond cell, topping off the liquid nitrogen, centering the cell in the laser beam, raising the pressure, and eagerly awaiting Hemley's analysis of each new spectrum. The process was repeated, with Rus Hemley alternately pounding the keyboard, making notes, and resting his head on his folded arms while waiting the few minutes for the machine to do its job.

At each higher pressure the new peak became stronger at the expense of the old. Gradually the weary researchers became convinced that they were seeing something completely new. The hydrogen had transformed.

Mao and Hemley repeated the experiment over and over in the next few weeks, confirming a dramatic change in hydrogen that begins at pressures as low as 1.5 megabars. By the end of May 1988, their manuscript, "Phase Transition in Solid Molecular Hydrogen at Ultrahigh Pressures," was received and almost immediately accepted by *Physical Review Letters*. The discovery of this transition has evoked considerable excitement, though its nature is still not completely understood. Some scientists think that the hydrogen may have become a bizarre clear and colorless metal composed of distinct molecules—a transitional form that precedes the predicted metallization with its isolated hydrogen atoms. Others suggest that hydrogen at ultrahigh pressure may represent a new state of matter, unlike anything seen before. Still others contend that the spectral changes simply reflect an unexpected change in atomic structure. Whatever the answer, science had taken one more critical step toward understanding the behavior of solid hydrogen.

17

✧

Metallization

The hypothetical metallic phase of monatomic solid hydrogen is the simplest possible metal. For years, this elegant material has been subjected to theoretical consideration ranging from the level of homework of a first-year graduate student to that of masters in the field of solid-state physics. . . . Recent high-pressure experimental results of hydrogen are full of surprises . . . In fact, most of the recent findings at ultrahigh pressures were unanticipated by theory.
—H.-K. Mao and R. J. Hemley, "Hydrogen at High Pressure," 1992

A letter from Ken Goettel is not soon forgotten. His missives are covered with exotic antiquated postage: colorful three-cent commemoratives, odd airmail issues, and obsolete stamps marked "Registry" or "Parcel Post." Foreign scientists must think it wonderful and strange to receive an envelope covered with an assortment of forty-year-old stamps honoring the Coast Guard, the discovery of anesthetics, Paul Bunyan, and Princeton University.

Ken Goettel's unusual envelopes reveal that he is a collector and likes to be noticed. As a graduate student at MIT, Goettel flirted with fame when his clever ideas about the possibility of the element potassium in the earth's core gained some hearing. But his biggest headlines came from his other business—philately. In the course of buying and selling rare stamps he purchased something rather different—an uncanceled 1797 bearer bond from the state of Connecticut for ninety pounds sterling at 3 percent interest. He obtained the small, faded document for a few dollars from an antiquarian book-seller's bin. But, if real, the two centuries of compound interest represented a staggering sum of more than $20 million—and Goettel was the sole bearer. His low-key letter of inquiry to the Connecticut treasury office created a panic, and the story made the front page of the Hartford newspaper. At first it appeared that Goettel's claim was valid, and that the 190-year-old bond would bankrupt the state, but a careful search of the state's early records seemed to indicate that the bond had, in fact, been canceled in the early 1800s. Still, Goettel retains the document, waiting for a chance to examine the records himself.

Ken Goettel learned the diamond-cell trade from Dave Mao during a two-year stint at the Geophysical Laboratory. While at the lab he was taught how to align, load, and operate the cell in the megabar range. He also joined Mao and Bell in research that set a number of high-pressure records—perhaps as high as five megabars—in the early 1980s. He then brought this megabar expertise to other high-pressure groups, first at Lawrence Livermore Laboratory and then at Harvard.

Knowing Goettel and his ambitions, I would have been keenly interested in his letter of September 1, 1988, even if it hadn't been plastered with more than thirty different commemoratives. I opened the colorful envelope with care, saving the postage, which came through uncanceled (old United States stamps don't have the fluorescent tags that trigger canceling machines). But the stamps were soon put aside in favor of the envelope's extraordinary contents: a manuscript describing the metallization of xenon gas. The Harvard University high-pressure group led by Isaac Silvera was perfecting its techniques, and hydrogen was next. "My diamond cell work is now focused on hydrogen," Goettel wrote. "My objective is to apply the principles developed . . . in the xenon paper to a serious attempt to metallize hydrogen."

The challenge was clearly stated. Ken Goettel intended to beat the Geophysical Lab at the hydrogen game.

✧ ✧ ✧

When I arrived at the lab early on Sunday morning, September 25, 1988, I knew something must have gone wrong. A billowing white cloud engulfed the left side of the building and rose from the liquid nitrogen storage tank to well above the roof of the three-story structure. Even from the bottom of the steep, winding driveway, it seemed obvious that the tank was leaking. Seen through a persistent cold rain, the dense artificial fog created an eerie effect.

I cursed at the hassle. Having just returned from a week-long lecture tour in England, I had planned a quick stop to pick up accumulated mail and messages, not to repair leaky gas lines. But no one would be around at that hour and something had to be done about the broken equipment. The leak didn't pose any danger—nitrogen gas makes up most of the earth's atmosphere, and a little more wouldn't make a difference. But a full tank of the refrigerant wasn't cheap, and the lab would need a supply on Monday morning. I had to check it out.

I parked on the west side of the building and jogged through the increasingly aggressive rain toward the two-story-tall tank. The telltale hiss of escaping gas seemed to confirm my fears. As I entered the cold vapor cloud, however, the sharp hiss abruptly ceased and a mist-shrouded figure approached. It was Dave Mao.

He presented a comic figure with his large black umbrella in one hand and large thermos of liquid nitrogen in the other. He was smiling and good-humored as he greeted me, but dark circles under his eyes betrayed a state of near exhaustion. It was Mao who had created the vapor cloud simply by pouring himself a bottle of the ultracold liquid. He and Hemley were working on hydrogen again.

"We started the experiment a week ago, but the diamonds still haven't failed," he explained. "We're over two megabars and the cell is really stable. But it's not metallic yet." Evidently, his latest diamond-cell design, sporting slightly modified diamond anvils and stabilized by $-200°C$ liquid nitrogen, worked better than any previous model.

But in the process of setting a new record for high-pressure hydrogen, the researchers had run into a serious new problem. Above the 2-megabar mark the diamond anvils began to fluoresce strongly, obscuring any signal from the tiny hydrogen sample. Above 2.2

megabars fluorescence swamped all other effects, with the result that there was no Raman signal at all from the solidified gas. And still the sample remained transparent to light, suggesting that no metal transition had occurred.

The exhausting routine of trying to measure spectra, calibrate pressure, raise pressure, and realign the system had taken its toll. Mao and Hemley had started joking that a broken diamond would be as much a relief as a disappointment, but they were determined to keep going as long as possible. Mao thought that the cell might exceed 3 megabars; metallization could be only a turn of the screw away.

By midweek the hydrogen-bearing diamond cell was above 2.4 megabars and holding. Even though the experiment was still in progress, Mao and Hemley had both promised to attend a meeting of mineral physicists on the West Coast. The two frustrated scientists left grudgingly, parking the cell in its nitrogen bath with instructions to their colleagues to keep the liquid topped off for a few days until they came back.

Within hours of their return to Washington the impatient scientists were back in the lab. They turned the screw of their diamond-anvil cell again. The hydrogen began to darken. At a pressure estimated to be greater than 2.5 megabars, hydrogen had begun to absorb visible light, one of the first signs of possible metallization. Mao and Hemley invited other members of the high-pressure group into the lab to look down the microscope to see the evidence for themselves. Although they cautioned us that many changes besides metallization could cause the subtle darkening, we had almost convinced ourselves that the dark phase appeared shiny, like a metal.

They repeated the whole experiment three times with new samples and new cells just to be sure, and then they wrote up the results. They included a dramatic color photograph of dark hydrogen in their *Science* article, which described the extraordinary changes in hydrogen's optical properties. The story of the unusual darkening of hydrogen under pressure made headlines around the world—headlines that almost immediately caused headaches for the discoverers.

✧   ✧   ✧

Isaac F. Silvera, leader of the Harvard high-pressure physics group, has spent more than two decades —most of his professional career—studying hydrogen at low temperatures. First at North American Rockwell in California, then the University of Amsterdam, and finally at Harvard's Lyman Laboratory, he measured its properties, the nature of its electrons, and the way it interacts with light. In the process, he became the acknowledged authority on hydrogen at liquid-helium temperatures—as low as one degree above absolute zero—and pressures up to about 10,000 atmospheres.

In 1988 his Harvard research group made a major effort to metallize hydrogen. After the arrival of Ken Goettel, they were able to achieve more than a megabar and confirm the 1.5 megabar change in the spectrum that Mao and Hemley had seen. Still, the higher pressures at which hydrogen darkened eluded them.

Silvera was not pleased at the way Mao and Hemley's 1989 observations of hydrogen at 2.5 megabars were received. The Carnegie scientists had phrased their *Science* paper with great care. They did not claim metallization of hydrogen; they simply provided evidence that pressure was a possible route to metallization, and their data agreed with many theoretical predictions. Unfortunately, the title of their paper included the words "Evidence for Metallization," leaving many readers with the mistaken impression that metallization had been achieved, and several prominent newspapers reinforced the misperception by announcing this erroneous news. Headlines in the *Los Angeles Times* proclaimed "Researchers Report Converting Hydrogen into Metal," while *The Washington Post* declared "Creation of Hydrogen Metal Reported."

The situation rankled Silvera, who submitted a letter to *Science* contesting Mao and Hemley's results. His intense communication was almost as long as the original article, but the message was pointed: "In my opinion the only appearance of evidence for metallization is in the title. . . . A claim of metallization of hydrogen must be accompanied by acceptable scientific evidence." Silvera's comments ignored the actual thrust of Mao and Hemley's paper, that optical-property measurements pointed to a specific mechanism for metallization.

Following journal protocol, the editor of *Science* forwarded Silvera's typewritten comments to Mao and Hemley with an apology about the tone of the letter. Only later did the Carnegie scientists learn that the first draft of Silvera's letter, seen only by his research students and postdocs, was even harsher. "We really had to sit on Ike to get him to tone down that letter," Ken Goettel recalls. After several months of argument and revision, a calmer version of Silvera's communication and Mao and Hemley's simple restatement of their observations and conclusions were printed as "Technical Comments" in *Science*'s February 16, 1990, issue.

But Silvera was not appeased and the situation came to a head a month later at the March 1990 meeting of the American Physical Society in Anaheim, California, where a program on high-pressure hydrogen brought all the key players together. At several technical sessions as well as at a press conference, Silvera went on the offensive, all but discounting the Carnegie scientists' experimental results at pressures above 2 megabars. Ironically, he then presented his own opinion that hydrogen turns to metal at 1.5 megabars—which was, coincidentally, the highest pressure that his group could obtain. Mao and Hemley continued to emphasize their numerous unique measurements well above 1.5 megabars and went back to work in Washington.

The highly publicized hydrogen research also drew an old adversary into the fray. Cornell materials researcher Art Ruoff, who a decade earlier had "disproved" Mao and Bell's megabar claim, once again disputed Carnegie Institution high-pressure work. Despite the fact that Ruoff's group had made no high-pressure measurements on hydrogen at all, he said: "Is the production of hydrogen . . . an extraordinarily important problem, i.e., the holy grail of physics? . . . [If so,] then we must conclude that claiming to have made metallic hydrogen is an extraordinary claim and therefore extraordinary efforts must be made to justify this claim."

In challenging the Carnegie work, Ruoff reminded listeners of the significant discoveries of his own team, notably his collaboration with Lawrence Livermore physicist Robin Reichlin in metallizing xenon gas—a major feat accomplished almost simultaneously by Isaac Silvera's Harvard group. These key studies marked the first time that a room-pressure gas had been turned into a metal, although the exotic silvery substance quickly vaporized when the pressure was released. Two years later, Ruoff and coworkers Serge Desgreniers and

Yogesh Vohra reported strong evidence for the metallization of oxygen at 1.3 megabars. Having achieved these two important results, Ruoff felt justified in dismissing the fuss over hydrogen entirely: "Unless you can show [hydrogen] has unique properties, it's no more exciting than if oxygen or xenon become metallic."

Various journalists who had been quick to publicize the original Geophysical Laboratory announcement seemed just as eager to pick up on the apparent disagreements among prominent high-pressure groups. *Chemical and Engineering News* sensationalized the issue in their story "Controversy Erupts over Hydrogen Metallization." *Science* correspondent Robert Pool took a more upbeat approach in "The Chase Continues for Metallic Hydrogen," his own account of the high-pressure drama.

The final verdict on metallic hydrogen is still out. Is the 1.5-megabar form of molecular hydrogen an exotic clear metal? Does the observed darkening above 2.5 megabars correspond to the metallization long predicted by physicists, or is it the sign of some other exotic material? When metallization is confirmed, will scientists be able to stabilize the metal at room pressure?

What does seem certain is that hydrogen, compressed to unimaginable pressures between the flat faces of diamonds, forms a substance that is quite unlike anything anyone has seen before. Soon—perhaps in a few years or even a few months—we will know the properties of this strangest of high-pressure materials.

Epilogue

So much work remains to be done. High-pressure research now consumes the lives of countless scientists and engineers, who know there are many breakthroughs still to be made. Some researchers are consumed by the quest for metallic hydrogen, while others continue to investigate minerals of the earth's deep interior. Chemists now search for valuable new materials, while physicists use pressure to probe the properties of matter. And for thousands of scientists, diamonds and other exotic forms of carbon still prove an irresistible lure.

Even after forty years of routine high-pressure synthesis, the diamond adventure is far from over. In the past two years an extraordinary discovery was made that has elated scientists and engineers and that may give rise to remarkable new high-tech products.

Just when it seemed that we had learned nearly all there was to know about diamond making—when synthesis of large, isotopically pure diamond crystals and vapor-deposited diamond films was redefining our mastery of carbon—scientists made a fantastic breakthrough, discovering a totally new way to make diamonds under pressure. The new approach was catalyzed by a discovery so remarkable and unexpected that it may take decades for scientists to sort out all of its implications.

In all the centuries of focused research on carbon and its compounds, nothing has caught scientists more off guard or has had a more immediate impact than the discovery of the buckeyball. For centuries carbon was known in only two basic forms—graphite and diamond. Now there are three.

Surprisingly, the serendipitous path to the new type of carbon began with studies of starlight. For more than half a century astronomers had puzzled over the distinctive light-absorbing properties of interstellar dust, which suggested the presence of clumps of carbon atoms—soot formed in the vicinity of stars. Several groups of scientists tried to simulate interstellar dust in their laboratories, vaporizing graphite in an effort to match the astronomers' spectra.

The first clear evidence of a new form of carbon came on September 4, 1985, when Harold W. Kroto of Sussex University, in collaboration with a group at Rice University led by Richard E. Smalley, discovered an unexpected concentration of molecules in their synthetic soot that weighed exactly 720 atomic mass units, corresponding to the weight of a cluster of sixty carbon atoms. An intense few days of study led them to conclude that these C_{60} molecules represented a particularly stable form of carbon that adopted the spherical form of a soccer ball, which is constructed from thirty-two panels—twelve pentagons and twenty hexagons that meet at sixty vertices. The distinctive alternation of these pentagonal and hexagonal rings, characteristic of the geodesic architecture of R. Buckminster Fuller, led Kroto's and Smalley's groups to name the new molecule buckminsterfullerene. Soon everyone was calling them buckeyballs for short.

Once scientists knew what to look for, they found that C_{60} clusters are ubiquitous. Under hundreds of different synthesis conditions researchers observed complex mixtures of C_{60} and various other carbon-rich molecules, including ordinary graphite. They found that while the sixty-carbon form is usually most abundant, there are also many other enclosed carbon molecules. The football-shaped C_{70} cluster is particularly common, but a staggering variety of fullerenes, from C_{32} to C_{600}, have also been identified.

From 1985 to 1990 many teams of chemists around the world studied the new carbon, but all were frustrated by their inability to purify the stuff. Richard Smalley and his colleague Robert Curl wrote, "We could not collect more than a few tens of thousands of these special molecules. This amount was plenty to detect and probe with the sophisticated techniques available in our laboratory, but there was not enough to see, touch or smell. . . . All we had to do was make more of them—billions and billions more."

German scientists Wolfgang Kratschmer and his graduate stu-

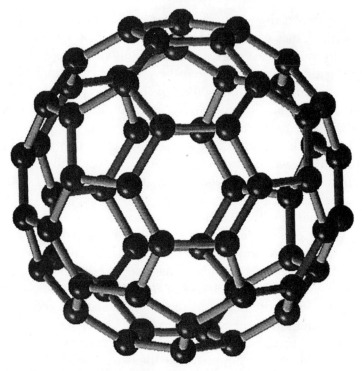

A buckeyball, the soccer-ball-like C_{60} molecule, forms crystals in which the round molecules are stacked like oranges at the grocery store. Other ball-like molecules containing from thirty-two to more than six hundred carbon atoms have also been identified. (Courtesy of Larry W. Finger.)

dent Konstantinos Fostiropoulos isolated pure buckeyballs at last on May 18, 1990, when they discovered that C_{60} dissolves in benzene, an ordinary liquid solvent. By washing their soot in the colorless liquid, the two scientists from the Max Planck Institute for Nuclear Physics in Heidelberg were able to produce a beautiful magenta solution of buckeyballs. Kratschmer immediately telephoned their longtime collaborator in fullerene research, Donald Huffman at the University of Arizona in Tucson.

Huffman vividly recalls the day. "Within minutes I was able to verify the solubility," he wrote. "Then came the ultimate 'Eureka' experience in my life as a solid-state physicist. With graduate student Lowell Lamb, I allowed a small drop of the red benzene solution to dry on a slide. Under the microscope [thousands of] beautiful little hexagonal platelets of apparently pure carbon were revealed—a brand new form of solid carbon." For the first time, humans could watch and study crystals of the unexpected substance.

In a matter of days they had learned to produce buckeyballs in quantity. The easiest way was to heat graphite in helium gas to produce a soot rich in C_{60} and other molecules, then to isolate the fullerenes with benzene. One of the earliest production devices at Arizona employed an old beer keg as the helium chamber. With their unique supplies of fullerenes, the Heidelberg and Arizona groups could finally measure many of the buckeyball's properties for the first time. The extraordinary results were presented to the world at a conference in Germany in early September and were published in their article "Solid C_{60}: A New Form of Carbon," which appeared in the September 27, 1990, issue of *Nature*.

An explosion of buckeyball research followed the September revelations. The stuff was easy to make, was easy to study, and possessed extraordinary chemical and physical properties. By mid-1991 thousands of scientists had jumped on the buckeyball bandwagon and hundreds of articles had appeared in record time. Pure C_{60}, it was found, is an electrical insulator, but add a little bit of potassium and it becomes a semiconductor. Add a little more and it becomes a superconductor. Buckeyballs mixed with other elements have achieved superconductivity at an amazing forty-five degrees above absolute zero—a record surpassed only by the so-called high-temperature copper superconductors. Buckeyballs are the most resilient of molecules: propel them at a diamond target at speeds of 20,000 miles per hour— a speed that would blast other molecules to pieces on impact—and they simply bounce off, undamaged. Some varieties of buckeyballs even become magnetic at low temperature, a phenomenon unique among carbon-based materials.

The buckeyball's chemistry is every bit as amazing as its physical properties. While the sixty-carbon cluster is physically tough, it is also quite reactive. Scientists at Rice University have synthesized buckeycages that enclose individual atoms or groups of atoms inside the carbon sphere. Chemists at Berkeley have created bunnyballs, which have a pair of earlike molecules branching off the main sphere. Northwestern University workers found that a layer of buckeyballs dramatically increases the speed of vapor deposition of diamonds—perhaps by a factor of ten. Chemists envision dozens of fullerene variants: $C_{60}H_{60}$ fuzzyballs with a hydrogen coating; $C_{60}F_{60}$ teflonballs that are predicted to have unusual lubricant properties; and fullerene hairyballs with elongated molecules that festoon the outside of the C_{60} sphere. Materials scientists have also synthesized a rich variety of buckeytubes, long cylinders of carbon atoms that produce incredibly strong fibers with the potential to revolutionize the field of lightweight construction.

When *Science* named buckeyballs its 1991 Molecule of the Year, the study of fullerenes was barely a year old, yet the round form of carbon stood poised to transform materials science. Almost buried in this avalanche of discovery was a short letter in *Nature* by Argentinean scientist Manuel Nuñez Regueiro and his coworkers Pierre Monceau and Jean-Louis Hodeau at Grenoble, France, who had performed the simplest of diamond-anvil cell experiments on buckeyballs. Having squeezed buckminsterfullerene to a modest 200,000 atmospheres, they had observed the transformation of the black material to a clear, yellowish solid. It was diamond—diamond formed at room temperature.

Many chemists predict that buckeyballs will soon be available for a few dollars per pound. If so, it may well usher in a new era of diamond making. As the French team wrote in their *Nature* article, "The high efficiency and fast kinetics at room temperature suggest the possibility of using this transformation for fabrication of industrial diamonds." Fast, cheap, no complicated heating requirements, just a simple squeezer to synthesize pounds of diamonds—buckeyballs could become a diamond maker's dream.

Much fame and fortune await the creative diamond maker. Thousands of investigators will spend years trying to figure out the best ways to grow isotopically pure diamond, to form semiconducting diamonds by vapor deposition, and to exploit fullerenes in the diamond-making business. The diamond gemstone industry is not about to collapse, and in all likelihood there will always be a demand for fine natural stones, but as diamond abrasives and thin films become more and more available to industry and commerce, they will play an ever-increasing role in our lives. Products that rely on futuristic high-pressure technologies and materials will come to affect every aspect of our lives, providing cheaper manufacturing, faster transportation, more reliable communications, stronger construction, and new forms of recreation.

The high-pressure adventure continues at an ever more intense pace, as research teams in a score of countries explore matter at extreme conditions. In the eighty years since Percy Bridgman first broke the 2,000-atmosphere mark in his makeshift laboratory, the range of routine research pressures has increased a thousandfold, and new records are set every few years. We have only just begun to discover the astonishing variety of new materials that pressure can provide—superhard abrasives, dense deep-earth minerals, exotic crystalline forms of ordinary liquids, and perhaps even metallic hydrogen, all created in the past quarter century. What new wonders await us? What unimagined substances will change our lives?

High-pressure scientists are always mindful of these extraordinary possibilities, yet what captivates us about pressure is not so much the hope of profit but rather the appreciation of nature's endless store of magic. Each trip to the laboratory begins an exploration into uncharted realms—each day holds the prospect of discovering fantastic materials and observing strange phenomena that no one has ever seen before.

For us, science remains the greatest adventure of all.

Additional Reading

Chapter 1: Mysteries

Balfour, Ian. *Famous Diamonds*. London: Collins, 1987.

Dickinson, Joan Younger. *The Book of Diamonds*. New York: Avenel, 1965.

Hahn, Emily. *Diamond*. New York: Doubleday, 1957.

Chapter 2: Attempts

Appleton, Victor. *Tom Swift Among the Diamond Makers*. New York: Grossett and Dunlap, 1911.

Appleyard, Rollo. *Charles Parsons: His Life and Works*. London: Constable & Co., 1933.

Crookes William. *Diamonds*. London: Harper & Brothers, 1909.

Davies, Gordon. *Diamond*. Bristol, UK: Adam Hilger, 1984. Davies provides an excellent overview of the science and technology of diamonds and diamond making.

Hershey, J. Willard. *The Book of Diamonds*. New York: Hearthside, 1940.

Moissan, Henri. *The Electric Furnace*. London: Edward Arnold, 1904.

Additional Reading

Chapter 3: Percy Bridgman

Bridgman, Percy. *The Physics of High Pressure*. London: G. Bell & Sons, 1958.

Walter, Maila L. *Science and Cultural Crisis: An Intellectual Biography of Percy Williams Bridgman (1882–1961)*. Stanford: Stanford University Press, 1990. I have relied heavily on Walter's biographical research and have quoted liberally from original documents she unearthed.

Chapters 4 and 5: ASEA and Norton

Wentorf, Robert (ed). *Modern Very High Pressure Research*. Washington: Butterworth's, 1962. This monograph includes important chapters by Baltzar von Platen on the ASEA device and by Loring Coes, Jr., on his work at Norton. Other chapters were written by scientists featured in this book. Among the distinguished authors are Francis Boyd, Francis Bundy, Harry Drickamer, John Jamieson, Andrew Lawson, Ellis Lippincott, Rustum Roy, Herbert Strong, Alvin Van Valkenburg, and Charles Weir.

Chapters 6–11: Diamond Synthesis

Banholzer, William. *Diamond Research at GE*. Schenectady: GE, 1991.

Derjaguin, B. V., and D. V. Fedoseev. *Diamonds Wrought by Man*. Moscow: MIR Publishers, 1985.

National Materials Advisory Board. *Status and Applications of Diamond and Diamond-Like Materials: An Emerging Technology*. Washington: National Research Council, 1990.

Suits, G. Guy. *Speaking of Research*. New York: Wiley, 1965.

277

Chapters 12–17: The Diamond Breakers

Hazen, Robert, and Larry Finger. *Comparative Crystal Chemistry.* New York: Wiley, 1982.

Manghnani, Murli, and Yasuhiko Syono (eds.). *High-Pressure Research in Mineral Physics.* Monograph 39. Washington, D.C.: American Geophysical Union, 1987.

Mao, Ho-Kwang, and Russell Hemley. "Hydrogen at High Pressure." *American Scientist* 80: 234–47.

Poirier, Jean-Paul. *Introduction to the Physics of the Earth's Interior.* Cambridge: Cambridge University Press, 1991.

Redfern, Martin. *Journey to the Center of the Earth.* London: BBC World Service, 1991.

Ross, Marvin, and Charles Shishkevish. *Molecular and Metallic Hydrogen.* Santa Monica, Calif.: Rand Corporation, 1977.

Sherman, W. F., and A. A. Stadtmuller. *Experimental Techniques in High-Pressure Research.* New York: Wiley, 1987.

Index

Index

Index

About the Author

ROBERT HAZEN, a graduate of MIT and Harvard, is a research scientist at the Carnegie Institution of Washington's Geophysical Laboratory, where he and his colleagues study the structure of minerals and their properties. He has written books and articles on a variety of subjects, including crystal chemistry and solid-state physics, geological poetry, the history of mining, and American brass bands. A part-time professional trumpeter, Hazen has performed with a number of ensembles including the National Symphony, the Metropolitan Opera, and the Royal Ballet. He lives in Potomac, Maryland, with his wife, author Margaret Hindle Hazen, and their two children, Benjamin and Elizabeth.